WEAPONS AND HOPE

Also by Freeman Dyson

Disturbing the Universe

Preface

In August 1960, I came back to America from Europe with my wife and eleven-month-old daughter. After thirty-six hours of traveling, we arrived at the old New York bus terminal and bought a carton of fresh milk for baby Dorothy. But we still had a problem. Dorothy could not drink out of the carton and her milk bottle was rancid in the August heat. I went to a public drinking fountain and began rinsing the bottle. Two tall crew-cut American soldiers stood nearby and watched my ineffectual efforts to get the bottle clean. Finally, one of them said, "Say, that's not the right way to clean a nipple. Let me show you how to do it. I happen to be an expert." He took the bottle and cleaned it out with the thoroughness and precision of a well-trained nurse. I thanked him and thought, Well, this is America and I am glad to be home. So was born the dream that the military establishment of my adopted country might serve a humanly comprehensible and ethically acceptable purpose. This book is an attempt to make the dream come true.

The first suggestion that I try to explain weapons to the public came from William Shawn at *The New Yorker*. The result was an article which appeared in *The New Yorker* in 1970 under the title "The Sellout." I am grateful to *The New Yorker* for permission to reprint it here as Chapter 10.

The more immediate origin of this book was a public meeting on the nuclear arms race organized by a group of churches in Princeton in September 1980. The talk which I gave at that meeting became the nucleus of the book. I am indebted to Pastor Wallace Alston of Nassau Presbyterian Church and Pastor John Crocker of

Trinity Episcopal Church for inviting me to talk and for infecting me with their concern.

An intermediate stage in the book's development was a set of Tanner Lectures given at Brasenose College, Oxford, in May 1982. I am indebted to the Tanner Foundation and to my hosts at Brasenose College for organizing the lectures and for their permission to incorporate them in this book. The lectures contained the substance of Chapters 11, 12, 18, 22, and 24. They are published under the title "Bombs and Poetry" in the annual volume of Tanner Lectures for 1983. Parts of Chapters 11 and 12 also appeared in *The Dial* in 1982.

My credentials as a military expert come mainly from being a member of Jason, a group of scientists who work on technical problems for the Department of Defense and other agencies of the American government. I am indebted to my Jason colleagues, especially Dick Garwin and Sid Drell, for my education in military technology and politics.

Others who have helped me are Hal Feiveson, George Kennan, Pierre Piroué, Clara Park, Genia Peierls, my wife, Imme, and my sister, Alice Dyson. Above all, I am indebted to Paula Bozzay for typing the manuscript and to Michael and Cornelia Bessie, my editors at Harper & Row, for persuading me to write the book and for helping at every stage with their advice and encouragement.

PART I

---❦---

QUESTIONS

Science is a match that man has just got alight. He thought he was in a room—in moments of devotion, a temple—and that his light would be reflected from and display walls inscribed with wonderful secrets and pillars carved with philosophical systems wrought into harmony. It is a curious sensation, now that the preliminary sputter is over and the flame burns up clear, to see his hands lit and just a glimpse of himself and the patch he stands on visible, and around him, in place of all that human comfort and beauty he anticipated—darkness still.

H. G. WELLS, 1891

1

Agenda for a Meeting of Minds

I chose the title *Weapons and Hope* for this book because I want to discuss the gravest problem now facing mankind, the problem of nuclear weapons, from a human rather than a technical point of view. Hope means more than wishful thinking. It means the whole range of positive human responses to intractable problems. Hope is a driving force of political action. The main theme of the book will be the interconnectedness of past and future. I will be exploring the historical and cultural context in which nuclear weapons grew, and at the same time looking for practical ways of dealing with the problem of nuclear weapons in the future. The cultural context provides a basis for hope that we can find practical solutions. Central to my approach is a belief that human cultural patterns are more durable than either the technology of weapons or the political arrangements in which weapons have become embedded.

The chapters of the book hang together as pieces of a broad panorama rather than as links in a logical chain of argument. Readers uninterested in technical or historical details may freely skip chapters or whole sections. Part I, "Questions," provides the frame for the picture. Part II, "Tools," describes weapons as they exist and as they are perceived by the public. Part III, "People," studies our involvement with weapons from a historical point of view, giving special attention to the national cultural patterns which have emerged in various countries from diverse historical experiences of war. Part IV, "Concepts," examines seven alternative strategic doctrines which have grown up around nuclear weapons, and tries to define a doctrine which may offer us hope of escape from the trap into which reliance on nuclear weapons has brought us. The last chapter, "Tragedy Is Not Our Business," looks at the problem of nuclear weapons in a wider context, as the contemporary manifestation of a human predicament which is as old as the *Iliad* and the *Odyssey*, the doom of Achilles and the survival of Odysseus. Each part of the book is arranged like an old-fashioned sermon, with exemplary stories at the beginning and a moral at the end.

Why should a scientist, a peaceful theoretician who has never seen a shot fired in anger, write a book about weapons and war? I write because I live in two worlds, the world of the warriors and the world of the victims, and I am possessed by an immodest hope that I may improve mankind's chances of escaping the horrors of nuclear holocaust if I can help these two worlds to understand and listen to each other.

The world of the warriors is the world I see when I go to Washington or to California to consult with military people about their technical problems. That world is overwhelmingly male-dominated. In spite of Joan of Arc and Margaret Thatcher, soldiering is still a game that only boys are supposed to play. The world of the warriors also includes many people outside the professional military establishments. It includes expert negotiators at the United States Arms Control and Disarmament Agency, and professors of International Affairs at the universities of Princeton and Oxford. It includes doves as well as hawks, scholars as well as generals. It includes the loyal opposition as well as the wielders of power. But all who belong to the world of the warriors share a common language and a common style. Their style is deliberately cool, attempting to exclude overt emotion and rhetoric from their discussions, emphasizing technical accuracy and objectivity, concentrating attention on questions of detail which can be reduced to quantitative calculation. They applaud dry humor and abhor sentimentality. The style of the warriors is congenial to professional scientists and historians, who also base their work on factual analysis rather than on moralistic judgment. The philosophical standpoint of the warriors is basically conservative, even when they consider themselves liberal or revolutionary. They accept the world with all its imperfections as given; their mission is to preserve it and to ameliorate its imperfections in detail, not to rebuild it from the foundations.

John von Neumann was a Princeton mathematician who felt a particularly strong affinity for the warriors' world and became a great expert on weaponry. He liked to shock his friends at Princeton with his version of the warriors' philosophy: "It is just as foolish to complain that people are selfish and treacherous as it is to complain that the magnetic field does not increase unless the electric field has a curl. Both are laws of nature." But Von Neumann was an extreme case, an academic outsider trying to be more military than the military. Real soldiers do not make dogmatic statements about the laws of human nature. Real soldiers know that human nature is unpredictable.

The world of the victims is the world I see when I listen to my wife's tales of childhood in wartime Germany, when we take our children to visit the concentration camp museum at Dachau, when we go to the theater and see Brecht's *Mother Courage*, when we read John Hersey's *Hiroshima* or Masuji Ibuse's *Black Rain* or any of the other books which truthfully record the human realities of war, when we sit with a crowd of strangers in church and hear them pray for peace, or when I dream my private dreams of Armageddon. The world of the victims is not male-dominated. It is, on the contrary, women-and-children-dominated. It is, like the Kingdom of Heaven, difficult to enter unless you come with a child's imagination. It is a world of youth rather than age. It pays more attention to poets than to mathematicians. The warriors' world describes the outcome of war in the language of exchange ratios and cost effectiveness; the victims' world describes it in the language of comedy and tragedy.

I also see the world of the victims when I attend meetings of our local citizens' peace movement in Princeton, the Coalition for Nuclear Disarmament. Our meetings are generally held in rooms belonging to one or another of the local churches. Occasionally we have public sessions with outside speakers. The most memorable of our meetings was an all-day affair which kept the Nassau Presbyterian Church packed from 11 A.M. till 9 P.M. The star of the show was Helen Caldicott, the Australian children's doctor who has become a full-time fighter against nuclear power stations and nuclear weapons. Her medical specialty is cystic fibrosis, but she has also some experience with victims of childhood leukemia, a disease which has a well-documented tendency to occur after children are exposed to excessive doses of nuclear radiation. She began her campaign against nuclear power as an exercise in preventive medicine. Even though childhood leukemia is in many cases a curable disease, the cure is uncertain and the treatment is long and debilitating. Every doctor who has to deal with such diseases knows that prevention is better than cure. In her own mind, Helen Caldicott did not cease to be a doctor when she switched from cure to prevention.

In Australia, Helen Caldicott concentrated her efforts on the local issues of nuclear power and the mining of uranium for export. After she came to America, she became aware that nuclear weapons and nuclear war are a graver public health hazard than nuclear power. "I realize now," she told us in Princeton, "that nuclear power is only the pimple on the pumpkin." She is now a prime mover in the worldwide organization of doctors against nuclear war, Physicians for Social Responsibility. As we listened to her talking in the Presbyterian church, it was easy to understand how she has captured the hearts and minds of people around the world. She is spontaneous, she is articulate, she is witty, and she communicates the anguish of a doctor struggling day after day to find help and comfort for desperately sick children. After you have heard her speak and shaken her hand, you cannot brush aside her message as the emotional outpouring of a fanatic. She speaks from a solid basis of medical experience. She speaks for the victims in a language which all of us should be able to understand.

And yet the world of the warriors goes on its way as if Helen Caldicott had never existed. One week I listen to Helen Caldicott in Princeton. The next week I listen to General So-and-so in Washington. Helen and the general live in separate worlds. In a few minutes of conversation I cannot explain Helen's message to the general or the general's message to Helen. If Helen and the general ever tried to talk directly to each other, it would be a dialogue of the deaf. And that is why I write this book. I know that there are not two separate worlds but only one. Helen and the general, whether they like it or not, live on the same planet. My task is to explain them to each other, to fit together the split halves of our world into a single picture.

Why is it so easy for the warriors to ignore Helen? The warriors do not feel inclined to take her seriously, because she does not play her game according to their rules. Both the style and the substance of her arguments violate the taboos of their profession. Her style is personal rather than objective. The substance of her argument is anecdotal rather than analytical. She is careless about technical details. She does not think naturally in quantitative terms. The qualities that make Helen convincing to an audience of concerned citizens in Princeton, her sincerity and seriousness and down-to-earth goodness, are outweighed in the world of the warriors by her weakness in arithmetic.

If it is difficult to translate Helen's message effectively into the language of the generals, it is even more difficult to translate the legitimate concerns of the generals into a language which pays some respect to ordinary human values and feelings. The deliberately impersonal style of the warriors' world gives outsiders the impression that the warriors are even more inhuman than they actually are. There is prejudice and antipathy on both sides. The military establishment looks on the peace movement as a collection of ignorant people meddling in a business they do not understand, while the peace movement looks on the military establishment as a collection of misguided people protected by bureaucratic formality from all contact with human realities. Both these preconceptions create barriers to understanding. Both preconceptions are to some extent true.

When I was seven years old, I was once reprimanded by my mother for an act of collective brutality in which I had been involved at school. A group of seven-year-olds had been teasing and tormenting a six-year-old. "It is always so," my mother said. "You do things together which not one of you would think of doing alone." That is a piece of my education which I have never forgotten. Wherever one looks in the world of human organization, collective responsibility brings a lowering of moral standards. The military establishment is an extreme case, an organization which seems to have been expressly designed to make it possible for people to do things together which nobody in his right mind would do alone.

Yet military people are, underneath their uniforms, human. The first high-ranking military officer with whom I came into close contact was Air Vice-Marshal Harrison, commanding Number 3 Group of the British Bomber Command in the later stages of World War II. I lived for some weeks at his headquarters in a lovely old country house in the village of Exning in Suffolk. At that time he commanded a force of 290 heavy bombers. His bombers took part in the constant heavy attacks on German cities and oil refineries, and suffered their full share of losses. But 3 Group never hit the headlines. While other bomber groups from time to time carried out individual operations of spectacular folly and heroism, 3 Group preferred to send its bombers to lay mines quietly in German coastal waters. In the pecking order of the six groups of Bomber Command,

3 Group by common consent came last. When I arrived at Harrison's headquarters in Exning, I understood why. I presented my credentials to Harrison as the newly appointed scientific adviser to 3 Group. I came prepared to discuss in detail the technical problems of operating a force of bombers. But Harrison did not want to talk about bombers. He talked only about silkworms. Since I was a scientist, he thought I would appreciate the fine points of silkworms. He took me out to his greenhouses, where his silkworms were feeding on carefully tended mulberry bushes. Silkworms were his passion. I could never get him to talk seriously about anything else.

At that time, when I was trying to give Air Vice-Marshal Harrison unwanted scientific advice, I found it shocking that a man who carried the responsibility for the lives and deaths of thousands should be wasting his time on silkworms. Now, thirty-eight years later, I look back and see Harrison as the wisest of the group commanders. He had probably understood earlier than the others that the area-bombing offensive against Germany was a misguided enterprise unworthy of the heroism of his air crews. He could not hope to challenge or change the overall direction of the campaign. The best he could do was what he did, to drive 3 Group with a light hand and shield his crews so far as possible from deeds of superfluous bravery. The cultivation of silkworms helped to keep him sane.

In every military establishment there are Harrisons to be found, men who obey orders without excessive efficiency, and quietly ameliorate evils which they cannot undo. A few weeks ago, on one of my visits to the warriors' world in Washington, I heard an American general say that he takes for his motto the words of the French diplomat Talleyrand, "Pas Trop de Zèle"—"Not Too Much Enthusiasm." There, I thought, walks the spirit of Air Vice-Marshal Harrison. But the Harrisons, no matter how numerous they may be and no matter how high they rise, are bound by the rules of their profession to keep their skeptical thoughts private. The public voice of the military establishment cannot be critical of its own purposes. The military machine is designed to carry out the missions which it has established for itself, irrespective of the thoughts and feelings of individual commanders.

The responsibility for criticizing and controlling military policies belongs to the political authorities of each country. The political arena is the place where, in theory, the warriors' world and the victims' world should come together, where the claims of generals and pediatricians should be compared and weighed in the balance. Political leaders have the opportunity to hear both sides. If the claims of the generals are found wanting, political leaders have the power to make drastic changes in weapon deployments and in military doctrines. But in the political arena as it actually exists, opportunities for deliberate weighing of alternative philosophical viewpoints rarely arise, and the power to make drastic changes is limited. Every politician knows that drastic change is troublesome and politically costly. Even in countries with a revolutionary political tradition, bureaucratic inertia usually prevails. In the United States, political decisions concerning military policy are almost always made piecemeal, in the course of routine budgetary hearings. Seldom do we see a decision made, as the decision to negotiate and ratify the Test Ban Treaty was made in 1963, with a full public debate allowing proponents and opponents to discuss the long-range historical consequences of the treaty rather than its immediate political costs and benefits.

The time is now ripe for a new public debate, placing in question the fundamental objectives of military policy. This time, the debate must be worldwide. It has already begun in Western Europe and in the United States. The argument centers around the question whether nuclear weapons have any longer a rational military purpose. Helen Caldicott and the European nuclear disarmament movement are a part of the debate. The efforts of my military friends in the Pentagon to find a secure basing mode for their new MX missile are also a part of it. But the argument remains sterile and disjointed because the two sides lack a common language. A debate can be politically effective, like the debate of 1963, giving political leaders courage and strength to make hard decisions which change the world, only if the two sides will listen to each other and understand each other's concerns. There must be an agreed agenda before a fruitful discussion is possible.

The purpose of this book is to help prepare an agenda for a fruitful nuclear debate. The debate is already in progress and will no doubt continue, with or without my help. But it will be of little benefit to the world if it remains politically polarized, with each side preaching only to its own true believers. For the debate to gain the serious attention of political leaders, it must be a real meeting of minds, with the two sides agreeing on the definition of the questions at issue. For the debate to result in practical steps toward a safer world, the two sides must find a middle ground where they can agree on some matters of substance. In this, as in all political endeavors, the preparation of a generally acceptable agenda is a big part of the battle.

The agenda which I am proposing is not narrowly defined. It consists of broad and general questions. The questions can be connected according to taste with current political issues, with historical examples, with technical analysis, or with abstract notions of right and wrong. My hope is that people coming from different backgrounds may find in these questions some points of contact through which they can communicate with one another. Here then is a list of thirteen questions with some preliminary comments.

Do nuclear weapons help to keep the world at peace? This is a loaded question. People from the warriors' world can answer it with a simple yes. People from the victims' world have to say "Yes, but." A large part of this book is devoted to explaining the "but."

If we continue forever to rely on nuclear weapons, is it inevitable that the weapons will sooner or later be used? This is another loaded question. Now the victims can answer yes and the warriors must say "Yes, but." Again the "but" requires some lengthy explanations. There is a widespread belief in the victims' world that the probability of nuclear war is inexorably increasing from year to year as a result of the continuing arms race. The warriors can argue that the probability of nuclear war is diminishing as a result of technical improvements in the design of weapons and their command and control apparatus. In reality, the probability of nuclear war depends more on political factors than on the numbers and technical characteristics of weapons.

How do we deal with the Russians? The implication of this question is that we deceive ourselves if we invent humanitarian solutions to the world's problems while ignoring the harsh realities of Soviet power. It is best to stipulate at the outset of our discussion that Soviet power is permanent and that it will remain harsh. There still remain many opportunities for us to influence Soviet power, to make it more dangerous or less dangerous to our survival. I do not pretend to be an expert on Soviet strategy and military doctrine. My picture of Soviet society is mainly derived from George Kennan and Richard Pipes, two experts who are supposed to represent the liberal and conservative wings of American opinion. Kennan's Russia and Pipes's Russia differ surprisingly little. They are both, after all, Russia. The feasibility of influencing Soviet nuclear policies does not depend crucially on whether Kennan's picture or Pipes's picture of Russia is the more accurate.

Is government an art or a science? I once spent a long evening on a mountaintop in the Caucasus, discussing this question with a young Russian astronomer. The astronomer was then living on the mountain, preparing to make observations with the new Soviet six-meter telescope, the largest telescope in the world. Since the sky was cloudy, we had plenty of time to wrestle with the problems of world politics. My Russian friend maintained that government is a science, that all questions of social organization, including the questions of war and peace, are scientific questions and can be answered by logical analysis. I argued the contrary view, that government is an art, resting my case on examples from Russian and Western history. But my friend's faith was not to be shaken. He admitted that his own government on numerous occasions failed to follow correctly the conclusions of scientific reasoning. Nevertheless, the science of human relations existed and would solve all our political problems if only we would study and apply it diligently. Now, the point of this story is not that my astronomer friend is a typical Russian. The point is just the opposite. He is, so far as I know, unique. He is perhaps the last survivor of the band of true believers in the possibility of a scientific utopia. There he sat on his mountaintop, surrounded by the glories of sky and snow, totally detached from the realities of earthbound humanity. Soviet society in the plains below his feet, like Western society, is run by people who practice the art of government, for better or for worse, without much help from scientific theory.

What is the appropriate time scale for discussion of strategic questions? People from different backgrounds are accustomed to thinking on different time scales, and the discrepancy of time scales is a serious obstacle to mutual understanding. Roughly speaking, the time scale for American politicians working with an annual budget cycle is one year, the time scale for Soviet politicians is five years, the time scale for military and industrial planners is ten years, the time scale for mothers of young children is twenty years, the time scale for grandparents is fifty years, the time scale for historians and science fiction writers is a hundred years. Which time scale is the most important? This question has no unique answer. All time scales are important. We have to deal with the future on all time scales. But we should say clearly, whenever we are discussing possible futures, which time scale we have in mind. Many things which are absurd on a time scale of five years are reasonable or even inevitable on a time scale of fifty years. My personal bias as a father is toward the longer time scales. I try to correct this bias by talking with students for whom the Vietnam War is ancient history and a decade seems like a lifetime.

Is the regulation of nuclear weapons best achieved by evolution or by revolution? This is one of the basic issues dividing warriors from victims. The warriors generally assume that the only safe road to a stable world lies through gradual change, with arms control achieved by carefully negotiated agreements while the balance of power is maintained by existing military forces. The victims generally assume that only a revolutionary shift in public attitudes can force the political authorities to undertake the drastic measures of disarmament which are needed to ensure mankind's survival. The argument often degenerates into a battle of slogans: "Ban the Bomb" against "Don't Rock the Boat." I shall argue that both sides are right, that the differences between them can be reconciled if we consider them to be looking at the same problem on two different time scales. We need both evolution and revolution. But revolutions are risky and should not be undertaken without careful preparation. In other words, it may be reasonable to believe in "Don't Rock the Boat" on a time scale of five years and in "Ban the Bomb" on a time scale of fifty years.

Is political influence exerted more effectively from inside or from outside a government? This question is similar to the previous one and has a similar answer. The answer depends on the time scale. In the short run, if you want to influence events, you must work within the establishment. In the long run, if you work within the establishment, you will not change anything fundamentally.

Do we wish to abolish war entirely or to prohibit only certain kinds of war? This has been a dilemma for pacifist movements all through history. If we wish to abolish war totally, we must accept some kind of world government; if we wish to prohibit only cer-

tain methods of waging war, we are making the world safe for war
as an institution. Einstein took his stand uncompromisingly for
world government. He said, in 1947: "War will be prevented only
when military power in the hands of individual nations is abol-
ished and is replaced by the military monopoly of a supranational
organization." But today neither the peace movements nor the
warriors look to world government as a practical solution to their
problems. There is a consensus that power, including the power to
make war, should remain in the hands of free and independent
nations. We differ only in the extent to which we would try to
place limits on the means employed by national governments to
defend their interests.

*Do we wish to make weapons more destructive and less usable, or less
destructive and more usable?* Each time a new weapon of great destructiveness is introduced, its inventors soothe their consciences
with the thought that this will finally make war impossible. It is
probably true that the least destructive nuclear weapons are the most
dangerous, because they make it easier for a nuclear war to begin.
But the ethical dilemma remains. Can we in good conscience follow
the slogan "The worse the better"?

Do intellectual theories of nuclear strategy have any real meaning?
James Fallows in his excellent book *National Defense* argues that the
theory of nuclear war is the modern equivalent of medieval theology. "Wars have been fought, empires built, heretics burned on the
basis of theology, and so, on the basis of the nuclear theology, are
missiles developed and war plans laid today." The experts who run
computer simulations of nuclear exchanges know how artificial and
dubious their input numbers are. Computer experts have a saying:
"Garbage in, garbage out." But the output of their calculations is fed
to generals and politicians who tend to believe the numbers and have
no time to study the tenuous web of assumptions on which the
numbers hang.

Can we survive nuclear war? This is a question of fundamental
importance, with no simple answer. It depends on what one means
by "we," what one means by "survive," and what one means by
"nuclear war." Following the terminology of Fallows, one may say
that this is a theological question. It nonetheless deserves a careful
discussion. Warriors generally answer the question affirmatively,

victims negatively. Even if they cannot agree, it would be useful for them to clarify the reasons for their disagreement.

What would be the effect on our national security if public opinion came to reject nuclear weaponry as politically and morally objectionable, in the same quiet, undramatic way in which the public has rejected bomb shelters? This is a question which our military authorities ought to be seriously pondering. We may already be approaching a time when further increases of offensive nuclear armament are no longer politically acceptable. A longer time must elapse before public opinion can be expected to turn against nuclear weaponry altogether. But shifts of public opinion are unpredictable, and sometimes happen more quickly than anyone expects.

Are we, as a society, prepared to face the risks and uncertainties of living in a non-nuclear world? In considering this, the last question on my agenda, it is important to say clearly what a non-nuclear world is and what it is not. A non-nuclear world is not a world with all nuclear weapons magically annihilated and all knowledge of their construction erased from human memory by a supernatural power. A non-nuclear world is a world where, after long and arduous negotiations supported by an aroused public opinion, a treaty has been signed and ratified by the nuclear powers, prohibiting possession and deployment of nuclear weapons; where the major nuclear delivery systems and the declared stockpiles of warheads have been publicly dismantled; where the good faith of the signatory powers is monitored by a substantial but imperfect verification system; where the existence of limited numbers of hidden nuclear weapons in unfriendly hands cannot be excluded; and where the knowledge and the technology for reassembling weapons are widely disseminated. It is not obvious that such a world would be more stable or less dangerous than the world we are living in now. Nevertheless, the non-nuclear world has important moral and political advantages, and its military hazards could be alleviated by a wise use of non-nuclear technological resources. Ultimately, there is no reason why the non-nuclear world should not be attractive to soldiers as well as to mothers and physicians. The sooner we all start thinking realistically about the challenges and difficulties of the non-nuclear world, the sooner we may have a chance to bring it into existence.

In the chapters which follow, I shall not limit myself to this agenda, nor shall I attempt to provide answers to all the questions on my list. The questions can have no definitive answers. Since the questions are concerned with politics and morality, it is not to be expected that everybody should agree about the answers. The purpose of the questions is to focus public debate on the broader issues of nuclear policy, in the hope that a genuine meeting of minds may become possible, with soldiers and citizens searching together for bold solutions to the problems of freedom and survival.

This book is a record of my personal effort to understand the nature of war and weaponry. In order to avoid a nuclear war it is not sufficient to be afraid of it. It is necessary to be afraid, but it is equally necessary to understand. And the first step in understanding is to recognize that the problem of nuclear war is basically not technical but human and historical. If we are to avoid destruction, we must first of all understand the human and historical context out of which destruction arises. We must understand what it is in human nature that makes war so damnably attractive.

Since I look to history as a source of understanding, a large part of this book is concerned with the past. History never repeats itself, but it offers wisdom to those who are willing to learn. It teaches its lessons in the form of parables. A parable is a story whose meaning is not obvious, illustrating by homely example and analogy some important moral principle. Jesus taught in parables because he knew that people would remember his lessons better if they had to think out his meanings for themselves. We still have much to learn from Jesus' style of teaching. When I look back into the past, I find in the two world wars the richest source of parables to help us see where we are going. That is why this book is filled with war stories. The most important lessons come from World War I. World War I, taken as a whole, is a gigantic parable of the war we are trying to avoid. It was a war of peculiar ugliness, fought with exceptional stupidity and brutality. It destroyed permanently a great part of European civilization. It was started for reasons which in retrospect seem almost trivial. The damage and loss suffered by all parties were utterly out of proportion to the pettiness of the initial quarrel between Serbia and Austria. In all these respects, the history of World War I holds up a mirror to us, showing us how small follies lead to great disasters, how ordinarily intelligent people walk open-eyed into hell.

2

The Question of Survival

On October 16, 1945, shortly after Robert Oppenheimer had resigned his position as director of the Los Alamos Laboratories, there was a ceremony in which General Groves handed Oppenheimer a certificate. It said: "This Certificate is awarded to Los Alamos Laboratories for valuable services rendered to the Nation on work essential to the production of the Atomic Bomb, thereby contributing materially to the successful conclusion of World War II. [Signed] Robert P. Patterson, Under Secretary of War, Henry L. Stimson, Secretary of War." Oppenheimer responded with the following speech:

> It is with appreciation and gratitude that I accept from you this scroll for the Los Alamos Laboratory, for the men and women whose work and whose hearts have made it. It is our hope that in years to come we may look at this scroll, and all that it signifies, with pride.
>
> Today that pride must be tempered with a profound concern. If atomic bombs are to be added as new weapons to the arsenals of a warring world, or to the arsenals of nations preparing for war, then the time will come when mankind will curse the names of Los Alamos and Hiroshima.
>
> The peoples of this world must unite, or they will perish. This war, that has ravaged so much of the earth, has written these words. The atomic bomb has spelled them out for all men to understand. Other men have spoken them, in other times, of other wars, of other weapons. They have not prevailed. There are some, misled by a

false sense of human history, who hold that they will not prevail today. It is not for us to believe that. By our works we are committed, committed to a world united, before this common peril, in law, and in humanity.

On the one side, these words of Oppenheimer. On the other side, memories of England in 1939. In 1939 in England, the younger generation was very sure that mankind must unite or perish. We had not the slightest confidence that anything worth preserving would survive the impending war against Hitler. The folk memory of England was dominated by the barbarities of World War I, and none of us could believe that World War II would be less brutal or less demoralizing. It was frequently predicted that just as World War I had led to the collapse of society and the triumph of Bolshevism in Russia, so World War II would have the same effect in England.

My uncle Oliver was a medical doctor who had spent his life building up public health services in the Sudan. In 1939 he was recalled from retirement and placed in charge of the emergency ambulance organization of London. He was a good man for the job, accustomed to tackling large medical problems under primitive conditions with improvised equipment. When he had time to spare from his ambulance work, he sometimes came to my parents' house in London and told us how the government was planning to deal with the catastrophic air attacks which were supposed to begin on the first day of the war. The first step, when England declared war on September 3, was to empty the London hospitals of all non-emergency patients. Uncle Oliver's job was then to take care of the air raid casualties, which were officially estimated at 100,000 killed and 200,000 wounded within the first two weeks, besides another 200,000 people who were expected to be mentally incapacitated by the bombing. These numbers were not based on fantasy; they were the estimates of military experts who extrapolated to the capability of the 1939 Luftwaffe the results achieved by smaller forces in Spain and Ethiopia. The experts did not all agree on those numbers, but they agreed on the general order of magnitude. Roughly speaking, the 1939 Luftwaffe could be expected to drop four hundred tons of bombs per day, and the experience of earlier wars indicated a civilian casualty rate of fifty physical and fifty mental casualties per ton. Why were these casualty estimates so wildly wrong? First of all,

when the war started, the Luftwaffe did not attack, and Uncle
Oliver had an additional year to organize his ambulances. During
that year the British government evacuated a substantial number of
children from London and established a rudimentary system of civil
defense. When the bombing began in September 1940, the total
daily tonnage was about as expected, but the casualties were less
than expected by a factor of twenty. Perhaps a factor of two reduction of casualties could be attributed to the inaccuracy of the bombing; only about half of the bombs fell in heavily built-up areas. The
remaining factor of ten reduction must be attributed to a law of
diminishing returns; as bombing becomes heavier, people rapidly
adapt themselves to it and learn how to stay alive. The law of
diminishing returns was confirmed later in Germany, where a bombardment much heavier than London's resulted in a casualty rate
lower by an additional factor of three. Both in England and in
Germany, the expected hordes of mental casualties failed to materi-
alize. The survivors of the London bombing, who included more
than 99 percent of the population, looked back afterward with some
nostalgia to the year of the Blitz as a time of public friendliness and
inner serenity. The ambulance drivers, usually pictured as young
and female and nonchalantly driving their battered ambulances over
rubble-choked streets, became a symbol of the city's toughness.

The experts who so grossly overestimated the effectiveness of
bombing in 1939 made many technical errors, but their major mistake was psychological. They failed to foresee that the direct involvement of civilian populations in warfare would strengthen their
spirit and social cohesion. The unexpected resilience and discipline
of civilians under attack was seen not only in England but even
more strikingly in Germany, Japan, and the Soviet Union. Would
the same qualities be shown in the United States by the survivors
of a nuclear attack? When one looks around today at the discordant
and unheroic aspects of contemporary American society, it is easy
to answer this question in the negative. Yet the English society of
1939 was just as discordant and unheroic.

So we come back to the simple and profound words of Oppenheimer. The peoples of this world must unite, or they will perish.
Many of us in England in 1939 believed these words so strongly that
we rejected altogether the morality of fighting, even for a just cause.
War and surrender to Hitler were both unacceptable, and we took
refuge in the doctrine of Gandhi, saying that only a nonviolent

resistance to evil could defend our ideals without destroying them in the process. What we said in 1939 did not prevail. We learned in the succeeding six years that a war could still be fought and won without destroying our civilization. We learned that yielding to threats is the greater evil; that is the lesson that most of us are still living by. When we in America in the 1980s apply this lesson to our dealings with the Soviet Union, are we misled by a false sense of human history? Is it a false sense of human history which teaches us that nationalism is still the strongest force in the world, stronger than the hydrogen bomb and stronger than humanity? These are some of the questions which Oppenheimer's words raise but do not answer.

Oppenheimer was right in his basic perception that history changed its course in 1945. Never again can a major war be fought in the style of World War II. And yet, after thirty-eight years, international politics are conducted on all sides as if the lessons of World War II still applied. History proceeds at its old slow pace, even if the course is changed. The transition from virulent nationalism to a world united must be stretched out over centuries. Meanwhile, we have to live in a precarious balance, between the apocalyptic warning of Oppenheimer on one side and a possibly false sense of human history on the other.

Ever since the destruction of Hiroshima, debates over nuclear strategy have continued, without producing agreement or mutual understanding among the participants. One reason for the sterility of these discussions has been the dogmatic positions held on both sides concerning the question of survival. On one side are people, generally regarded as conservative and including a large contingent of military officers and government officials, who believe that nuclear war is not fundamentally different from other kinds of war and that the old-fashioned military virtues, preparedness, endurance, and discipline, will enable us to survive it. On the other side are people, generally regarded as liberal and including a large contingent of scientists and academic military experts, who believe that survival is impossible and that any preparations designed to improve our chances of survival are a dangerous delusion. The true believers on each side consider themselves to be not only right but morally superior. They consider the other side to be not only wrong but morally deficient.

Not all preachers of the opposing doctrines are narrow-minded and self-righteous. Two classic statements of the arguments on each side were published twenty years ago, Herman Kahn's *On Thermonuclear War* arguing for survival and Tom Stonier's *Nuclear Disaster* arguing against it. Both books are eloquent, fair-minded, and technically accurate. Both base their argument on a deep study of human history as well as on technical assessments of damage and casualties produced by nuclear weapons. Anybody wishing to understand the problem of survival in all its complexity would be well advised to read both books. Unfortunately, few people wish to hear both sides of the case. The majority of scientists became aware of Kahn's book only through a review by James Newman published in *Scientific American*. Newman wrote a brilliant and scathing essay, first casting doubt on Herman Kahn's existence and then passionately denouncing him while ignoring the substance of his arguments. Stonier's book also failed to receive the attention it deserved, perhaps because the liberal establishment in the 1960s was preoccupied with Vietnam and had no time to spare for greater disasters.

How could it happen that Kahn and Stonier, two intelligent and well-informed thinkers, could reach such opposite conclusions? Partly the explanation comes from their different backgrounds. Kahn was a physicist, Stonier is a biologist. Kahn took his evidence from politics and diplomacy, Stonier from ecology. Kahn looked at war from the point of view of the warrior, Stonier from the point of view of the victim. But these differences would not have driven them to opposite conclusions if the question of survival had been objectively answerable. The fact of the matter is that Kahn's and Stonier's conclusions are subjective, based upon their personal judgments of human and social behavior, based in the last resort upon intuition and faith. After I have weighed their evidence, my verdict is that both their arguments are emotionally convincing, neither is logically compelling. The only logical conclusion which I can draw from their books is that nuclear war is incalculable. Whether or not we can survive depends on unknowable human responses to unimaginable tragedy. We cannot, despite the best efforts of systems analysts and social psychologists, know in advance whether any functioning social and legal and economic fabric would emerge from a catastrophe without historical parallel. Historical and ecological analogies provide us with suggestive evidence, but they cannot give us certainty.

The debate concerning survival took a fresh turn in 1982 with the appearance of a special issue of *Ambio* entitled "Nuclear War: The Aftermath." *Ambio*, a professional journal of the Royal Swedish Academy of Sciences, normally publishes analyses of environmental problems caused by peaceful economic activities. The special issue contains fourteen technical articles, all concerned with environmental effects of nuclear war. Many of the effects described in these articles were already discussed by Tom Stonier twenty years earlier, but the *Ambio* authors raise a number of new questions. Whereas Stonier had assumed that the heaviest effects of nuclear war would be largely confined to the belligerent countries and their near neighbors, the *Ambio* writers find that disturbances of the natural environment could be severe enough to destroy human societies over the entire northern hemisphere of the earth. Twenty years of experience with the recalcitrance of environmental problems have made the experts doubtful of the ability of the earth to heal the wounds inflicted by human folly. One of the new questions raised by *Ambio* is the global effect of smoke produced by burning cities and forests. The pall of smoke might be dense enough to darken the sky over much of the earth for several months, bringing winter weather in midsummer and destroying a year's growth of food crops. Poor countries with subsistence economies might starve to death thousands of miles away from the nearest nuclear explosion. The editorial advisers for the special issue summarize its message by saying: "One of the conclusions that may be reached from this study is that the short-term effects for which we have relatively reliable calculations—fire, blast and radioactive contamination—may be matched or even vastly overshadowed by longer-term, less-predictable environmental effects."

The *Ambio* study has stimulated a new wave of calculations of climatic and chemical processes triggered by nuclear explosions in the atmosphere. The newer calculations may or may not confirm the *Ambio* estimates. In either case, the results of the new calculations will not put an end to uncertainties. The science of climate-modeling has not yet progressed far enough to predict with certainty, in the absence of a nuclear war, whether next winter will be mild or severe; it is unreasonable to expect the same science to give us reliable descriptions of the meteorology of a nuclear holocaust. The meteorological uncertainties of nuclear war will remain at least as great as the uncertainties of peacetime weather prediction. The psychological and sociological uncertainties will remain even greater. The *Ambio* summary says: "About one-third of the urban survivors will be in a state of acute anxiety, and about 20 per cent of the other survivors will be so incapacitated by psychological and patho-psychological conditions that they will be unable to care for themselves or others." These estimates of psychological casualty rates are similar to the estimates made by the civil defense experts in London in 1939. All such estimates are pure guesswork. The fact that the 1939 guess was wrong does not prove that the 1982 guess was wrong.

The *Ambio* study is important, even if one does not believe its numerical conclusions. All of its assumptions, and all of its detailed results, are open to challenge. Alternative and equally plausible assumptions give widely different results. The study does not, as some of its authors claim, make our knowledge of the effects of nuclear war more precise. The study is important for the opposite reason. It has shown us that our ignorance of the effects of nuclear war is even greater than we had realized. It has confirmed in our own era the judgment which Tolstoy expressed in *War and Peace* a century ago, that war is in its nature incalculable and unpredictable and uncontrollable.

Jonathan Schell's book, *The Fate of the Earth,* goes even further than the *Ambio* study in its apocalyptic description of the effects of nuclear war. Schell asserts that a nuclear war might cause the total and final extinction of the human species. His book is an eloquent protest against the moral blindness of the present generation of mankind, against our arrogance in endangering the existence of all future generations for the sake of our petty and transient political concerns. I do not agree with all the technical details of Schell's argument. I am unable to imagine any chain of events by which our existing nuclear weapons could destroy mankind and leave no remnant population of survivors. But I fully share Schell's moral indignation and I believe his major thesis is valid independently of the technical details.

On a deeper level, Schell is certainly right. Although it may be technically impossible for a single nuclear exchange to exterminate the human species, a succession of nuclear wars might well do so. The ultimate danger to our species comes not from the destructive effects of our existing stockpiles but from the possibility that the fighting of nuclear wars might become a habit, that we might find ourselves adapting too well to the fighting of nuclear wars. The effects of the first nuclear war might be severe enough, not to exterminate mankind, but to leave our species in some sense incurably insane. Hatred and suffering on an unparalleled scale might lock us into a cyclical pattern of war and rearmament and revenge which would in the end make our planet uninhabitable. As it was said long ago: Whom God wishes to destroy, He first makes mad. Jonathan Schell may be right in saying that a single nuclear war can destroy our species, if we interpret his words as meaning that a single nuclear war could leave us so psychologically scarred that we would be unable afterward to escape from the vicious cycle of hatred and revenge. If a species becomes collectively insane, then it becomes in the Darwinian sense unfit, and in the long run it is unlikely to survive. A sequence of ten nuclear wars, each one more desperate and more insane than the one before, could plausibly result in our final disappearance from this planet. I have too much respect for the sanity of our species to believe that such an outcome is probable, but I cannot discount it as a technical impossibility. To the extent that our collective sanity is endangered by nuclear war, Schell's nightmares have a basis in reality.

In opposition to the *Ambio* authors and to Jonathan Schell stands an extensive literature written by experts in the technology of civil defense. Advocates of civil defense can demonstrate that simple protective measures would substantially reduce the lethality of almost any nuclear attack. Their calculations, like the *Ambio* calculations, are based on unproved assumptions. Whatever factual information we have about the global effects of nuclear explosions is mainly derived from analysis of the bomb tests carried out in the atmosphere by the United States and the Soviet Union during the 1950s and 1960s. These bomb tests had an aggregate yield of about three hundred megatons, about one-thirtieth of the megatonnage of a full-scale nuclear war. People who believe in survival can argue that our planet survived the bomb tests with only minor damage and that even the thirty-times-greater stress of a full-scale war should not strain the planetary ecology to its breaking point. People who do not believe in survival can argue that the extrapolation of damage estimates from the hundred-megaton range of the bomb tests to the thousand-megaton range of full-scale war is illegitimate, and that there is no reason to expect ecological damage to be proportional to megatonnage. So the argument goes on, with no end in sight.

Since the believers in survival and in nonsurvival have failed for

thirty-five years to convince each other, I propose to break the
deadlock by adopting dogmatically a third position. My dogma is
that the question of survival is undecidable. There is no way, short
of actually fighting a nuclear war, to find out whether anything
worth preserving would survive it. This dogma of undecidability is
consistent with all available evidence. And it may help us to escape
from the doctrinal rigidities which have frustrated our efforts to
negotiate nuclear disarmament. The dogma of undecidability is not
just an abstract proposition. It has immediate practical consequences. It implies two fundamental rules of conduct for the nuclear
age. It says, since survival may be possible, it makes sense to try to
save lives. It says, since survival may be impossible, it makes no sense
to count the lives saved.

The rule that it is meaningless to count the lives saved impacts
directly upon some of the urgent political problems of the 1980s. If
we understand this rule, we shall be able for the first time to deal
rationally with the issue of counterforce. Irrational fear of counterforce has been one of the main causes of failure of arms control
negotiations. Counterforce means a policy of aiming nuclear weapons only at military targets and not at civilian populations. The
detailed implications of this policy will be examined in Chapter 20.
Counterforce has been for many years the official policy of the
Soviet strategic rocket forces. It is also, to some extent, in spite of
theoretical ambiguities, the policy of the United States; the number
of strategic warheads on each side far exceeds the number of significant nonmilitary targets, so that the majority of weapons must be
aimed at military targets if they are aimed at anything at all. The
military officers of my acquaintance who have anything to do with
the targeting of weapons prefer the counterforce policy; they accept
the fact that weapons aimed at military targets will incidentally kill
vast numbers of civilians, but they still feel a strong moral repug-
nance against killing civilians deliberately. Unfortunately, their ethical preference for counterforce tends to bring us into a potentially
unstable situation. The theorists of arms control strongly oppose the
counterforce policy on the ground that counterforce leads to strategic instability. In simple words, the arms controllers' argument is
that if I aim my weapons at your weapons instead of at your population, then I have a greater incentive to strike first. This argument
against counterforce is theoretically valid. It would be a decisive
argument in a theoretical world where the effects of nuclear war

could be calculated. In the real world, the world where survival of nuclear war is undecidable and unpredictable, the argument is less cogent. No matter how my weapons are aimed, I have no way to count the lives that I might save by striking first. In the real world, the only way I can be sure of saving lives is not to strike at all.

The arms controllers' argument against counterforce has had the unfortunate effect of misleading the American people and government into a paranoid fear of the Soviet counterforce policy. It is reasonable to be afraid of Russian weapons, but it is unreasonable to regard the Soviet counterforce policy as evidence of particularly evil or murderous intentions, and it is unreasonable to suppose that the dangers of nuclear war would be much reduced in the unlikely event that the Soviet authorities could be induced to change their policy by arguments based on a theoretical view of strategic instability which they do not share. It is more likely that the dangers of nuclear war could be reduced by an explicit recognition on both sides that counterforce targeting is inevitable as long as nuclear weapons continue to exist.

If we could all accept the Soviet view that counterforce targeting is a lesser evil than direct targeting of populations, one of the serious sources of misunderstanding in disarmament negotiations would be removed. We might then find it easier to reach agreement on specific measures of arms reduction. We might, for example, have ratified the SALT II treaty after it was signed in 1979, if some important American senators had not been convinced that the possession of accurate SS-18 missiles gave the Soviet Union a dangerous counterforce advantage. We might be able to negotiate substantial reductions of intermediate-range weapons in Europe, if we did not insist that the most accurate Soviet missile, the SS-20, must be removed first. Both the SS-18 and the SS-20 arouse disproportionate anxiety in the minds of American politicians because they are effective counterforce weapons. They are valued highly by Soviet leaders for the same reason. If we wish to make serious progress in negotiations, common sense would suggest that we leave these particular weapons aside and concentrate our attention on others. There are plenty of other missiles which we might agree to dismantle. But to make this possible, Americans must first understand that SS-18s and SS-20s are no better and no worse than other kinds of missile, that in nuclear war the effects of accurate and inaccurate weapons are equally incalculable. In a world where we cannot count the lives saved, there is no reason to distrust the naive human instinct which tells us that it is better to aim our weapons at things than at people.

The rule that it is meaningless to count the lives saved has other consequences. It applies to the enemy's lives as well as to our own. Both applications of the rule are important. Applied to the enemy's lives, the rule says that it is absurd for Americans to react with paranoid anxiety to reports that the Soviet government is building bomb shelters and planning the evacuation of cities in an attempt to protect some fraction of the Soviet population. The Soviet government is acting reasonably in doing whatever it can to save the lives of Soviet citizens, but neither they nor we have any reason to feel confident of the effectiveness of such efforts. Applied to our own lives, the rule says that it is absurd for Americans to oppose the building of active defenses against nuclear bombardment because of an assumed incompatibility between defense and deterrence of nuclear war. There are other valid reasons for opposing active defense; one may reasonably oppose defense because it is expensive or because it is ineffective or because it is forbidden by treaty, but it is unreasonable to oppose defense on the ground that it would weaken deterrence. The theoretical antagonism between defense and deterrence disappears as soon as it is understood that all counting of the lives saved by defense is illusory. The practical and moral issues raised by active defense and by bomb shelters will be discussed in detail in Chapters 7 and 8.

I recently watched a documentary film about nuclear weapons, which included a short scene showing a class of American schoolchildren being taught to take quick shelter under their desks when the teacher blew a whistle. The schoolroom scene was photographed around 1960, when civil defense was briefly popular. The 1982 audience reacted to the scene with contemptuous giggles. This in spite of the fact that the audience had seen, a few minutes earlier, a scene of Hiroshima schoolchildren horribly burned. If those Hiroshima children had been sitting under their desks when the bomb exploded, they would probably not have been burned. But the 1982 audience did not look at it this way. One of the 1982 audience expressed the feelings of the majority: "Well, if the bomb comes, we're all dead anyway, so why bother to save a few children?"

Who was right, the 1960 teacher or the 1982 audience? This is a deep ethical problem, with strong arguments to be made on both sides. But one thing at least is clear. The response "We're all dead anyway, so why bother?" is inadequate. We cannot know in advance that we are all dead. Nuclear war is incalculable. It could happen that a single nuclear weapon might explode a few miles away from the school, with no general holocaust to follow. In that case, the children trained to slip quickly under their desks might be saved from months of pain and disfigurement. Does the remote chance of an irrational event justify the taking of special precautions? Such questions are not easy to answer.

Americans have grown up in a cultural background which leads them to expect practical questions to have answers. They tend to believe numerical predictions and calculations. A conspicuous example of this tendency is the American style of strategic analysis, both in the military establishment and in the academic arms control community. Even in congressional committee hearings, which are supposed to be intelligible to laymen, discussions of strategic issues are generally conducted in quantitative terms, with frequent reference to calculations of kill probabilities, cost effectiveness ratios, and survival rates. With this background, it is difficult for American policymakers to grasp the central fact about nuclear war, the fact that survival cannot be calculated. They want a calculable answer to every question.

Perhaps the best answer to the question of active defense and all the other ethical questions of nuclear policy is to be found, not in the professional literature of twentieth-century strategists, but in an Indian poem written two thousand years earlier, the *Bhagavad-Gita:*

> You have the right to work, but for the work's sake only.
> You have no right to the fruits of work.
> Desire for the fruits of work must never be your motive in working.

This was the answer of the god Krishna to the warrior Arjuna, who asked whether it was right to engage in war. The same answer can be given to the modern warrior who asks whether it is right to try to defend a country against nuclear weapons. You have the right to defend, but you have no right to count the fruits of defense. You have the right to try to save lives, but you have no right to count the lives saved. This answer is not easy for Americans to digest. We are accustomed to making Indians think like Americans. It is more difficult to persuade Americans to think like Indians.

PART II

---❦---

TOOLS

Out of the libraries come the killers.
Mothers stand despondently waiting,
Hugging their children and searching the sky,
Looking for the latest inventions of professors.
Engineers sit hunched over their drawings:
One figure wrong, and the enemy's cities remain undestroyed.

BERTOLT BRECHT, 1940

3

Paradoxes of the Arms Race

We base our recommendation on our belief that the extreme dangers to mankind inherent in the proposal wholly outweigh any military advantage that could come from this development. Let it be clearly realized that this is a super weapon; it is in a totally different category from an atomic bomb. The reason for developing such super bombs would be to have the capacity to devastate a vast area with a single bomb. Its use would involve a decision to slaughter a vast number of civilians. We are alarmed as to the possible global effects of the radioactivity generated by the explosion of a few super bombs of conceivable magnitude. If super bombs will work at all, there is no inherent limit in the destructive power that may be attained with them. Therefore, a super bomb might become a weapon of genocide. The existence of such a weapon in our armory would have far-reaching effects on world opinion: reasonable people the world over would realize that the existence of a weapon of this type whose power of destruction is essentially unlimited represents a threat to the future of the human race which is intolerable. . . . In determining not to proceed to develop the super bomb, we see a unique opportunity of providing by example some limitations on the totality of war and thus of limiting the fear and arousing the hopes of mankind.

These words were written by James Conant, president of Harvard University and member of the General Advisory Committee to the United States Atomic Energy Commission, on October 30, 1949. They were signed by Conant and five other members of the committee, including Robert Oppenheimer. They were attached as an annex to the formal report of the committee, which recommended unanimously against proceeding with a high-priority program to develop hydrogen bombs. The formal report dealt with narrower technical issues. The annex allowed the six men who signed it to express the broader moral grounds for their opposition. Enrico Fermi and Isidor Rabi, the two other members of the committee, wrote an annex of their own, which says almost the same thing in even stronger words:

> The fact that no limits exist to the destructiveness of this weapon makes its very existence and the knowledge of its construction a danger to humanity as a whole. It is necessarily an evil thing considered in any light. For these reasons we believe it important for the President of the United States to tell the American public, and the world, that we think it wrong on fundamental ethical principles to initiate a program of development of such a weapon. . . .

The text of the General Advisory Committee report with its majority and minority annexes remained secret until 1974, but the general drift of its argument became publicly known in 1950 after President Truman had announced that work on the development of a hydrogen bomb would be continued. In the public statements as well as in the secret debates of the early 1950s, the phrase "unlimited destructive power" constantly recurs. The peculiar horror of the hydrogen bomb was seen to be the fact that its cost would be almost independent of its size. Once you had built a workable bomb, you could increase its destructive power without limit by adding deuterium fuel, which would cost about sixty cents a kiloton at 1950 prices. The cost of adding the equivalent of another Hiroshima to the destructive power of a hydrogen bomb would be only about ten dollars.

The nightmare, which caused Conant and Oppenheimer to oppose the hydrogen bomb so passionately, was an arms race driven by the forces of economics and deliverability toward monstrously large bombs. They expected that each bomb would require a large investment of scarce and expensive tritium to ignite it, so that no country could afford many such bombs. Economics would then dictate that each bomb be fueled with a huge quantity of cheap deuterium to justify the initial investment. The bombs would then become so large that they could barely be carried in airplanes; Oppenheimer remarked in a letter to Conant shortly before the 1949 committee meeting: "I am not sure the miserable thing will work, nor that it can be gotten to a target except by oxcart." The problem of deliverability would then dictate that the bombs be installed in submarines or surface ships and detonated offshore, devastating great areas of country with tidal waves and radioactive fallout. But then the installation of shore defenses would force the bomb designers to move the point of detonation farther out to sea, and the bombs would have to be made still larger to do the same damage from a greater distance. The vicious cycle of the arms race would then continue, bombs growing less deliverable as they became bigger, and growing bigger as they became less deliverable. The only end to such an arms race would be bombs the size of submarines, each having a yield of many thousands of megatons. The cheapness of deuterium makes the construction of such bombs technically and economically feasible. They were called "gigaton mines" by the people who worried about them in the 1950s. A gigaton is the technical term for a thousand megatons. The construction of gigaton mines would indeed be, in Conant's words, "a threat to the future of the human race which is intolerable."

This nightmare produced a literary response which has continued to reverberate ever since. In 1957, only two years before his death, the novelist Nevil Shute Norway published *On the Beach*, a description of mankind wiped out by radiological warfare. Norway's poignant translation of apocalyptic disaster into the everyday voices of real people caught the imagination of the world. His book became an international best-seller and was made into a successful film. The book and the film created an enduring myth, a myth which entered consciously or subconsciously into all subsequent thinking about nuclear war. The myth pictures nuclear war as silent inexorable death from which there is no escape, radioactive cobalt sweeping slowly down the sky from the northern to the southern hemisphere. The people in Australia, after the rest of the world is dead, live out their lives quietly and bravely to the end. There is no hope of survival; there is no talk of building an underground Noah's Ark to keep earth's creatures alive until the cobalt should have decayed. Twenty-five years before Jonathan Schell, Nevil Shute imagined the human species calmly acquiescing in its own extinction.

The myth of *On the Beach*, like Jonathan Schell's myth, is technically flawed in many ways. Almost all the details are wrong: radioactive cobalt would not substantially increase the lethality of large hydrogen bombs; fallout would not descend uniformly over large areas but would fall sporadically in space and time; people could protect themselves from the radioactivity by sheltering under a few feet of dirt; and the war is supposed to happen in 1961, too soon for even the most malevolent country to have acquired the megatonnage needed to give a lethal dose of radiation to the entire earth. Nevertheless, the myth did what Norway intended it to do. On the fundamental human level, in spite of all the technical inaccuracies, it spoke truth. It told the world, in language that everyone could understand, that nuclear war means death. And the world listened.

If the hydrogen bomb had led to an arms race of the kind which Conant and Oppenheimer most feared, with undeliverable bombs growing bigger and bigger until they became gigaton mines, then the scenario of *On the Beach* might ultimately have come close to reality. Gigaton mines could, one way or another, make our planet uninhabitable. This is the truth which Norway's story brought home to mankind. And it is a truth which we must never forget.

Gigaton mines were also in Herman Kahn's mind when he published his book *On Thermonuclear War* in 1960. In that book he created a new myth, the Doomsday Machine, which was intended to be a *reductio ad absurdum* of the idea of deterrence. The Doomsday Machine is a device designed to deter nuclear war with absolute certainty by making the cost of aggression infinite. It is the final theoretical step in an arms race which begins with hydrogen bombs and runs in the direction of gigaton mines. Let Herman Kahn describe it in his own words:

A Doomsday weapons system might be imaginatively, and entirely hypothetically, described as follows: Assume that for, say, ten billion dollars we could build a device whose only function is to destroy all human life. The device is protected from enemy action, perhaps by being put thousands of feet underground, and then connected to a computer which is in turn connected, by a reliable communication system, to hundreds of sensory devices all over the United States. The computer would then be programmed so that if, say, five nuclear bombs exploded over the United States, the device would be triggered and the earth destroyed. . . .

Table 29 lists some desirable characteristics of a deterrent. 1.

Frightening. 2. Inexorable. 3. Persuasive. 4. Cheap. 5. Non-accident-prone. 6. Controllable. As far as the first five characteristics are concerned, . . . Doomsday Machines are likely to be better than any current or proposed competitor for deterrence. . . . The difficulties lie in item 6. . . . The Doomsday Machine is not sufficiently controllable. Even though it maximizes the probability that deterrence will work, . . . it is totally unsatisfactory. One must still examine the consequences of a failure. In this case a failure kills too many people and kills them too automatically. . . .

I have been surprised at the unanimity with which the notion of the unacceptability of a Doomsday Machine is greeted. I used to be wary of discussing the concept for fear that some colonel would get out a General Operating Requirement or Development Planning Objective for the device, but it seems that I need not have worried. Except by some scientists and engineers who have overemphasized the single objective of maximizing the effectiveness of deterrence, the device is universally rejected. It just does not look professional to senior military officers, and it looks even worse to senior civilians. The fact that more than a few scientists and engineers do seem attracted to the idea is disquieting, but as long as the development project is expensive, even these dedicated experts are unlikely to get one under way.

Herman Kahn's *On Thermonuclear War* may have been a classic, but it was not a best-seller. His historical erudition and ironic style were not designed to appeal to a wide audience. The public learned about Doomsday Machines through the art of Stanley Kubrick, whose film *Dr. Strangelove or: How I Learned to Stop Worrying and Love the Bomb* presented Kahn's idea in the language of black comedy. Here is Soviet Ambassador De Sadeski, speaking to American President Muffley:

"A Doomsday Machine, gentlemen. That's what I said and that's what I meant. When it is detonated it will produce enough lethal radioactive fallout so within twelve months the surface of the earth will be as dead as the moon. . . . There were those of us who fought against it, but in the end we could not keep up in the Peace Race, the Space Race and the Arms Race. Our deterrent began to lack credibility. Our people grumbled for more nylons and lipsticks. Our Doomsday project cost us just a fraction of what we had been spending in just a single year. But the deciding factor was when we learned your country was working along similar lines, and we were afraid of a Doomsday Gap."

"That's preposterous. I've never approved anything like that."

"Our source was the *New York Times.* "

President Muffley turned to his Director of Weapons Research and Development. "Doctor Strangelove, do we have anything like this in the works?" Doctor Strangelove spoke with Germanic precision. He emphasized his point with abrupt movements of his right hand. "Mister President, under the authority granted to me as Director of Weapons Research and Development, I commissioned a study of this project by the Bland Corporation last year. Based on the findings of the report, my conclusion was that this idea was not a practical deterrent for reasons which at this moment must be all too obvious." . . . Strangelove turned so he looked directly at De Sadeski. "There is only one thing I don't understand, Mister Ambassador. The whole point of the Doomsday Machine is lost if you keep it a secret. Why didn't you tell the world?" De Sadeski turned away. He said quietly but distinctly, "It was to be announced at the Party Congress on Monday. As you know, the Premier loves surprises."

The end of the story is told in the epilogue: "Though the little-known planet Earth, remotely situated in another galaxy, is admittedly of mere academic interest to us today, we have presented this quaint comedy of galactic pre-history as another in our series, 'The Dead Worlds of Antiquity.' "

Meanwhile, on the real planet Earth, the arms race was proceeding in quite a different direction. For technical reasons which Conant and Oppenheimer in 1949 did not foresee, hydrogen bombs became smaller and smaller instead of larger and larger. The two factors, economics and deliverability, which in 1949 appeared likely to push the hydrogen bomb toward monstrously large sizes unexpectedly turned around and pushed the other way. First, in 1951 Teller and Ulam discovered a practical design for hydrogen bombs which would not require large quantities of tritium, and it rapidly became clear that hydrogen bombs would be cheap and easy to manufacture; the constraints of economics and tritium supply no longer forced hydrogen bombs to be few and large. Second, in 1954 a committee under the chairmanship of the mathematician John von Neumann examined the state of the art of rocketry and concluded that intercontinental ballistic missiles would provide a reliable means of delivery of hydrogen bombs to any target on earth. There was no longer any reason to think of the hydrogen bomb as an undeliverable monster which could only be detonated offshore. And since the cost of the rocket would be greater than the cost of the bomb, the peculiar rules of nuclear economics which make big bombs as cheap as small ones would no longer be relevant. When costs of rocket delivery are included, the normal rules of economics apply, and small bombs are substantially cheaper than big ones.

The first generation of hydrogen bombs which were tested in 1952 and 1954 had yields running from ten to fifteen megatons. They were, from a modern point of view, absurdly and inconveniently large. Looking back on them with the advantages of hindsight, one is at a loss to understand why they were built so large. Probably the reason is that they were a psychological holdover from the era of the superbomb. The people who designed them had spent many years struggling with the old pre-Ulam-Teller superbomb, the superbomb which Conant and Oppenheimer had so strongly disliked. The old superbomb was huge and cumbersome; it was usually described as having a yield a thousand times greater than the Hiroshima bomb. So the first hydrogen bombs were built huge and cumbersome, with thousand-times-Hiroshima yields, for the same reason that the first automobiles were built to look like horse carriages. By the time I paid my first visit to Los Alamos, in the summer of 1956, hydrogen bombs of the twenty-megaton class were already considered technologically obsolete; all the experts I spoke to were working on smaller bombs with lower yields. The big first-generation bombs were manufactured and stockpiled for a few years longer. But it is now many years since the last of them were withdrawn from active service, their nuclear ingredients refabricated and incorporated into smaller weapons.

A similar evolution seems to have occurred in the Soviet Union, even though Soviet weapons are generally more massive than ours and the pace of their development was slower. The Soviet bomb tests of 1961 were like our 1954 tests, a series of huge explosions, with many in the ten-megaton class and one with a yield of fifty-seven megatons. That fifty-seven-megaton bomb was the closest the world has yet come to a Doomsday Machine, although it was carefully designed to produce a relatively small quantity of fallout. After 1961, the Soviet weapons program has moved, less rapidly than ours

but just as steadily, toward lower yields. There is no evidence that
any bomb with a yield larger than twenty-five megatons was ever
made into an operational weapon. Their newest weapons, like ours,
are substantially smaller.

The race toward smaller bombs has been driven by three factors
which gradually became dominant in the 1960s and 1970s. First, as
the numbers of weapons on both sides increased, the military planners rapidly ran out of targets for huge bombs. There is not much
satisfaction, even for the most bloodthirsty general, in using ten
megatons to wipe out an airfield or a city when a tenth of a megaton
would do the job just as well. Second, the accuracy of missiles
improved dramatically. So long as missiles were inaccurate, with
aiming errors measured in miles, it made sense to use high-yield
weapons on small targets. As soon as the errors were reduced to a
small fraction of a mile, small targets could be attacked more effectively by accurate low-yield weapons than by inaccurate monsters.
Third and most important, new means of delivery were developed
which tilted the balance of costs decisively toward low-yield weapons. The new delivery systems were the cruise missile and the
MIRV (Multiple Independently-targeted Reentry Vehicle). The
cruise missile is a small pilotless airplane which can be carried in
large numbers by a manned bomber. The MIRV is a small ballistic
missile which can be carried in large numbers by a single booster
rocket. Both the cruise missile and the MIRV make it possible to
deliver low-yield weapons in large numbers accurately and cheaply.
As soon as cruise missiles and MIRVs are available, high-yield weapons rapidly become obsolete. The last high-yield weapons in the
United States arsenal are carried in our oldest vehicles, the manned
B-52 bombers and the Titan missiles. The bombers will soon be
converted from high-yield bombs to low-yield cruise missiles. And
the only reason the Titans are not converted to low-yield MIRV
warheads is that they are too old and too few to justify the effort of
manufacturing a special MIRV system to fit them.

The arms race has thus led to the paradoxical result that, at least
as far as United States forces are concerned, the hydrogen bomb has
become almost irrelevant. The precise meaning of this statement is
as follows. Suppose that in 1949 the hopes of Conant and Oppenheimer had been fully realized, that President Truman had decided
to accept their recommendation not to build hydrogen bombs, that
a solemn treaty had been signed by the United States and the Soviet

Union and the other nuclear powers banning the building of hydrogen bombs, that the treaty had been ratified and faithfully observed by all parties; and suppose that no other disarmament agreements had been concluded going beyond those which exist in the real world: then the weapons deployed by the United States in that hypothetical world without hydrogen bombs would not have been noticeably different from those which we are now deploying. The technical reason for the irrelevance of hydrogen bombs is that, except in the large sizes which we are now phasing out, the costs and performance of modern fission bombs and modern hydrogen bombs are essentially the same. Conant and Oppenheimer were right in saying that the hydrogen bomb had little military value and that the continued development of fission weapons was strategically more important. Thirty years later, the United States military establishment, after rejecting and bitterly resenting their advice, has been pushed by the logic of the arms race into a position close to theirs. The essence of the Conant-Oppenheimer doctrine was that superbombs with multimegaton yields were not only immoral but militarily uninteresting. Thirty years ago, this doctrine was a subversive heresy. Now, thanks to the cruise missile and the MIRV, heresy has become orthodoxy. The same Strategic Air Command which clamored so loudly for the big bombs thirty years ago is now quietly withdrawing them from service.

There is a curious similarity between the history of the hydrogen bomb and the history of commercial nuclear power. In both cases, a new technical development became the center of a passionate controversy, with exaggerated hopes on one side and exaggerated fears on the other. In both cases, the protagonists of the new technology won the initial battles and enthusiastically pushed ahead to the construction of bombs and power stations of the largest feasible size. In both cases, the big units turned out to be inconvenient and uneconomical. In both cases, the advantages and the dangers of the new technology turned out in the end to be smaller than the protagonists and antagonists had claimed. The hydrogen bomb and nuclear power stations are not, as they were once thought to be, the driving forces of history. History has, in its ironic and unpredictable way, passed them by.

The obsolescence of the hydrogen bomb was not achieved without cost. The cost of getting rid of the big bombs was a large increase in the numbers of small ones. We must never allow ourselves to forget that the word "small" is here used only in a comparative sense. A typical modern "small" strategic weapon will have a yield of a tenth of a megaton, seven times the yield of the Hiroshima bomb. Such weapons are "small" in comparison with the monsters they replaced, but they are still big enough to destroy people and buildings over an area of many square miles. Opinions differ as to whether a large number of smaller weapons is more or less dangerous than a smaller number of large weapons. One fact which speaks in favor of small weapons is that the replacement of one large weapon by a cluster of small ones has resulted in a substantial decrease in total megatonnage. For example, the single-warhead Minuteman missile with a yield of one megaton was replaced by a three-warhead MIRV with a total yield of half a megaton. The B-52 bomber which used to carry bombs with a total yield of twenty megatons will soon be carrying cruise missiles with a total yield of about four megatons. When the conversion of bombers to cruise missiles is complete, the total megatonnage of the United States strategic forces will be less than half what it was ten years ago. This will remain true, even if the contribution from the new MX missiles which may be deployed during the next ten years is added in. Similar large reductions in megatonnage are occurring at a slower pace in the Soviet strategic forces.

From the point of view of mankind as a whole, the shift from large to small weapons with the concomitant decrease in total megatonnage was a significant step in the direction of sanity. Large weapons are worse for mankind than small ones, because, while the local military effects of a nuclear attack are roughly proportional to the number of weapons, the long-range fallout and the global effects are more nearly proportional to the total megatonnage. When the nuclear powers replaced large weapons with small ones, they increased the intended damage they could do to each other and decreased the unintended damage to the rest of mankind.

The central paradox of the arms race is the discrepancy between public perception and reality. The public perceives the arms race as giving birth to an endless stream of weapons of ever-increasing destructiveness and ever-increasing danger. The reality is more complicated. In the 1950s there was indeed a race to produce weapons of mass destruction, to assert technological superiority by exploding the largest possible firecracker. But that race came to an end with the Soviet fifty-seven-megaton explosion in 1961. Since then the arms race has been running strongly in other directions, away from weapons of mass destruction toward weapons of high precision. While bomb technology has stagnated, there have been three successive revolutions in the technology of computers and information handling. The computer revolutions made possible the accurate delivery of small weapons, non-nuclear as well as nuclear. One consequence of the computer revolutions has been the replacement of big hydrogen bombs by the MIRV and the cruise missile. Another consequence has been the appearance of accurate non-nuclear missiles. The computer revolutions are not yet over. If the arms race continues in the same direction, toward cheaper and more capable non-nuclear technology, then there is a chance we may see not only hydrogen bombs but nuclear weapons of all kinds gradually becoming obsolete.

It would be absurd to claim that technological development by itself could rid the world of nuclear weapons. The two primary agents for abolishing nuclear weapons must be international negotiation and the aroused conscience of mankind. But the success of negotiation and moral indignation in bringing about nuclear disarmament will also depend upon technical factors. We will have a far better chance of achieving nuclear disarmament if the weapons to be discarded are generally perceived to be not only immoral and dangerous but also obsolescent. An intelligently conducted arms race, leaving nuclear technology further and further behind, could help mightily to sweep nuclear weapons into the dustbin of history.

Up to the year 1982, six countries had acquired nuclear status: the United States, the Soviet Union, Britain, France, China, and India. It was certainly true in the first four cases, and possibly true in all six, that scientists rather than generals took the initiative in getting nuclear weapons programs started. In each case of which we have knowledge, scientists were motivated to build weapons by feelings of professional pride as well as of patriotic duty. The construction of a bomb was a technical challenge which aroused their fiercest competitive instincts. In each case, the scientists felt themselves to be in competition with the scientists of some other country. The Americans at Los Alamos, imagining a nonexistent bomb project in Germany, were in competition with the Germans. The Russians were in competition with the Americans. The British, after having contributed substantially to the wartime effort at Los Alamos, were ungraciously pushed out as soon as the war was over;

this made the British scientists angry and roused them to prove that the British could make just as good bombs as the Americans. The French, who had contributed substantially to the wartime effort in Canada, were likewise pushed out and likewise angry; the French scientists were determined to show that they could do as well as the British. It is no great exaggeration to say that the British and French programs were driven by the professional pique of scientists rather than by a careful consideration of strategic needs. The same thing might also be said of the American hydrogen bomb program. The nuclear arms race from 1940 to 1960 was powerfully reinforced by the professional ambitions of scientists who saw nuclear weapons technology as a grand arena for the exercise of their talents. The walls of official secrecy which surrounded these exercises made professional rivalries more intense and gave a false glamour to the new technology.

But now no more. During the years from 1960 to 1980, the walls of secrecy came tumbling down. Since 1964, anybody who wanted to know the general principles of fission weapon design could find them explained by Robert Serber in the declassified *Los Alamos Primer*. Since 1979, anybody who wanted to know how hydrogen bombs work could refer to Howard Morland's article in the November 1979 issue of *The Progressive*. Nuclear weapons design has been stripped of its mysteries, and there is no longer any scientific glory attached to it. Since the essential knowledge has become public, nobody with pretensions to be considered a serious scientist finds professional fulfillment in proving that he can design a bomb as competently as the Americans. From now on, there will be no more first-rate scientists driving the nuclear arms race with their rivalries. Even in scientifically backward countries, young people of talent now know that nuclear weapons have ceased to be a scientific challenge.

It is probably no coincidence that the nuclear club ceased to expand at the same time as nuclear secrets ceased to be secret. Twenty years ago, many of us were predicting that by 1980 the nuclear club would have grown to at least a dozen members. We have been pleasantly surprised to see only one new member overtly join the club since 1964. And the Indian entry into the club has been only a token entry, probably because the Indian scientists have been wise enough not to push their weapons program ahead with excessive enthusiasm. Nuclear weapons proliferation has slowed down noticeably since scientists all over the world became aware that weapons design is a scientific backwater. It is possible that the next ten years will bring a big new wave of accessions to the club. But it is also possible that the tide has turned, that after the leading scientists have lost interest in promoting nuclear weaponry, the generals and the politicians will lose interest in it too.

There are many different ways in which one may try to discourage nuclear proliferation. One way is to negotiate nonproliferation treaties. Another way is to establish nuclear-free zones. Another way is to place embargoes on the export of nuclear apparatus to countries which are unwilling to submit their nuclear activities to international inspection. Another way is to organize political opposition to commercial nuclear power stations. Another way is to sabotage or demolish by air attack facilities which are believed to be incipient nuclear weapons projects. All these ways have been tried, and all have been partially successful. But all of them have the disadvantage of treating symptoms rather than the underlying disease. The only way to cure the underlying disease is to extinguish desire for nuclear weapons. To extinguish desire, it is necessary to convince political leaders that possession of nuclear weapons brings trouble and danger rather than strength and safety. Most of the rulers of non-nuclear countries were wise enough to learn this lesson long ago. For those who are not yet convinced that nuclear weapons are more trouble than they are worth, the arms race itself may be a good teacher. After the experience of the past thirty-five years, every government contemplating entry into the nuclear club must be aware that the club demands more than a down payment, that after the first euphoria of a successful test explosion comes an unending commitment to delivery systems and modernization programs which are far more expensive than the bombs themselves. In the end, the miseries and burdens which the nuclear arms race imposes upon the nuclear powers may be the most effective deterrent in dissuading others from walking into the same trap.

So the arms race remains, as it has always been, a bundle of paradoxes, a Pandora's box with hope at the bottom. On the one hand, it is a monstrously wasteful and mindless outpouring of resources for destructive ends. On the other hand, it sets limits to destruction and opposes brute force with discrimination and intelligence. It made superbombs possible and it made them obsolete. It made nuclear weapons cheap and it made the means of their delivery expensive. It made big countries overwhelmingly strong and it made them powerless to fight one another. Many people believe that "stopping the arms race" would lead us to a more stable and peaceful world. Perhaps they are right, perhaps not. The arms race is a tool which can be used for either good or evil purposes. To stop it altogether may be a worthy long-range goal. But our more urgent need is to guide the arms race intelligently, to use it, in conjunction with moral outrage and diplomatic negotiation, to hasten the obsolescence and retirement of weapons of mass destruction.

4

David and Goliath

And there went out a champion out of the camp of the Philistines, named Goliath, of Gath, whose height was six cubits and a span. And he had an helmet of brass upon his head, and he was armed with a coat of mail; and the weight of the coat was five thousand shekels of brass. . . .

And the Philistine said to David, Come to me, and I will give thy flesh unto the fowls of the air, and to the beasts of the field. . . .

And David put his hand in his bag, and took thence a stone, and slang it, and smote the Philistine in his forehead, that the stone sunk into his forehead; and he fell upon his face to the earth.

The story of David with his slingshot slaying the clumsy giant has delighted children for three thousand years. David was an early example of a common type of folk hero, the boy who fights with skill and daring against superior force and wins. Some time before David's triumph in the valley of Elah, Odysseus was in Sicily winning his battle of wits against the Cyclops. Similar stories are found in the folklore of nations all over the world.

A modern version of the same story might run as follows: One fine day, out of a blue sky, a monster ballistic missile carrying a megaton warhead comes falling toward its target at a speed of three miles per second. Five minutes before the missile is due to arrive, a little rocket weighing a few pounds goes up from the ground to meet it. The little rocket carries no warhead and does not move very fast. It carries only a telescope and a microcomputer and an accurate servosystem to bring it onto the missile's track. The missile crashes into the rocket at three miles a second, at which speed the rocket tears through the warhead and rips it apart. The missile is destroyed by its own speed; the rocket has to do nothing except to be there at the right place at the right time. The dead missile falls upon its face to the earth.

This little story might come true, at some experimental missile-testing range, with the megaton warhead replaced by a suitable dummy. It might happen at an American range, or at a Soviet range, or both. Let us suppose for the sake of the story that it happens at an American range. Then the experiment does not remain secret for long. Films of the encounter appear on television. There are articles in *Aviation Week* describing the event and making exaggerated claims for the effectiveness of the interceptor. There are articles in more sober magazines, pointing out that a successful demonstration of an interception of a single missile over a test range does not prove the feasibility of non-nuclear defense against a real attack by hundreds or thousands of missiles. Experts testify before congressional committees that the development of non-nuclear interceptors is a waste of money, that the staging of the test interception is a propaganda exercise calculated to deceive the public. But the public is not deceived. The public understands well enough the difference between a test interception and an operational defense. The public also understands, better perhaps than the technical experts, that the test interception is an event of some importance.

A successful David-and-Goliath experiment, with a two-pound rocket killing an intercontinental missile, even under the artificial conditions of a test range, could be a historical turning point. It could mark the beginning of a change in the way people think about nuclear weapons. It would show nuclear weapons in a new light, as clumsy brutish things outwitted by a cheaper and more agile adversary. The death of Goliath could be the death of an era, the end of the unquestioned technical supremacy of nuclear weapons. It would make clear to everybody that we have a choice, either to continue relying on the old technology of nuclear weapons, or to switch our emphasis to the newer and more versatile technology of sensors and computers. The victory of the two-pound interceptor could be a signal to the world that nuclear weapons are at last on their way down, that the complete abolition of nuclear weapons is technically thinkable.

The point of the David-and-Goliath story is not that David will always win. On the contrary, it is easy to imagine Goliath winning if he uses suitable countermeasures against David's tactics—for example, by redesigning his helmet of brass so that it covers his vulnerable forehead more effectively. The point of the story is that David won once, and that was enough to make Goliath a laughingstock for three thousand years. After Goliath's defeat, giants no longer commanded respect. After the technological supremacy of nuclear weapons has once been challenged, their moral and political unattractiveness will stand revealed clearly to the eyes of the world.

Another modern version of the David legend would put a bomber airplane or a cruise missile in the role of Goliath. David would again be a small agile rocket with the ability to intercept and kill by direct impact. David's task in this case would be technically more demanding, because bombers and cruise missiles do not fly straight. Again, David will not always win, but if he is small enough and cheap enough, he can make his enemies look like blundering fools.

A third variation on the David-and-Goliath theme could be staged in the ocean. In this version of the story, Goliath is a billion-dollar nuclear submarine carrying long-range missiles with enough warheads to destroy a whole country. David is a little mechanical suckerfish, programmed to attach itself to the skin of a submarine, imitating the remora suckerfish, which attach themselves by suction to the skins of sharks. David lurks in the water until Goliath approaches, then swoops down and quietly sucks. Once attached to Goliath, David computes his exact location and is ready to transmit this information to headquarters, either at predetermined times or upon demand. The trick of using suckerfish to catch submarines is not a modern invention. It has been known to the Australian aborigines of Cape York since time immemorial. The aborigines used the trick with captive suckerfish (gapu) to catch sea turtles. "The same gapu will catch three or four turtle," reports a nineteenth-century observer. "When they have brought it up, they take the gapu off and put it out to catch another."

This story of the suckerfish raises troublesome questions. Both the United States and the Soviet Union have invested enormous resources in their fleets of missile-carrying submarines. The strategic doctrine of the United States relies heavily on the ability of submarines to remain undetected. According to the orthodox doctrine of deterrence, the undetectability of submarines provides our strongest guarantee of strategic stability; so long as we have a major part of our offensive force securely concealed in the ocean, nobody can hope to gain any decisive advantage from an attack on our more vulnerable land-based forces. Conversely, if submarines become detectable, the existence of stable deterrence is endangered and the peace of the world becomes precarious. This is the orthodox doctrine which has guided United States policies for the last twenty years. Many of our experts in arms control believe so firmly in this doctrine that they look to the missile-carrying submarine as a uniquely benign form of strategic armament. Whether or not we agree with the official doctrine, we must recognize that the missile submarine has many technical and political advantages. The loss of submarine invulnerability would force us to make radical changes in our strategic assumptions. In short, the story of the suckerfish may be not merely troublesome but dangerous. Perhaps it is irresponsible of me to mention it as a possibility.

What can I say in defense of the suckerfish? I will say three things. First, the story is only a story. So far as I know, no such animal exists, even as a diagram on the desk of an inventor. I tell the story only as an example of the consequences which the technology of microcomputers may bring to military operations in the ocean as well as on land. Second, I am not suggesting that anybody should attempt to attach suckerfish to operational Soviet submarines; this would indeed be a highly provocative and dangerous thing to do. Third, it would take enormous numbers of suckerfish distributed over huge areas of ocean to ensure that all missile-carrying submarines were located; such a massive deployment of mechanical fish could not be carried out quickly, cheaply, or secretly; the technology of suckerfish is not about to take the world by surprise. But after these disclaimers have been made, it remains true that the technology of suckerfish, or some similar non-nuclear technology, could in the long run put an end to the popularity of missile-carrying submarines. For David to defeat the submarines, it would not be necessary for him to locate all the submarines all the time. He needs only to throw serious doubt upon the ability of submarines to remain concealed. If submarines cannot rely on concealment, the military advantage of using them as missile carriers disappears. A successful demonstration of suckerfish technology would reveal the missile-carrying submarine for what it is, a vulnerable Goliath carrying far too many lethal eggs in one fragile basket.

When mankind decides, as I believe we must ultimately decide, that missile-carrying submarines are intolerably dangerous, the task of eliminating them will be carried through sooner or later, with or without the help of suckerfish. The task will be made easier if the military virtues of submarines have already been discredited. A robust technology of submarine location will allow an international agreement banning sea-based missiles to be effectively monitored. As always, the primary requirement for carrying through any act of nuclear disarmament is the political will to do so, but the formation of such a will can be powerfully helped by a technological development deliberately aimed toward making nuclear weapons unattractive.

Let me now return from fantasies to facts. There exists a vigorous and rapidly advancing area of military technology known as precision guided munitions or PGM. PGM are small accurate missiles with non-nuclear warheads, mainly designed to kill tanks or airplanes. They are of many kinds, some small enough to be fired by infantry soldiers, others carried in armored cars, helicopters, airplanes, and ships. They were first seen in action on a large scale in the 1973 Middle East war, when PGM supplied by the Soviet Union to Egypt and Syria caused heavy losses to Israeli tank forces. Since 1973 the technology of PGM has been pushed much further, not only in the Soviet Union and in the United States but in other countries too. Experts disagree concerning the extent to which PGM have revolutionized land warfare. Some say that PGM will defeat tanks in the 1980s as decisively as airplanes defeated battleships in World War II. Others say that tanks will still survive provided that they are supported by friendly PGM and infantry. Nobody doubts that PGM have put an end to the era in which tank armies won easy victories.

The existing PGM technology fits well into the David-and-Goliath tradition. The PGM themselves are light and agile and comparatively cheap; the tanks which they destroy are heavy and clumsy and expensive. The PGM exploit the new technology of accurate sensors and servos and computers; the tanks are stuck with the old technology of armor and guns. The PGM are likely to prevail in the end because they are more cost-effective. But there is always a chance that PGM will fail, especially if the people who design them succumb to the temptation to improve them until they become as complicated and expensive as tanks.

The emergence of PGM technology has raised questions of fundamental importance for the feasibility of nuclear disarmament. Can PGM be an effective substitute for tactical nuclear weapons? Is it possible to use PGM as the basis for a credible non-nuclear defense of Western Europe? In answering these questions, it must be said at the outset that the success of PGM in stopping a Soviet tank army from rolling across Germany cannot be guaranteed. Effective use of PGM requires large numbers of competent and brave soldiers. If equipment alone could guarantee a successful defense, France would not have been overrun by a numerically inferior force of German tanks in 1940. Warfare is always a gamble, for the defenders as well as for the attackers. It makes no sense to demand that PGM provide a defense with zero risk of failure. The question we should be asking is whether the risks of a PGM defense would be smaller than the risks of our present reliance on tactical nuclear weapons. This question cannot yet be answered with certainty, but there are strong reasons to believe the answer will be affirmative.

The chief virtue of tactical nuclear weapons is that they make a European war unthinkable and allow the Europeans to avoid worrying seriously about defense. So far as Germany is concerned, the tactical weapons are almost the equivalent of a Doomsday Machine; in case of any major trouble, Germany is destroyed almost automatically. Like a Doomsday Machine, the nuclear weapons bring stability and tranquillity to the political life of Europe, and save us a great deal of money which would otherwise have to be spent on non-nuclear armaments. Sudden withdrawal of the nuclear weapons would be politically upsetting and militarily risky. Nevertheless, the argument which Herman Kahn used against his Doomsday Machine applies with equal force against tactical nuclear weapons; they are not acceptable as a permanent solution of the problem of European security because a failure of the system kills too many people and kills them too automatically. In the long run, the risks of a PGM defense are smaller. The problem is how to manage the transition from nuclear to non-nuclear defense without running into worse risks in the intermediate stages.

It is not likely that the denuclearization of Europe can be achieved by substituting PGM for tactical nuclear weapons directly. The substitution will probably come about indirectly, through a sequence of preliminary steps. One preliminary step might be a partial replacement of tanks by PGM in the Warsaw Pact forces as the Soviet authorities become aware that tanks are no longer cost-effective. Another intermediate step might be a negotiated trade-off of Soviet tanks against NATO nuclear weapons. A third step might be an agreement to eliminate the remaining tactical nuclear weapons on both sides. It is easy to invent other possible sequences of steps leading to nuclear disarmament. The essential point is that the decisive last step, the agreement to get rid of the nuclear weapons, will be made much easier by the preliminary downgrading of tank forces in response to PGM development.

If the elimination of tactical nuclear weapons proceeds in this indirect fashion, we are not at any stage left in a situation where the existing Soviet tank armies are in Central Europe and only a few NATO soldiers with PGM stand between them and the Rhine. Instead, we have a situation in which tank armies on both sides diminish as PGM become more capable. Our aim must be to achieve simultaneously the withdrawal of nuclear weapons and the obsolescence of tank armies. It is important to understand that this program cannot succeed if only the Western armies deploy PGM. A heavy Soviet investment in PGM is also essential. In other words, if we want to free both East and West from addiction to tactical nuclear weapons, the best way may be to engage both sides in a PGM arms race.

The mathematician John von Neumann played a leading part in the development of nuclear weapons and an even larger part in the development of computers. He said in 1946, when both these developments were just beginning, that the computers would be more important than the bombs. The impact which computers have made upon civilian society has already proved him right. And now the advent of PGM promises to prove him right in the military sphere also.

The computer revolution transforms war into a contest of information rather than of brute force. It enables small cheap devices with brains to overwhelm big expensive vehicles. It favors David against Goliath. At sea, aircraft carriers become vulnerable to small boats carrying torpedoes or cruise missiles. On land and in the air, tanks and airplanes become vulnerable to PGM. In space, it is no longer absurd to imagine smart little non-nuclear rockets killing nuclear missiles. In all four places, the computer revolution is chipping away at the supremacy of nuclear weapons, providing the technological foundations for a world in which weapons of human scale and purpose take the place of weapons of mass destruction.

Another hopeful aspect of the computer revolution is that it tends in the long run to shift the balance of forces away from offensive and toward defensive weapons. The qualifying phrase "in the long run" is here essential; two of the first fruits of the computer revolution were the cruise missile and the MIRV, two weapons which further strengthened the supremacy of the offensive. But in the long run, as war becomes increasingly a contest of information rather than of firepower, defense becomes easier and attack more difficult. Already today the effects of PGM in land warfare are favorable to defense. In land warfare, offensive units must be mobile and visible, hence vulnerable to PGM, while defensive units can be concealed and relatively invulnerable. The fundamental reason why the computer revolution favors defense is that in a battle of information, the defenders fighting in their own territory can see what is happening better than the attackers fighting in exposed vehicles. Even in the strategic contest of missile against antimissile, the same principle should be valid in the long run. If the antimissiles are numerous enough and agile enough, they can destroy any missile which they can clearly see, and the defenders directing the antimissiles over their own territory will have a clearer view of the battle than the attackers sitting five thousand miles away.

The slow shift of technological advantage toward defense does not imply that a country will be able to survive a nuclear attack without catastrophic damage. It implies only that there will be some economic and strategic incentives for transferring resources from offensive to defensive deployments. Defensive technology cannot by itself ensure our survival. But it can give useful support to the political movements and arms control treaties which will finally put an end to the technology of mass destruction.

All through human history, military technology has appeared in two guises, with the face of Goliath and with the face of David. The contrast between the two faces of weaponry became sharper than ever with the advent of modern technology. Our century has provided spectacular demonstrations of Goliath and David in action. Many observers of the human situation, seeing what our technological Goliaths achieved in the two world wars and later in Vietnam, have come to believe that all modern weapons and military establishments are instruments of enslavement, natural enemies of the independent rational soul, and that a morally responsible person should have nothing whatever to do with them. Einstein expressed this view eloquently in his writings and in his actions. Yet one cannot begin to understand the deep involvement of American scientists in military technology if one does not examine the contrary view, that freedom and military inventiveness are natural allies.

John von Neumann was the most brilliant and the most articulate of the scientists who consciously devoted their talents to the improvement of weaponry in the cause of freedom. Von Neumann's generation saw free societies obliterated all over Europe, not by internal forces of oppression but by Hitler's armies. Freedom survived in England in 1940 because the technological Davids, the coastal radars and the fighter airplanes, were there when they were needed. Many people at that time believed that freedom's survival was made possible by the willingness of British and American scientists to apply their skills wholeheartedly to the problems of war. Even Einstein shared this belief in 1939 when he helped his friend Leo Szilard to launch the American nuclear energy enterprise. After Hiroshima, Einstein changed his mind, but the majority of American scientists did not. Their experience of World War II left behind it a widespread feeling that a permanent alliance between freedom and military science was right and proper. The alliance was evidently beneficial to both parties; a free society needed superior military technology to withstand the superior discipline of a totalitarian enemy, and the military establishment needed a free society to allow scientists and soldiers to work together in an informal and creative style which a totalitarian state could not match. In the context of the Soviet-American arms race, the free scientists of America carried a responsibility to stay ahead in the quality and variety of their inventions, so as to compensate for the larger military expenditures and the advantages of secrecy on the Soviet side. This picture of the arms race sounds naive and old-fashioned today, but it was dominant in von Neumann's thinking; it still flourishes in Israel and in the less sophisticated regions of America. For every scientist who believes with Einstein that modern weapons in the hands of modern governments are an absolute evil, there is another who believes with von Neumann that modern weapons rightly used can help David to survive in freedom in a world of Goliaths.

The root of the moral dilemma of our age lies in the fact that both Einstein's and von Neumann's viewpoints contain a large element of truth. Einstein was right in saying, "Mankind can gain protection against the danger of unimaginable destruction and wanton annihilation only if a supranational organization has alone the authority to produce or possess these weapons." Von Neumann was right in believing that the old political realities of national power and the old tribal imperatives of fighting for survival would remain essentially unchanged even in a world armed with hydrogen bombs. So long as nation-states continue to base their security on threats of general annihilation, there can be no escape from the moral dilemma. But a way of escape may lie open if nation-states can find military means which are effective both in defending tribal interests and in diminishing reliance on nuclear weapons. Each nation is exposed to two kinds of danger, the danger from particular international conflicts and the danger from nuclear weapons in general. An optimum strategy should be designed to deal with both dangers simultaneously. We should recognize explicitly in our military doctrine that our own reliance on nuclear weapons creates a threat to our security which is as serious as any external threat. This being accepted, the appropriate weapons to implement our military doctrine will be the weapons of David, weapons which are capable of defending territory without destroying it in the process. The way out of the moral dilemma is to demand that our weapons answer mankind's need for deliverance from nuclear threats as well as our tribal need for defense of our friends' territory.

All our military arrangements should be designed with two purposes in mind: the short-range purpose of discouraging aggressive countries from overrunning their neighbors, and the long-range purpose of achieving a gradual transition to a non-nuclear world. The two purposes are not incompatible. The weapons which are most effective in wars of local territorial defense are likely also to be helpful in the global political war against nuclear annihilation.

Einstein believed in no such compromises. He said, "I would unconditionally refuse all war service, direct or indirect, and would seek to persuade my friends to adopt the same position, regardless of how I might feel about the causes of any particular war." On another occasion he said, "I appeal to my fellow scientists to refuse to co-operate in research for war purposes." Perhaps he was right. Perhaps the hope of using non-nuclear technology to make nuclear weapons obsolete is an illusion. But the example of David keeps the hope alive.

Nobody can predict the future of technology over a long time scale. But it may be possible to make predictions which will be valid for a decade or two. It seems likely that the rapid development of microcomputer and sensor technology will result in a growing proliferation of sophisticated non-nuclear weapons of the kind which I described in my David stories at the beginning of this chapter. The dissemination of David weapons will cause armies to take a step back into an older, more professional style of warfare. The new weapons need elite, highly trained soldiers to use them effectively. They do not need the mass armies which provided the cannon fodder of the two world wars. The Falklands campaign of 1982 provides some additional evidence that the winds of change are blowing in this direction. The Argentine air force, a small elite force using precise weapons with daring and skill, did great damage to the invading forces, while the Argentine army, a mass army of conscripts, was crushingly defeated. It seems that modern technology is taking us back toward the eighteenth century, toward the era when small professional armies fought small professional wars.

How lucky it would be for humanity if the new David weapons were to make obsolete both of the two great monstrosities of the twentieth century: the nuclear mass-destruction weapons and the great cannon-fodder armies! That would be an unbelievable stroke of luck, as if David were to slay two Goliaths with one stone. History teaches us not to expect such luck, and common sense teaches us not to rely on it. Nevertheless, the obsolescence and ultimate abolition of nuclear weapons and mass armies is a worthy political goal which we should strive to reach by all available means. The technology of David weapons is only one of the available means, and probably not the most important, for reaching this goal. If the David weapons can help even slightly to make the goal politically attainable, they will have served a useful purpose. What the world needs in order to be saved is not technological magic but a rebirth of hope.

5

Technical Follies

The most effective weapons are usually simple. Once in a while, advanced technology gives rise to new weapons which are simple and effective. For example, the decisive victories of the German army in the early years of World War II were largely due to a simple technical innovation. General Guderian added a radio and a radio operator to each tank in his tank divisions. As Hermann Balck, one of Guderian's tank commanders, reported forty years later: "This allowed both small and large tank units to be commanded and maneuvered with a swiftness and flexibility that no other army was able to match. As a result, our tanks were able to defeat tanks that were quite superior in firepower and armor." But Balck also reports proudly that he himself had the foresight, before the beginning of the war, to buy for German army reconnaissance units the mules which the British army was then selling at bargain prices. The British were mechanizing their army and believed that mules were obsolete, old-fashioned, unsuited to the conditions of modern warfare. Balck knew better. His secondhand mules performed splendidly as long as the supply lasted. "As the war progressed," he reports, "the infantry divisions simply didn't get any reconnaissance units at all, mostly for lack of equipment. . . . And of course, the mules were running out, too."

Professional soldiers, especially those with experience of land warfare, look with a skeptical eye at the claims of technology to solve military problems. They know that technology sometimes helps. The jeep, after all, proved in the end to be a better reconnaissance vehicle than the mule. But soldiers have a well-justified distrust of technological gadgets which come accompanied by exaggerated promises. Precision guided munitions are a case in point. It is all very well for an armchair strategist like me to sing the praises of precision guided munitions, to describe how they will revolutionize warfare, to call them by the poetic name of David weapons. The professional soldier asks merely, "Will the damned things work?"

Precision guided munitions come in many shapes and sizes. Some of them are already battle-tried; those unquestionably work, until the enemy finds an effective countermeasure. Some of them are in process of development, having the electronic and mechanical bugs shaken out of them. Others are still only gleams in the eye of the inventor. It is not to be expected that all of them will be successful. For them to fulfill their promise, it is only necessary that a few of the many available designs turn out to be effective, rugged, and cheap, like Guderian's radios and Balck's mules. The development of precision guided munitions is a constant seesaw between two opposing trends. On the one hand, the technology of weapon components, of microcomputers and sensors and memory units and software, improves from year to year in cheapness and reliability. On the other hand, as the components improve, the designs of the overall weapon systems tend to become more elaborate and expensive. If the tendency of designers to improve and embellish is not held in check, precision guided munitions may become one more item in the long list of technical follies which overenthusiastic engineers have inflicted on soldiers throughout the long history of warfare.

The first technical folly which I encountered in my career as a military expert was a system called AGLT, automatic gun-laying turrets. This was in 1944. The British Bomber Command, suffering heavy losses in night operations over Germany, had appealed for help to the engineers in our weapons research establishments. We knew that the main cause of bomber losses was the German night fighters. We knew that the majority of bombers were shot down in surprise attacks before the gunners in the bomber's gun turrets had a chance to see the fighter. Our research engineers came up with a magnificent technical solution to this problem. AGLT was a gun turret combined with a high-performance search-and-track radar and a gyroscopic gun sight which automatically compensated for the motion of the aircraft. The radar could detect and track a fighter well beyond visual range. The information from the radar was fed through the gun sight to a servosystem which aimed the turret and the guns. All the gunner had to do was wait until the fighter came to an appropriate distance, still beyond visual range, and then pull the trigger. The system was installed in a bomber and tested against pilotless drone targets in trials over England. It worked brilliantly. Drones venturing within half a mile of the bomber were shot down more reliably by the AGLT at night than by the gunner using his eyes to aim the guns in daylight. The problem of the German night fighters was solved. The Ministry of Aircraft Production launched a crash program with the highest priority, to mass-produce AGLT and install it in the operational squadrons of Bomber Command. As a result of heroic efforts, the modified bombers were coming off the production lines in 1944, and were beginning to appear in the squadrons, when I was called in to help prepare plans for their operational use.

AGLT had one little snag. Before it could be used on operations, the whole of Bomber Command had to be equipped with an IFF system (Identification Friend or Foe), which would stop the AGLT bombers from shooting down other bombers which happened to come within range. Bombers already carried a radio IFF system which was supposed to stop friendly antiaircraft gunners on the ground from shooting at them, but we had learned by bitter experience that the radio IFF was only about 90 percent effective. From my knowledge of the densities of bomber streams and the frequency of interceptions during operations over Germany, I calculated that on the average, if AGLT was allowed to fire blind without either visual or IFF identification of the target, we would shoot down four hundred times as many bombers as fighters. If the existing 90 percent effective IFF was used for identification, we would still shoot down forty bombers for each fighter. When this difficulty was understood, the Ministry of Aircraft Production launched a second crash program, to produce and install in the bombers a brand-new IFF system using coded infrared transmitters and receivers. The performance of the new IFF was disappointing; it turned out to be only about 95 percent effective under operational conditions. That meant that if we relied on it, we would still shoot down twenty bombers for each fighter. Frantic efforts were made to improve the IFF and the training of the crews who had to operate it. But the highest performance that was ever achieved fell short of 99 percent reliability. If the IFF could have been made 99 percent reliable over the whole bomber force, AGLT aircraft using it for identification would have destroyed only four bombers for each fighter.

At that point, Bomber Command gave up the struggle. It was clear that AGLT could never be used as it had been intended to be used, to destroy fighters at long range. Gunners using AGLT could not be permitted to open fire without first seeing the target and counting its engines. After the huge efforts that had been expended in designing, producing, and deploying it, AGLT was only slightly better than a conventional gun sight. In the official British history of the strategic air offensive, the AGLT fiasco is concealed in a brief and inconspicuous footnote: "A new and remarkable device, the Automatic Gun-Laying Turret, known to Bomber Command as Village Inn, was under development. It automatically sighted and fired at enemy aircraft, but by the time of the German surrender it had been used on such a limited scale as to make no difference."

AGLT was a typical example of a common variety of technical folly. It is always tempting, when a new weapon performs well under the artificial conditions of a test firing, to rush it into production with the expectation that it will do equally well on the battlefield. The thing usually fails on the battlefield, not because it does not work technically, but because the criteria for being useful on the battlefield are different from the criteria of a test firing.

During the months when Bomber Command was struggling in vain to salvage something of value from AGLT, we were being bombarded by the Germans with their V-1 and V-2 missiles. We were delighted to see that the Germans were engaged in a salvage operation at least as hopeless as ours. The V-1 and V-2 missiles were technical follies, as useless as AGLT, and considerably more costly to the Germans than AGLT was to us. The Germans had expended irreplaceable resources in bringing these follies into mass production, without any realistic test of their operational effectiveness. In 1944, when the Allies invaded France, the Germans were compelled to use the missiles or lose them. They tried to salvage something from their investment by firing the missiles off in the general direction of London, and later in the direction of Antwerp. The only real benefit the Germans derived from this operation was that the Allies diverted to the bombing of V-1 and V-2 launch sites large numbers of airplanes which might otherwise have been bombing German trucks and trains.

But the V-1 and V-2 missiles were not the greatest technical follies of World War II. Considered on a larger scale, the whole strategic air offensive of Bomber Command against Germany was a technical folly too. The origins of the British bomber offensive go far back into history. Already in 1928, Sir Hugh Trenchard, founding father of the Royal Air Force and Chief of the Air Staff, wrote a memorandum for the Chiefs of Staff Subcommittee on the War Object of an Air Force. "I would state definitely," he wrote, "that in the view of the Air Staff the object to be sought by air action will be to paralyse from the very outset the enemy's productive centres of munitions of war of every sort and to stop all communications and transportation." Sir George Milne, the Army Chief of Staff, raised strong objections to Trenchard's statement. "As regards the ethical aspect of his proposals," Milne concluded, "it is for His Majesty's Government to accept or refuse a doctrine which, put into plain English, amounts to one which advocates unrestricted warfare against the civil population of one's enemy. On the military side I have demonstrated that it is clearly to our national disadvantage to subscribe to the policy he advocates, while the adoption of a doctrine by the Royal Air Force which is independent of that under which the other two services are trained to wage war will inevitably lead to their attempting to wage war independently. In war, concentration of effort alone can bring about success, and my main anxiety, after studying the Air Staff Memorandum, is lest the acceptance of the views advanced may lead us in exactly the opposite direction." The memoranda of Trenchard and Milne are classic statements of the arguments for and against the doctrine of strategic bombing. The Navy Chief of Staff added a shorter memorandum, concurring with Milne.

So far as the British government was concerned, Trenchard won the argument. He retired from the air force in 1929 but played the role of elder statesman for almost thirty years longer. His successors in the air force lived in his shadow and followed his policies. No political leader dared compel the air force to subordinate its strategic objectives to the plans of the army and navy. The Trenchard doctrine remained, from 1928 until the end of World War II and beyond, the official doctrine of the Royal Air Force. The strategic air offensive of Bomber Command was carried out according to Trenchard's plan.

After the bomber offensive had run its bloody course, after the six years of heroism and sacrifice were over, one could see in retrospect that all Trenchard's expectations had proved false and all Milne's expectations had proved true. Trenchard said in 1928, "paralyse from the very outset the enemy's productive centres." Bomber Command failed for five years to achieve this objective, succeeding only in the final months of the war, when Germany was already defeated and invaded by the Allied armies. Milne's fear that the pursuit of an independent air force strategy would damage the cohesion of British military operations proved abundantly justified. If the tremendous resources devoted to Bomber Command had been available to support the strategic objectives of the army and navy, we could have concentrated our efforts on the two campaigns which were strategically decisive, the invasion of France and the fight against the U-boats in the Atlantic. Bomber Command by itself absorbed about one quarter of the entire British war effort. All through the war the operations of the Allied armies were delayed and prolonged by our chronic shortage of ships. Had England decided at the beginning to build fewer bombers and more ships, we would probably have ended the war in Europe at least a year sooner.

Trenchard had been commander of the Royal Flying Corps in World War I. The Royal Flying Corps was a part of the British army; it worked under army directives in support of army operations. Trenchard was himself an army officer, and as commander of the Royal Flying Corps he waged war brilliantly in the style recommended by Sir George Milne, subordinating his strategic objectives to the needs of the army. The operations of his squadrons were effective and helpful to the army; the story of the Royal Flying Corps is one of the few bright pages in the dismal history of World War I. But Trenchard saw the army stuck in the mud of Flanders and felt that the efforts of his airmen were being wasted. After years of frustration, in April 1918 he at last got what he wanted; the Royal Flying Corps was renamed the Royal Air Force, and became an independent service with the freedom to follow its own ideas. Trenchard was ready to begin at once with a strategic air offensive against Germany; only the armistice in November 1918 stopped him. This personal history explains why Trenchard for the rest of his long life fought so passionately for the independence of Bomber Command and for the primacy of strategic bombing. Deep down, he believed that if the Royal Air Force were to follow the advice of Sir George Milne, England would be condemned to bleed again in the mud of Flanders. He could not foresee that in the next Great War the army would learn to be agile while his beloved independent bomber force would become trapped in a costly campaign of attrition.

The apparatus of Bomber Command as it developed in World War II, with its inflexible strategy and its huge outpouring of men and machines, had the three salient characteristics of a technical folly. First, it was incapable of doing the job, paralyzing the enemy's production, for which it had been designed. Second, it was incapable of adapting itself effectively to any other job. Third, it was inordinately expensive. These are the same three characteristics which we saw on a smaller scale in the story of AGLT.

During the years since 1945, the military services of the United States have been guilty of many technical follies, several of which are well documented in James Fallows's book *National Defense*. But the services may also take credit for having frequently said no to enthusiastic inventors and salesmen. A number of bizarre projects were promoted by government and industrial research laboratories but never sold to the military services. They were brought to a halt before they could do any real harm. Since these abortive projects had no military consequences, they hardly deserve the name of follies. They could more charitably be described as welfare programs for scientists and engineers. A notorious example of such a welfare program was the nuclear-propelled airplane, an airplane which was supposed to be able to stay in the air for weeks at a time because it was driven by a nuclear reactor. It never flew. There were two snags, a major and a minor. The minor snag was the fact that the reactor could not be adequately shielded within the weight limitations of an airplane, so that the thing would have become a perpetual radiation hazard as soon as it started to fly. The major snag was the fact that nobody could think of anything useful to do with it. A less well-known but technically more interesting project was Pluto, a nuclear-propelled supersonic cruise missile. Pluto was promoted by the Livermore nuclear weapons laboratory. It had at least the virtue of being spectacular. The missile was supposed to scream along at two or three times the speed of sound, a few hundred feet above the ground, generating shock waves strong enough to flatten buildings on either side of its track. It would do so much damage while cruising around over an enemy country that it hardly mattered whether it carried a warhead or not. This looked as if it might be a militarily useful device until one began to ask practical questions. Where could it be based and tested? What specific missions would it be good for? After asking a few such questions, the air force wisely decided to leave it alone.

But alas, the air force was not so wise when it came to deal with the problem of the MX missile. The MX program reminds me in many ways of AGLT. The air force has bought the MX missile and speeded its development, without having discovered a satisfactory place to put it. The problem of where to put the MX is called the basing problem. The basing problem is for MX what the IFF problem was for AGLT. The AGLT itself was such a technical tour de force that nobody expected to be stymied by the comparatively simple job of building a reliable IFF. Then it turned out that the IFF was not a simple job after all. The MX with its ten accurate and independently targetable warheads is likewise a technical tour de force, and its designers did not expect to be stymied by the comparatively simple job of building a base for it.

The origins of MX and AGLT were also similar. The MX program was started because our existing force of a thousand land-based intercontinental missiles, the Minuteman force, was becoming vulnerable to a Soviet surprise attack as the opposing force of Soviet missiles became more numerous and more accurate. The primary purpose of MX was to solve this Minuteman vulnerability problem, just as the purpose of AGLT was to solve the problem of the vulnerability of bombers to surprise attack by fighters. To solve the Minuteman vulnerability problem, the MX had to be put in bases which were protected or concealed so that Soviet missiles could not attack them effectively. To solve the bomber vulnerability problem, the AGLT had to be able to shoot blind at long range, so that fighters should not get close enough to attack effectively. The MX without a secure basing system is only a fancier and more expensive Minuteman, just as AGLT without a reliable IFF was only a fancier and more expensive gun sight. We have seen one attempt after another to design a secure MX basing system. We have tried tunnels, trenches, deep underground burial; dispersal of mobile missiles on roads, on train tracks, and in airplanes; the multiple protective shelter or race track system, which threatened to cover large areas of Nevada and Utah with concrete; and the dense pack system, which would squeeze all the MX missiles together into a small area in Wyoming. All these attempts ran into snags of one kind or another. The search for a good basing system still continues, and it is as frustrating to those engaged in it as the search for a good IFF was in 1944.

Perhaps the analogy between MX and AGLT goes deeper. AGLT was a small technical folly embedded within the grand technical folly of Bomber Command. MX is a small technical folly embedded within the grand technical folly of nuclear missile forces. Bomber Command had its roots in the Trenchard doctrine, the doctrine that a strategic bomber force operating independently of armies and navies could by itself be a decisive weapon of war. Nuclear missile forces have their origin in the doctrine of deterrence, the doctrine that offensive nuclear forces of overwhelming destructive power will preserve our security by deterring our adversaries from hostile actions. The deterrence doctrine is not identical with the Trenchard doctrine, but it grew historically out of the Trenchard doctrine and it has the same basic weakness. Both Trenchard and the theorists of deterrence believed that they could predict the course of history by rational calculation. Hitler and the German night fighters proved Trenchard wrong. The recalcitrance of the MX basing problem has not quite proved the theorists of deterrence wrong, but it has at least thrown serious doubt upon their credibility. If we look at the story of Bomber Command and the story of MX as variations upon a common theme, we are led to ask whether our reliance on the theory of deterrence as a permanent guarantee of our survival may not be the greatest technical folly of all.

6

Star Wars

Why was the *Star Wars* film such an outstanding box office success? Perhaps it was only because the public responded to the fairy-tale humor, to the pair of sweetly bumbling robots, to the avuncular Alec Guinness with his beneficent magic force. But it is also possible to interpret the success of the film in a more sinister fashion. It is, after all, a film about war. The public has learned from the disasters of the twentieth century that war in our time is too tragic to be a suitable theme for light entertainment. But the public is still, consciously or subconsciously, in love with war. Perhaps the true reason for the film's phenomenal success was the fact that it made war seem innocent; the remote location in space and time allowed the public to indulge its secret love of war with a clear conscience.

Twenty years earlier, I witnessed another Star Wars fantasy which was closer to us in space and time and also closer to being real. I was at that time engaged in the design of a spaceship called Orion. We intended Orion to be a large and ambitious spaceship, driven by nuclear explosions and capable of traveling rapidly from planet to planet. All the civilian scientists and engineers who worked on the design, including our leader, Ted Taylor, who invented it, had come to it with peaceful intentions. We wanted to build a ship which could carry mankind peacefully from one end of the solar system to the other. But our work was funded by the United States Air Force, and some people in the air force had other purposes in mind. There was one air force captain in particular who had grand ideas for the future of Orion. Orion was to become a space battleship. Great fleets of space battleships were to patrol the ocean of space. The captain had read Admiral Mahan's classic work, *The Influence of Sea Power upon the French Revolution and Empire*, and his imagination had been fired by Mahan's famous description of the British navy in the years of the Napoleonic Wars: "Those far distant, storm-beaten ships, upon which the Grand Army never looked, stood between it and the dominion of the world." The captain's Deep Space Bombardment Force was to preserve the Pax Americana in the twenty-first century, as the far distant storm-beaten warships of England had preserved the Pax Britannica in the nineteenth. Cruising majestically in orbits beyond the moon, manned by air force captains as brave as the English sea captains of old, the ships of the Deep Space Bombardment Force would stand between the tyrants of the Kremlin and the dominion of the world.

The captain worked hard to convince us of the practicality of his plans. He drew big charts of cislunar and translunar space, depicting the maneuvers of the Deep Space Bombardment Force and the various subsidiary forces required for provisioning, communication, and reconnaissance. But few of his colleagues in the air force took his ideas seriously. The charts of the Deep Space Bombardment Force were presented only once in a briefing to the senior air force dignitaries who were responsible for the funding of our project. The dignitaries made it clear that they wished no more of their funds to be spent on dreams of imperial glory. The captain's dream fleet, the ghostly armada of Orion ships silently keeping watch over our planet, did not impress them favorably. After the briefing, the captain's charts disappeared into a drawer, and the captain's dreams remained dreams.

It is easy to dismiss the success of *Star Wars* as inconsequential; after all, the whole point of the film was that it was not supposed to be taken seriously. And it is easy to dismiss as a dreamer anybody who, like our friend the air force captain, believes seriously in space battleships. But behind the flummery and absurdity lies a real and important question. Is it possible, as a practical matter, that the perennial squabbles of mankind could be made less dangerous to our health and welfare by a displacement of military activities from the earth into space? If this is possible, the move would bring great relief and benefit to humanity. Warfare in space could become, as naval warfare traditionally has been, a comparatively decent and humane method of settling political disputes. Space battles, like sea battles, would be fought by professional elites, with minimal damage to noncombatants. Even a few thousand megatons exploded here and there in deep space would be a harmless display of fireworks for the spectators on Earth, doing as little damage to civilians as the distant thunder of the guns of Jutland in 1916. Is this picture, the earth being made safe for humanity by a shift of warfare into space, only a childish fantasy? Or is there some possibility that it could really happen?

To answer these questions we must turn away from fantasy and look at the realities of military operations in space. When we examine missions and machines in detail, the analogy between naval and space operations immediately disappears. The physical properties of ocean and space are quite dissimilar, and as a result the functions of a water navy and a space navy are totally different. Space is transparent, the ocean largely opaque. From space we can see almost everything, from the sea almost nothing. At sea we can stop and wait, in space we are perpetually on the move. From the sea we can touch land and go ashore, from space we can touch nothing. The exercise of sea power has historically required a navy to perform four functions: protection of merchant shipping, blockade of enemy ports, movement of armies overseas, and protection of coasts against invasion. None of these functions, nor any functions analogous to them, can be performed from space. Instead, military space vehicles as they now exist perform four equally important but quite different functions: reliable radio communication among military units on the ground, provision of reference signals for accurate navigation of ships and airplanes, collection of intelligence by interception of signals from foreign military forces, and reconnaissance of foreign territory by direct photography from space. In short, the functions of existing military space forces are concerned entirely with the collection and transmission of information. Sea navies can influence military operations on land by the interposition of brute force; space forces at present can influence operations on the ground only by supplying information. So long as all the physical violence remains on the ground and only data processors are put in space, a space navy will bear no resemblance to a sea navy.

Humanity derives great benefit from the existence of military space vehicles performing their present function of information gathering. Photographic reconnaissance from space is the essential tool for verifying arms control treaties, for diminishing threats of surprise attack, and for quietening exaggerated fears and rumors of secret weapons. *Aviation Week* and other magazines are constantly spreading stories, some true and some false, of Soviet activities in advanced weapon technology. We read about giant Soviet lasers and particle beam experiments, and we are supposed to be duly frightened. Fortunately, we can rely upon photographic reconnaissance from space to give us timely warning if ever any of these alleged superweapons reaches the stage of serious deployment. Without the reconnaissance satellites, it would be far more difficult for us to resist the scaremongers. And without the reconnaissance satellites for verification, it is unlikely that we could negotiate any serious arms control agreements at all.

The unarmed military satellites of the Soviet Union do not do much harm to us, and our satellites do not do much harm to the Soviet Union. In fact, if peaceful coexistence is our goal, the satellites of both sides are beneficial to both sides. Soviet satellites benefit us by reducing the intensity of Soviet paranoia, and our satellites benefit the Soviet Union by reducing the intensity of our paranoia. The American arms control community believes strongly that this happy state of affairs ought to be perpetuated, and therefore urges the American government to negotiate a formal satellite protection treaty with the Soviet Union, forbidding both countries to deploy or test any apparatus designed to destroy or damage each other's spacecraft. During 1978 and 1979 the two governments started to negotiate such a treaty. The negotiations began well but failed to make progress after the first few months. We do not know how seriously the Soviet leaders regarded the negotiations. On the American side there was an evident lack of seriousness. The American negotiators were unable to negotiate effectively because they received no coherent guidance from Washington. The American government never pulled itself together to decide what kind of a treaty it wanted. President Carter, discouraged by his failure to achieve the ratification of the SALT II treaty and distracted by the Iranian hostage crisis, allowed the negotiations to peter out. But the possibility lies open that the two sides will one day return to the negotiating table and agree to legislate a permanent ban on all forceful action in space. Space would then become, not totally peaceful, but a privileged sanctuary for military spacecraft of all nations going about their business of collecting and transmitting information. This is one possible future for the military utilization of space. Since the arms controllers consider it desirable, I call it the arms controllers' future. In the arms controllers' future, space is a sanctuary and weapons stay on the ground.

There are other possible futures. The Soviet Union has already developed and tested a satellite with the ability to hunt and kill other satellites. If a satellite protection treaty is not concluded, the United States will also experiment with satellite killer systems. After that, we may see a proliferation of military spacecraft carrying the weapons which *Aviation Week* publicizes, high-energy lasers and particle beam generators of various kinds. This possible future I call the technical-follies future. In the technical-follies future, space becomes the arena of a technological arms race pursued without much regard for military utility. Both sides may decide to launch space battleships, in spite of the fact that space battleships are militarily as obsolete as sea battleships. Space battleships, like sea battleships, are chiefly valued by officers of high rank as platforms for the ceremonial exercise of command. In space, even more than on the ocean, big ships are vulnerable and cost more than they are worth. Real military advantage in space will lie with numbers and concealment. In space there is no place to hide, but concealment is possible if active units are small and are deployed among a large number of decoy units of similar appearance. Cheap and many will have the advantage over expensive and few. Unmanned will have the advantage over manned. If we choose the technical-follies future, we shall see a proliferation of military spacecraft of all shapes and sizes. But this display of technical proficiency will probably affect very little the realities of military and political power on the ground.

Enthusiasts for space weaponry, like my friend the air force captain, have always dreamed that one day their space weapons could dominate ground weapons, that their space forces could impose peace on ground forces. The concrete expression of this dream is a space-based antimissile system which could reliably destroy any ground-launched or sea-launched missiles in the vulnerable early stages of their flight. In the dream, the space force constantly patrols the planet, ready to kill in a second or two, with a lightning bolt of laser or particle beam energy, every missile which rises from the earth without due notification and authorization. It is a beautiful dream, the weapons of high precision rendering impotent the weapons of mass destruction. The celestial lightning bolts, without hurting a single hair of a human head, purge the earth of mass-destruction weapons by the controlled and localized force of a superior technology.

Unfortunately for humanity, the purging of nuclear weapons from the earth is too big a job for technology to do alone. The dream of the omnipotent celestial laser beam patrol fails on technological grounds. The space-based antimissile system has many technical weaknesses. Even if death-ray weapons could be aimed and focused with perfect accuracy and could deliver a sufficient concentration of energy to destroy a missile, they would still be at a great disadvantage in terms of vulnerability. A missile is vulnerable to death-ray attack only for a few minutes while it is in flight; a death-ray machine in space is vulnerable all the time. A death-ray machine is a large and delicate piece of apparatus; a single pebble colliding with it at orbital velocity would have a good chance of putting it out of action. The same technology which allows us to aim the death ray with the necessary precision also allows us to aim the pebble. When the experts play their little games, with ground-based missiles on one side and death-ray machines in space on the other, the ground-based side almost always wins. It is of course possible to adjust the numbers of weapons on the two sides so as to make it an even game, but then the cost of the space weapons is outrageously high compared with the cost of the ground weapons. These imaginary battles ignore many aspects of the real world, but they lead us to a clear conclusion: So long as large land-based or sea-based missile forces exist and are not subject to severe political constraints, there is no technological magic by which space-based weaponry can disarm them. The extension of the technological arms race into space cannot by itself make ground-based missiles obsolete or ineffective. For this reason I call the future in which space weapons proliferate without end the technical-follies future. It is an extension into the future of the same folly which gave us AGLT and MX. It is a future of double folly, the small-scale folly of militarily useless weapons, and the large-scale folly of unattainable strategic objectives.

The arms controllers' future makes space a peaceful sanctuary and leaves us to deal as best we can with our strategic problems on the ground. The technical-follies future makes space a battleground and does nothing to make the problems on the ground more tractable. But there is a third possible future, a future in which nuclear weapons are legally banned from the earth and from space, and in which the resources of non-nuclear technology are used in an energetic fashion to help make the ban effective. This third future I call the defense-dominated future. In the defense-dominated future, weapons of mass destruction are disarmed, not by defensive technology alone, but by legal and political restraints strengthened by the active intervention of technology.

So long as we maintain overwhelmingly destructive nuclear forces on earth, we would be wise to keep space disarmed so far as possible. But if we can ever achieve drastic disarmament on earth, a deployment of appropriately designed space weaponry may help us to push the negotiated reduction of nuclear arsenals all the way to zero. These are the premises of the defense-dominated future: the earth becomes a non-nuclear sanctuary stabilized by substantial military forces in space; space forces are specifically designed to allay fears and to diminish incentives for secret or open nuclear rearmament. To achieve these purposes, the space forces would not need to attempt the almost impossible task of nullifying a full-scale onslaught of the present-day Soviet or American missile forces. It would be sufficient for the space forces to be capable of nullifying much smaller threats. The smaller threats which would exist in a non-nuclear world would be either residual nuclear forces concealed by a country secretly violating a disarmament treaty, or embryonic nuclear forces deployed by a country openly abrogating the treaty, or forces belonging to smaller countries which had never acceded to the treaty. Space forces which could defeat these smaller threats are not beyond the realm of technical possibility. Such forces would not by themselves remove all danger of breakdown of the non-nuclear regime, but they would powerfully strengthen the political and institutional structures on which the durability of the regime would depend.

What kind of space forces would the defense-dominated future require? Certainly not space battleships, and probably not death-ray generators or high-energy lasers. One of the primary requirements for an effective space force is to be itself inconspicuous and invulnerable. The most likely shape for the space force would be a multitude of small vehicles, scattered in orbits around the earth, carrying telescopes and sensors of various kinds. The purpose of these vehicles would be to collect accurate and timely information. In a defensive battle, information is more important than exotic kill-mechanisms. If the defense has adequate information, it can relay the information to small non-nuclear interceptors, either ground-

launched or in orbit, which can use their own sensors to home onto
a flying missile and kill it by direct impact. The idea of a space force
of this kind is not new. It was proposed in the 1950s and given the
name Bambi (Ballistic Missile Boost Intercept). It was then rejected
as technically impracticable and prohibitively expensive. During the
subsequent twenty years, sensors and microcomputers have become
enormously more capable and also cheaper. If the world ever decides to move along the road toward the defense-dominated future,
it is possible that space forces of the Bambi type can be built at
reasonable cost, and that they can be effective enough to help stabil-
ize the world against backsliding into nuclear terror.

In the defense-dominated future as I have described it, the space
forces play a modest role, patrolling the earth inconspicuously and
serving as an adjunct to earthbound political arrangements. These
forces could probably operate most efficiently without a single air
force officer in orbit. It is a far cry from the Deep Space Bombardment Force, or from the Galactic Empire space force which we saw
in the *Star Wars* film. And that is all to the good. If space forces have
a constructive role to play in our future, it is the role Sir George
Milne envisaged in 1928 for the Royal Air Force, not the role Sir
Hugh Trenchard demanded. Space forces, like air forces, should be
firmly harnessed to the strategic needs of earthbound humanity.

In the end, the goals of the arms controllers' future and the
defense-dominated future are the same, and only the means are
different. The goal of both futures is a stable world with a minimum
of nuclear armament. The arms controllers' future chooses first to
disarm space and to leave nuclear offensive forces on the ground
intact, in the hope that a stable regime of nuclear deterrence will
allow gradual steps toward disarmament. The defense-dominated
future chooses first to disarm nuclear forces on the ground and to
let space forces grow, in the hope that a disarmed world will settle
down more comfortably if it has space forces providing substantial
protection against the risks of surprise attack. Both futures, if they
fulfill their promise, converge to a common end. The real future, if
we are wise, will probably lie somewhere in the middle between the
arms controllers' and the defense-dominated extremes. If we are
unwise, the technical-follies future is there, waiting for us to stumble
into it.

7

The ABM Problem

ABM, short for antiballistic missile, is one of the few military acronyms which have passed into civilian language and are generally understood by people not expert in military jargon. Since "antiballistic missile" is an ugly phrase, I shall use the abbreviation ABM without further apology. The fact that ABM has become a familiar concept outside military circles is itself significant. It signifies that the public has been more deeply involved in the political debate over ABM deployment than in other strategic debates of the past twenty years. To me it was always puzzling, and saddening, that the public reacted with such vehemence against the defensive ABM and yet accepted without serious concern the deployment of our far more murderous offensive nuclear systems, the Minuteman missiles and the Polaris and Poseidon submarines. It is a fact that the public, whether wisely or unwisely, prefers offensive to defensive weapons. This fact lies at the heart of what I choose to call "the ABM problem." The problem is how to deal with the contradiction between old-fashioned ethics and new-fashioned strategic doctrines. Old-fashioned ethics say that self-defense is good and mass murder is evil. The strategic doctrine of deterrence, supported not only by government experts but by the multitude of ordinary citizens who rose in protest against ABM, brings us into a world of upside-down logic which considers weapons of self-defense evil and weapons of mass murder good. There are two possible responses to the contradiction. One may simply reject the old-fashioned ethics as naive, impractical, irrelevant to the complex realities of modern weaponry. This is the response of the majority of my friends both inside and outside the government establishment. Or alternatively one may stubbornly struggle, as I do, to be faithful to the old-fashioned ethics, and look for an evolution of our strategic doctrines that will allow old-fashioned ethics to be once again relevant and practical.

The ABM problem has a long history, which I will not attempt to summarize here. Many well-documented historical studies are available. So far as the general public in the United States was concerned, the history began in the late 1950s when political opposition to nuclear bomb tests became serious. Military leaders opposed to a test ban then invoked the development of an ABM system as one of the justifications for continued testing. By 1963 the worldwide outcry against radioactive fallout from nuclear tests in the atmosphere had become so loud that governments were forced to respond; in that year the atmospheric test ban treaty was signed. After the signing of the treaty came the debate over its ratification by the United States Senate. In the ratification debate, most of the military witnesses supported the treaty, saying that they were satisfied with the opportunities left open by the treaty for continued testing underground. At that point, the victory of the treaty was assured, and the opponents became a beleaguered and unpopular minority. The only serious military development program which could not be accommodated by underground testing was the nuclear ABM program as it then existed. So, in the closing phase of the debate, the discussion centered almost exclusively around the ABM issue, the opponents of the treaty using the necessity of atmospheric tests for ABM as their main argument for rejecting a test ban. In the end, as could have been foreseen from the beginning, the treaty won and ABM lost. The general public was introduced to ABM in the context of the test ban debate, and learned to identify ABM with the unpopular cause of continued atmospheric bomb tests. This was a blow from which ABM never recovered. Neither side in the test ban debate had any incentive to tell the public that ABM need not be nuclear.

The next phase in public awareness of ABM came in 1969, when President Nixon proposed to deploy around American cities a nuclear ABM system called Sentinel. Opposition to the deployment was widespread and stormy. The cause of defeating Sentinel brought together people from widely diverse backgrounds: suburban housewives who objected to the stationing of nuclear-armed interceptor missiles in their neighborhoods; young political activists who opposed Nixon's war policy in Vietnam and were automatically against anything that Nixon wanted; distinguished scientists and military experts who had well-founded technical arguments against Sentinel. The combination of environmental, personal, and technical opposition was strong enough to convince Nixon that this was a fight he could not win. He withdrew the proposal to deploy Sentinel before it came to a vote in Congress. In an effort to pacify the suburban housewives, he retreated to a new proposal. Sentinel was to be moved away from cities and converted into a system concentrated around offensive missile bases in Montana and North Dakota. Its name was changed from Sentinel to Safeguard. The scale of the proposed deployment was considerably reduced. In the end the Safeguard system was approved in a halfhearted fashion by Congress, and a small fraction of it was actually deployed. But it was understood by all concerned that the Safeguard system as it finally emerged was only a token deployment, not a real ABM defense. Nixon had lost the battle for a real ABM deployment, and the public knew it. The public had learned a second time to identify ABM with a losing and unpopular cause.

The third and last time that ABM came to the attention of the public was in 1972, when Nixon successfully negotiated the SALT I treaty with the Soviet Union. The substance of the treaty was an agreement by both sides not to deploy serious ABM defenses. In order to accommodate the token Safeguard deployment and a small ABM system which the Soviet Union had already deployed around Moscow, each side was allowed to build systems with up to two hundred interceptors. The allowed limit was intentionally made so low that the treaty puts an end to all possibility of real ABM defense as long as it remains in force. During the process of negotiation and ratification, the treaty received overwhelming public support. It was the first major arms control agreement since the test ban treaty of 1963, and it was generally acclaimed as a large step forward toward the goal of bringing the nuclear arms race under control. Even Nixon's bitterest enemies did not care to oppose him on this issue. The Sentinel fiasco was fresh in everyone's memory. So far as the general public was concerned, ABM meant the discredited Sentinel and Safeguard proposals, and opposition to the treaty meant trying to revive Sentinel and Safeguard. The few generals and politicians who opposed the treaty had no hope of stemming the tide of popular approval. Arms control was popular. ABM was worse than unpopular; it was politically a dead issue, and the treaty was only hammering a few more nails in the lid of its coffin. When the United States Senate met to ratify the treaty, the vote was eighty-eight in favor and two opposed. For a third time, the public condemned ABM with a clear conscience. In the mood of public joy which accompanied the easy ratification of the treaty, nobody voiced misgivings about the awkward ethical implications of putting a permanent ban on self-defense.

After 1972 the general public ceased to be seriously concerned with ABM. In the view of the public, ABM was a troublesome political problem which was finally settled by the 1972 treaty, and there is no reason to worry about it further. But I still worry about it, and I still wonder whether the ethical foundations of the 1972 treaty are sound. As a practical matter, I wonder whether some form of non-nuclear ABM may not be an essential part of the environment within which humanity can make the difficult transition from a nuclear to a non-nuclear world. I am unable to put an end to the ABM debate in my own mind. So I will first examine as fairly as I can the case against ABM, and then try to come to a verdict, to decide whether ABM can or cannot play a helpful role in various possible versions of the future.

The case against ABM begins with a story. I am invited to supper by a scientist friend at the University of Illinois. My friend is a computer addict. He has a home computer with a collection of computer games. One of his games is a simulated ABM battle. He plugs it in and invites me to play. At the bottom of the television screen appears a row of six cities: Richmond, Washington, Baltimore, Philadelphia, New York, Boston. I have to defend these cities with my ABM. I have my hands on a pair of switches which control the movement of my interceptors on the screen. Out of the top of the screen comes a sporadic stream of incoming warheads, some single and some multiple. I am a naive beginner and have never played such a game before. I am quickly caught up in the excitement of the battle. My skill with the switches improves. My interceptors zip from side to side of the screen and catch more and more of the warheads. Each time a warhead is killed, a gratifying fireball appears on the screen. More and more interceptions, more and more fireballs. I am learning fast and doing well. Then suddenly the action stops and the game is over. I look down to the bottom of the screen and see to my dismay that the cities are all destroyed. Nothing is left.

The screen announces: "Your score is 452." That is the number of seconds it took for the attack to penetrate my defense and finish off my cities. My host says that is not bad for a beginner. When he is in good form he sometimes scores over 800.

A game is only a game. But this game teaches a serious lesson. It shows how easy it is to become totally absorbed in the shooting match in the sky, so totally absorbed that one does not notice the disappearance of six cities with their twenty million inhabitants on the ground. The game is a true parable, teaching us about the way people behave in the real world of nuclear weaponry. Our human frailties are the same, whether we are playing a computer game, or planning to defend the territory of Western Europe with tactical nuclear weapons, or planning to defend the cities of the United States with ABM. In all these situations, the defenders think they are doing well when they destroy a high percentage of the attackers. The defenders become so absorbed in doing well that they fail to notice the disappearance of whatever it was that they were supposed to be defending.

The public rejected ABM for many reasons, but the first and fundamental reason for rejection was that people never believed the thing would work well enough to save their lives. The ABM game mirrors accurately the ultimate futility of ABM as seen by the public. What difference does it make whether the attack gets through in four hundred or in eight hundred seconds, if in the end we are all dead? But a computer game is not admissible evidence in a court of law. The game may mirror accurately the public image of ABM, and still the public image may be false. So I now proceed to state the case against ABM in a more formal fashion, dividing the case into eight counts.

Count 1. ABM is technically ineffective. In the ABM debates of 1969, the expert witnesses made it clear that the Sentinel and Safeguard systems were technically inadequate to defend anything against large-scale Soviet attacks. Safeguard had a much easier job to do than Sentinel, since Safeguard was to defend missile sites while Sentinel was to defend cities. Missiles are easier to defend than cities, for two reasons: first, missile sites are small and tough, whereas cities are large and vulnerable; second, a defense of missile sites is considered effective if it can save half the missiles, whereas a defense of cities has to try to save them all. But it turned out that Safeguard could not do even the easier job. Safeguard depended for its functioning on a small number of large fixed radars. It could not defend its own radars against a concentrated attack, and once its radars were gone it could not defend anything else. This weakness of the Safeguard system as it existed in 1969 could be corrected by adding more radars, and especially by adding mobile radars. But it is a general weakness of all ABM systems that they are enormously complicated, and if a few central elements fail, the whole system is likely to collapse.

Count 2. ABM is destabilizing. This is the classic argument brought against ABM by the professional experts in arms control. It applies equally to nuclear and non-nuclear ABM. The argument starts from the orthodox doctrine of deterrence, which assumes a world held in equilibrium by the balance of invulnerable offensive forces of overwhelming destructive power. According to the deterrence doctrine, the strategic equilibrium remains stable so long as nobody tries to defend himself against attack. But if one country deploys a serious ABM system, the opposing country is obliged to respond with a large increase of offensive forces to nullify the possible effect of the ABM; the arms race is accelerated, and the equilibrium is no longer stable. This argument is convincing to people who believe in the doctrine of deterrence. When the negotiators of SALT I decided to include non-nuclear ABM within the scope of their treaty, they did so mainly because they believed ABM of all kinds to be destabilizing.

Count 3. ABM creates a dangerous illusion of safety. This count suggests that a country might feel so safe under the protection of an ABM system that it would consider itself invulnerable and blunder into rash adventures. It is hard to imagine anybody feeling safe under the protection of Sentinel or Safeguard or any other ABM system that could be built in the near future. The illusion of safety might become a serious problem in a future non-nuclear world, just as it was in the real world of the past before nuclear weapons were invented.

Count 4. ABM is forbidden by treaty. The SALT I treaty is a major achievement of arms control, and any serious attempt to revive ABM would require abrogation or renegotiation of the treaty. The treaty, irrespective of its technical merits, must be preserved for political reasons, because it is an expression of Soviet-American willingness to cooperate in the control of the arms race.

Count 5. ABM is unreasonably expensive. So long as ABM is

nuclear, each interceptor carrying a nuclear warhead will cost about as much as the warhead which it is supposed to intercept. Since many interceptors will miss, and many must be held in reserve, an effective defense must have several interceptors for each incoming warhead. In addition to the interceptors, the defense must have large numbers of radars, computers, and communication channels. Altogether, a nuclear ABM system is likely to cost several times as much as the offensive missile system which it is designed to defeat. In principle, a non-nuclear ABM system using very small interceptors might be radically cheaper than a nuclear system. But in practice, non-nuclear ABM designs using existing components appear to be as expensive as nuclear ABM.

Count 6. ABM cannot be realistically tested. There is no way in which a full-scale ABM system could be given an operational test under conditions resembling a real attack. Fatal flaws in the coordination of the system are likely to remain undetected until the real attack reveals them. This count against ABM applies to non-nuclear systems to some extent, but much more strongly to nuclear systems. A non-nuclear ABM could at least be exercised with live ammunition from time to time. A nuclear ABM could never be test-fired so long as the atmospheric test ban treaty remains in force. And even if the test ban treaty were broken, other political and environmental constraints would not permit a nuclear ABM to be test-fired on the scale required for a realistic trial of the system as a whole.

Count 7. ABM means a vast proliferation of nuclear warheads. This count and the next apply only to nuclear systems. Any ABM designed to defend against present-day missile forces must employ thousands of interceptors. If the interceptors are nuclear, the ABM requires thousands of nuclear warheads to be deployed in sites scattered over the defended territory. Such a proliferation of warheads is particularly troublesome because the interceptors must be ready to fire at a moment's notice in case of a surprise attack. Large numbers of ready-to-fire nuclear weapons in scattered sites are undesirable for many reasons: they arouse local political opposition, they bring real risks of nuclear accident and nuclear theft, and they presuppose a command-and-control system of improbable reliability.

Count 8. ABM is easily converted into an offensive system. This count is important if one is hoping, as I am, that the world will one day shift its weaponry from predominantly offensive to predominantly defensive purposes. We might, for example, negotiate a treaty prohibiting offensive missile systems and allowing each country freedom to defend itself with ABM as insurance against possible violations of the treaty. Count 8 says that nuclear ABM is not acceptable for this purpose. The components of a nuclear ABM system are still weapons of mass destruction and can too easily be converted into offensive missiles. If the shift of the world from offensive to defensive weaponry is to be permanent, all mass-destruction weapons must be forbidden and any permitted ABM systems must be non-nuclear.

That is the case against ABM. In the opinion of most knowledgeable people, the case is so overwhelmingly strong that no further discussion is necessary. And still I stubbornly refuse to consider the case closed. I am not suggesting that it would make sense to deploy ABM systems in the world as it now exists. But for the long future, the ethical imperative of moving from offense to defense compels me to take ABM seriously.

The case against ABM divides itself into two halves. The first half, counts 1 to 4, says that ABM is ineffective, destabilizing, deceptively reassuring, and forbidden by treaty. The second half, counts 5 to 8, says that ABM is unreasonably expensive, untestable, conducive to nuclear proliferation, and easily diverted to offensive purposes. The first half of the indictment applies equally to nuclear and non-nuclear systems, the second half to nuclear systems only. I do not attempt to rebut the second half. So far as I am concerned, counts 5 to 8 make an unanswerable case against nuclear ABM. I concede that nuclear ABM deserves the public contempt into which it has fallen. Nuclear ABM failed, as many other military projects have failed, because it used bad means to achieve good ends. Bad means corrupt good ends and finally make good ends unachievable. The good end, in this case the defensively oriented world, cannot be achieved by means of nuclear weapons, which are in their nature weapons of mass destruction. Count 8, which did not figure prominently in the public debate, is to me the final and conclusive argument against nuclear ABM.

The case against non-nuclear ABM consists of counts 1 to 4 only and rests on much weaker ground. Each of these counts is to some extent valid. Each may become invalid or unimportant as the state of the world changes. I will attempt to rebut each of these counts in turn, and then summarize the conditions under which it may still be possible to conceive of non-nuclear ABM as a good means to a good end.

Rebuttal to Count 1. Effectiveness is a concept with many meanings. If effectiveness means saving with high probability all the targets which are attacked, then ABM is certainly ineffective against large attacks. If effectiveness means saving those targets which are not attacked, then ABM is highly effective. The true function of ABM lies somewhere between these two extremes. It forces an attacker to concentrate a large number of weapons onto each target which he intends to destroy, thereby reducing greatly the number of targets which can be attacked at all. It increases substantially the cost of an attack, and it increases even more substantially the uncertainties faced by the attacker. In summary, an ABM system may be militarily effective in complicating, discouraging, and deterring attacks, even if it cannot claim 100 percent technical effectiveness.

In addition to the most difficult mission of defeating large-scale attacks, for which the effectiveness of ABM must always be uncertain, there are easier missions for which ABM can be highly effective. The most important easier mission is defense against possible attack by small forces of concealed weapons after major offensive forces have been disarmed by treaty.

Rebuttal to Count 2. ABM was in fact destabilizing in the 1960s, when the United States reaction to early Soviet ABM experiments was a multiplication of offensive warheads. This experience of the 1960s caused the arms control experts and the public to believe that ABM is always destabilizing. But the reaction to ABM under different circumstances might be quite different. For example, if the numbers of offensive weapons were firmly limited by treaty, the warhead-multiplying reaction would be prohibited.

At a deeper level, the belief in the destabilizing nature of ABM rests on the belief that a stable equilibrium of offensive forces without defense is possible and desirable. This latter belief is the orthodox doctrine of stable deterrence. The continuing offensive arms race, and the increasing worries about vulnerability of land-based missiles to surprise attack, make the doctrine of stable deterrence less plausible in the 1980s than it was in the 1960s. It may be true, as I believe, that stable deterrence is an illusion, that the only truly stable balance of forces is a defense-dominated equilibrium. If this is so, then ABM becomes more and more stabilizing as we move further toward the reduction and elimination of offensive forces.

An additional reason for rejecting the doctrine of stable deterrence is the fact that the balance of terror becomes more complicated and delicate as the number of nuclear powers increases. Already the existence of Chinese and British and French nuclear forces complicates the negotiation of agreed limits on Soviet and American forces. As we move from a bilateral to a multilateral balance of terror, the equilibrium becomes more liable to disruption by unforeseen events. In a multilateral nuclear world, non-nuclear ABM would be stabilizing in two ways. It would substantially reduce the ability of small nuclear powers to threaten their neighbors. And it would reduce the incentive for additional countries to join the nuclear club.

Rebuttal to Count 3. Only a madman could succumb to illusions of safety induced by ABM. If a political leader is crazy enough to plunge his country into war under the protection of an ABM system, he is probably crazy enough to plunge into war without an ABM system. Neither ABM nor the doctrine of stable deterrence provides any real protection against madmen. The only real protection is to get rid of weapons of mass destruction altogether. And in a non-nuclear world, the margin of safety provided by ABM may cease to be an illusion.

Rebuttal to Count 4. The existence of the SALT I treaty is the strongest argument for consigning ABM to oblivion. I would not under any circumstances advocate the unilateral abrogation of the treaty. So long as the Soviet Union wishes to maintain the treaty in force, it should be maintained. I would also not advocate renegotiation of the treaty until we have succeeded in negotiating firm and permanent limits on offensive weapon deployments. So long as offensive deployments are open-ended, we must not complicate the negotiation of limits by reopening the discussion of ABM. But after we have an effective limit on offensive forces, and especially if we are successful in reducing offensive forces by treaty to far below their present size, then the time might be ripe for a reconsideration of SALT I. There is no reason why the Soviet Union should not find it advantageous to join us in a transition to a defensively oriented world. We might, for example, offer for negotiation a treaty reducing nuclear weapon deployments step by step toward zero and concurrently opening the door to deployment of non-nuclear ABM. If such a proposal were acceptable to both sides, it would be foolish to let the SALT I treaty stand in its way.

We have now heard the testimony against ABM and the rebuttal in favor of non-nuclear ABM. What is to be the verdict? Neither guilty nor innocent is to me a reasonable verdict. I prefer the verdict of not proven, which is allowed in Scottish criminal law. History alone can decide whether or not ABM may have a useful role to play in human affairs. It would be equally wrong to accept the verdict of the SALT I treaty as final or to try hastily to overturn it.

The future of ABM depends on many unpredictable developments, in technology, in politics, and in public morality. Nobody knows, and nobody will know for many years, whether the technology of non-nuclear ABM can be developed into a practical system. I will not go here into the details of ABM technology. In the United States there is a non-nuclear ABM research program directed toward a system called Overlay, which is intended only to be an adjunct to a nuclear ABM system. Overlay cannot stand by itself as a serious non-nuclear ABM system; as a system it is inconsequential. But the technology now being developed for Overlay is impressive. It is possible that the Overlay technology may point the way to an effective non-nuclear ABM. If not, then some other technology may turn out to be effective. Alternatively, we may find that no non-nuclear technology is adequate to meet the demands which ABM imposes. If non-nuclear ABM turns out to be technically impossible, then its political and moral advantages will not do us any good.

The political and moral uncertainties surrounding the future of ABM are even greater than the technical uncertainties. ABM is only a tool, and a tool can be used either wisely or unwisely. In this respect, ground-based ABM is like the space-based Bambi antimissile system which I described in the previous chapter. For ABM on the ground, just as for antimissile armaments in space, there are three possible futures. The first is the arms controllers' future, in which the SALT I treaty is held inviolate forever, ABM of all kinds is forbidden, and the world continues to rely for its survival on the doctrine of stable deterrence. The second is the technical-follies future, in which offensive weapons continue to increase while ABM systems proliferate; in this future the ABM cannot bring safety or stability, but only an arms race without purpose and without end. The third is the defense-dominated future, in which nuclear weapons are drastically reduced or prohibited and non-nuclear ABM provides reassurance against the danger of nuclear surprise. One version of the defense-dominated future is the situation described at the end of Chapter 6, where we supposed the apparatus of strategic defense to be removed from the ground and entrusted to space forces in orbit. The political difficulties which must be overcome to reach the defense-dominated future are the same, whether the job of strategic defense is done by space forces or by ground-based ABM.

In the arms controllers' future, ABM is a tool unused. In the technical-follies future, ABM is a tool used unwisely. In the defense-dominated future, ABM is a tool used wisely. Nobody can know today whether the arms controllers' future or the defense-dominated future will be in the end the safer goal for humanity to follow. ABM, so long as it is non-nuclear, may be a good tool to keep handy in case the defense-dominated world should come within our grasp.

It is essential to distinguish ends from means. Means are important, but ends are more important. The non-nuclear world is a worthy end for mankind to strive for. The means to reach it must be firstly moral, secondly political, thirdly technical. Moral means are peace movements and public campaigns arousing the conscience of mankind against weapons of mass destruction. Political means are treaties and military doctrines and deployment decisions. Technical means are precision-guided munitions, non-nuclear ABM systems, and other clever gadgets still to be invented. Technical means come last, but they still may be helpful.

8

Shelters

The ethical problems associated with bomb shelters are similar to the ethical problems associated with crash helmets for motorcyclists. If you force cyclists to wear crash helmets, you save some riders' lives. But many cyclists still prefer to ride without crash helmets. And if you are a pedestrian on a narrow road and a gang on motorcycles is coming at you at fifty miles an hour, the sight of crash helmets does not make you feel any safer.

Some years ago I was teaching physics for a few weeks at the Swiss Federal Institute of Technology in Zurich. While I was there, two officials from the Swiss civil defense authority came to see me. They invited me to meet with them for an unofficial consultation. We had lunch together and they told me about their problems. They were responsible for writing the performance standards of bomb shelters for the population of Switzerland. According to Swiss law, every new house or public building must have a bomb shelter. The law was originally imposed in 1950 and was made more comprehensive in 1963 and 1978. The specifications for shelters have been gradually stiffened as the danger shifted from old-fashioned high-explosive bombs to nuclear and then thermonuclear weapons. The law has been enforced for thirty years, and during that time the construction of new homes, suburbs, schools, shops, and factories has never stopped. As a result, a high percentage of the Swiss population has immediate access to a shelter. All through the 1950s and 1960s and 1970s, the Swiss have been quietly building shelters.

The quality of Swiss shelters is even more impressive than their quantity. These are not the makeshift shelters which one used to see in public buildings in the United States, intended to give protection only against radioactive fallout. Swiss shelters are massive reinforced-concrete structures built into the foundations of buildings. They are intended to protect people against blast and fire as well as fallout. The civil defense authority makes sure that they are kept in working order, with air filters, food, water, sanitary facilities, and medical supplies adequate to give the inhabitants a reasonable chance of survival. The civil defense authority, like the Swiss army, takes its job seriously. The financial cost of the program is about one tenth of the Swiss military budget. No other country has a civil defense system of comparable size and sophistication.

The two officials explained how they calculated the specifications for shelters. They started from the information published by the United States Atomic Energy Commission about physical and biological effects of nuclear weapons. The United States handbook on weapon effects is not secret and is readily available. It gives detailed descriptions of nuclear explosions, and includes graphs of pressure, heat flux, earth shock, and radiation dose at various distances from bombs of various sizes. The Swiss officials had used these graphs to calculate thicknesses of concrete walls and steel doors, heat resistance of air intake pipes, and other technical characteristics of shelters to be specified by law. I found nothing wrong with their calculations. The overall effect of their standards could be summarized in two sentences. So far as the effects of blast are concerned, the area within which people in Swiss shelters would be killed by a given bomb is less than a quarter of the area within which people without shelters would be killed by the same bomb. So far as the effects of radiation are concerned, people in Swiss shelters anywhere outside the area of lethal blast damage would have a reasonable chance of survival. These two statements are worded in such a way as to be true independently of the size of the bomb.

What does "a reasonable chance of survival" mean? The Swiss officials were careful not to claim any exact knowledge of the probability of survival. A reasonable chance means, simply, as good a chance as can be expected in the circumstances of a nuclear war. The local and immediate effects of a bomb are calculable; the large-scale and long-term effects of nuclear war are not. A Swiss shelter, if you are not too close to the bomb, gives you efficient protection against local and immediate effects. After you dig yourself out of the shelter and survey the surrounding sea of rubble, your survival depends on finding a functioning society to support you. Nobody can guarantee that you will find a functioning society when you emerge. The Swiss officials said only that, if any society in Europe is still functioning after a general nuclear war, Switzerland will be functioning.

At the end of our meeting, I asked them why they had wanted to talk to me. So far as I could see, they already knew everything I had to tell them. Then they finally explained the purpose of the meeting. They had been worried because their shelters seemed too good to be true. It was hard to believe that simple shelters could really be as effective as their calculations indicated against the mighty hydrogen bomb. And all their calculations had been based on the American weapons-effect handbook. Perhaps they had been foolish to trust the American numbers. Perhaps the Americans had been misleading everybody by publishing overoptimistic numbers in the open literature and keeping the correct numbers secret. Perhaps the published numbers were correct for old-fashioned bombs but not for the more modern American designs. There had been rumors that the Americans were working on cobalt bombs and neutron bombs and other new horrors which would make the published handbook obsolete. The Swiss officials knew that I had been to Los Alamos and was privy to American secrets, and that was why they had invited me. They asked me whether I could, without betraying the secrets of Los Alamos, settle their doubts about the reliability of the American handbook. I said this would not be difficult to do. I said, first, that Americans working inside the security fence used the same weapons-effect graphs which were published in the handbook. Second, that the numbers in the handbook might be inaccurate, but the uncertainties depended far more on local topography and weather conditions than on details of bomb design. Third, that there were plenty of competent Swiss physicists who could independently check the accuracy of the published numbers. Fourth, that the introduction of cobalt bombs or neutron bombs would change the details of the radiation-dose curves but would not change the overall picture significantly. So they thanked me and said good-bye. I do not know whether their doubts were completely resolved by my remarks. It is an old tradition in Switzerland that one does not trust foreigners unnecessarily. That is, after all, the reason why the Swiss build shelters.

A few days later, I went to a construction site where a house was

being built for one of my Swiss friends. My friend proudly showed
me the half-finished house, and I was able to see for myself how a
Swiss bomb shelter is built. Swiss building codes, even for ordinary
construction, are far more stringent than American codes. Every
part of the house was made of reinforced concrete and looked as if
it was built to last five hundred years. The shelter looked as if it was
built to last five thousand years, like a pharaoh's grave.

The Swiss shelter handbook begins with a couple of sentences
describing the Swiss view of the shelter problem: "As inhabitants of
a small country, we recognize that we shall have no influence on the
choice of weapons used by the belligerents in a major conflict. We
must start from the presumption that we cannot know in advance
which weapons may or may not be launched against our country
at the decisive moment." Switzerland is a small country, stubbornly
determined to do whatever is possible to increase its chances of
survival. Two aspects of the Swiss shelter program are extraordinary: its technical thoroughness and its political quietness. The
Swiss have built a shelter system comprehensive enough and rugged
enough to save a large fraction of their people in many possible
contingencies of nuclear warfare. And they have done this without
noise, without hysteria, without threatening their enemies or scar-
ing their friends.

After I came back from Switzerland to the United States, I began
to talk to some of my friends about my impressions of the Swiss
shelter program. I quickly learned that this is not an acceptable topic
of conversation in polite society. Almost nobody in the United
States wants to hear about shelters. If you persist in talking about
shelters, people excuse themselves and move away. According to the
majority opinion in American academic circles, anybody who takes
shelters seriously must be either an idiot or a lunatic.

The history of shelters in the United States has been the exact
opposite of the history in Switzerland. In the United States, efforts
to persuade people to build shelters have resulted in a lot of noise,
a lot of hysteria, and no coherent action. There was never the
slightest chance that the American people would support a massive
and sustained shelter-building program on the Swiss model. Shelter
programs were started spasmodically in response to transient war
scares, and then gradually petered out after the scares subsided. The
end result of this history is that we have in the United States two
kinds of shelters: a rudimentary public system of fallout shelters in

public buildings, and a scattering of domestic shelters built with private funds and belonging to private homes. The public shelters are poorly maintained and do not usually provide enough shielding to give protection against heavy fallout. The private shelters are too few to protect more than a tiny fraction of the population. Neither public nor private shelters come close to meeting Swiss standards of performance. Everybody in the United States knows that the existing shelters are pitifully inadequate, and almost everybody is fiercely opposed to any serious effort to improve them.

The antipathy toward shelters in the United States has a strong ethical component. Shelters are not merely unpopular; they are perceived by the public to be unethical. This is paradoxical, because civil defense is in its nature the most gentle and humanitarian of all forms of defense. The evil reputation of shelters arises from two main sources. First, the building of private shelters created an image of the rich home-owner sitting comfortably in his shelter and locking his doors against the homeless refugees dying of radiation sickness outside. Second, the building of public shelters, by a government heavily armed with nuclear missiles, created an image of a country setting out to massacre its enemies while keeping its own population safe from retaliation. Both images are exaggerated nightmares, but both also contain an element of truth. If rich people have shelters and poor people have none, or if governments build shelters while simultaneously building offensive missile forces, then shelters are inextricably linked in our imagination with murderous intentions. Shelters have lost their innocence. So far as the United States is concerned, the gentle and humanitarian aspects of shelter-building are overshadowed by nightmares of selfishness and aggression. The ethical justification for shelter-building is turned upside down.

This overturning of ethical perceptions is the fundamental reason why shelters are right for Switzerland and wrong for the United States. In Switzerland the shelter program is public and universal; in theory, and to a large extent in practice, shelters are equally available to all residents, to Italian migrant workers as well as to Zurich bankers. In the United States, shelters are perceived to be socially divisive because housing patterns are socially divisive; no shelter system in the United States could claim to be universal unless it included a public housing program of unprecedented scope and quality. In Switzerland there are no nuclear weapons and no strategic missiles; however effective or ineffective the Swiss shelter system

may be, it threatens nobody. In the United States there are large
missile forces whose official reason for existence is the doctrine of
assured destruction. Assured destruction means that these missiles
are capable of destroying any country which might attack the
United States, whether or not the attacking country has a shelter
system of its own. Shelters are perceived to be futile because the
assured destruction strategy demands that they be ineffective. Shelters are perceived to be threatening because they suggest an intention to make the operation of assured destruction unilateral. If the
United States ever wishes to build shelters in a serious fashion, two
preconditions are essential. Equal right of access to shelters for
everybody must be established as a legal principle, and the doctrine
of assured destruction must be abandoned. Even after these conditions are fulfilled, it is unlikely that Americans will want to spend
large sums of money on civil defense. But they could then do so,
if they wished, without running into ethical entanglements.

While the American public was expressing its opposition to
shelters mainly in moral and emotional terms, military experts and
academic intellectuals were discussing the same issues in a more
analytical style. The public reaction was decisive in determining
government policy; it is impossible for any American government
to force civil defense upon an unwilling population. The debate
among the experts had only a minor influence. But it may still be
useful to examine the analytical arguments for and against shelters,
to see whether they support the Swiss or the American perception
of the problem.

The intellectual case against shelters rests on two counts, analogous to the first two counts of the case against ABM. Shelters are
alleged to be technically ineffective and strategically destabilizing.
Both counts are to some extent valid. A shelter system built in a
halfhearted and desultory fashion, like the existing American shelter
system, would undoubtedly be technically ineffective. And a major
American commitment to a Swiss-style shelter system, if accompanied by the usual American political rhetoric of nuclear confrontation, would scare everybody to death and would undoubtedly be
destabilizing. It is unlikely that any major civil defense program
could be launched in the United States without scare tactics and
public hysteria. But these arguments for the ineffectiveness and the
destabilizing effects of shelters assume present-day American habits
and customs. The arguments may or may not still be valid under

other circumstances and over a longer time scale. American moods and political mores are always subject to change.

If we disregard present-day political constraints and consider the effectiveness of shelters as a purely technical question, the charge of technical ineffectiveness is not supported by the evidence. Properly constructed shelters are, from a technical standpoint, remarkably effective. This does not mean that any feasible shelter system would guarantee the survival of a society after a full-scale nuclear attack. It means that, in any situation short of a direct full-scale attack, a properly constructed shelter system has a good chance of making the difference between the life and the death of a society. And in any situation, up to and including a full-scale attack, a properly constructed shelter system has a better chance of saving your life than any other weapon system which you could buy for the same money. Shelter systems are, in the jargon of the experts, cost-effective. A dollar's worth of shelters gives better protection than a dollar's worth of anything else. The case for technical ineffectiveness of shelters is much weaker than the case for technical ineffectiveness of ABM. The major problems in building an effective shelter system are human and not technical.

The professional arms control community generally concedes that shelters may be technically effective, but fears that they may be destabilizing. Arms controllers usually have no objection to modest shelter systems intended only as disaster insurance. Fallout shelters are strategically innocuous. Blast shelters may be strategically disturbing. What worries the arms controllers is the possibility that a shelter system may be effective enough, or may appear to be effective enough, to upset the balance of strategic deterrence. Shelters, according to the orthodox doctrine of deterrence, are destabilizing insofar as they imply a serious intention to make a country invulnerable to attack. In a situation of stable deterrence, the building of a serious shelter system by one side compels the other side to respond with an increase of offensive forces. The argument is the same as the analogous argument against ABM. And the rebuttal to it is also the same. The doctrine of stable deterrence need not always be true. If ever the world should start moving toward a defensively oriented equilibrium, with offensive forces substantially reduced by treaty, then the effect of shelters will be stabilizing rather than destabilizing. Shelters may be destabilizing in some places and at some times, but there is no law of nature which makes them so.

In summary, the intellectual arguments against shelters are no more conclusive than the intellectual arguments against non-nuclear ABM. And shelters have the advantage of not requiring renegotiation of the SALT I treaty. The decisive rejection of shelters by the American people is based on emotion and historical accident rather than on strategic analysis. The Swiss and the American perceptions of shelters grew out of the different historical experiences of the two peoples. Both perceptions are equally ethical and equally logical.

Perhaps the deepest roots of the American rejection of shelters lie in the cultural tradition of America, the tradition of freedom under the open sky. Americans seem to acquire from their native landscape an aesthetic revulsion against the whole idea of burrowing underground in pursuit of safety. Aesthetic revulsion is the dominant theme in contemporary American writing about shelters. Americans can never share the feelings of warmth and friendliness which Europeans of my generation associate with our experiences of shelters in World War II. I still remember vividly the London underground stations as they were then, with three-tiered bunks stretching from end to end of the platforms on both sides. People loved to come down there to sleep. It was noisy and not very clean, but you met your friends there and played cards, and the atmosphere was cozy and cheerful. Most memorable of all is the feeling of comradeship which prevailed during the bad nights of bombing, when you sat down there out of harm's way and listened to the racket of guns and bombs overhead. People kept on coming down to the shelters at night long after the bombing stopped. They kept on coming down because it was friendlier down there than up above. They kept on coming down even after the war was over, until the bunks were finally removed.

Londoners were left with a persistent nostalgia, which sometimes hits them unexpectedly when they travel by underground and contemplate the platforms now stripped of bunks and of friendliness. Nostalgia is an emotion which grows stronger as the years go by. This shelter nostalgia can never be understood, much less shared, by Americans. But the Swiss were close enough to World War II to understand. Switzerland remained neutral all through the war, but was bombed accidentally from time to time by British and American airplanes. Schaffhausen, close to the German border, was bombed heavily. The Swiss expect, if ever nuclear war rages in Europe, to stay neutral. Neutral or not, they expect to receive their share of the bombs and the fallout. They are prepared for the possibility that they may be attacked deliberately. There is nothing they can do to diminish the probability that these disasters will happen. All they can do is to mitigate the consequences of disaster as far as possible. They carry in their cultural tradition, as Americans do not, the knowledge that when the bombs begin to fall, there is nothing so comforting as a group of friendly faces in a deep hole underground.

It is difficult to imagine any circumstances in which it would make sense for the United States to embark upon a program of nationwide shelter-building in the Swiss style. Aesthetics, ethics, and common sense all argue against it. So long as our land is loaded with nuclear weapons, serious shelter-building is ethically unacceptable. If we succeed in negotiating ourselves into a non-nuclear world, we shall probably feel even less inclined to build shelters than we do today. But the nature of a non-nuclear world is hard to discern from where we stand now. It is possible that a non-nuclear world will be stable and peaceful, but it is more likely that it will be as full of international turbulence and crisis as the world of today. The threat of a relapse into nuclear armament will always be present. The non-nuclear world will at least have one advantage over the world of today: it will allow any country which feels itself threatened to build shelters as an insurance against nuclear surprise, without coming into conflict with the principles of ethics or of strategic stability. If the non-nuclear world brings with it no relief from chronic stress and conflict, even the United States might one day be glad to make use of this possibility. Americans might ultimately come to look upon shelters as the Swiss do now, as tools of survival rather than as symbols of paranoia.

Shelters are the last item on the list of topics which occupied the "Tools" section of this book. "Access to Tools" is the slogan of the *Whole Earth Catalog,* the bible of rugged individualists seeking independence from big organizations and mass society. The Statement of Purpose of the *Whole Earth Catalog,* written by its founder, Stewart Brand, says: "We are as gods and might as well get good at it. . . . A realm of intimate, personal power is developing, power of the individual to conduct his own education, find his own inspiration, shape his own environment, and share his adventure with whoever is interested. Tools that aid this process are sought and promoted by the *Whole Earth Catalog.* " With the tools of modern technology, used in a humane and intelligent fashion, the rational soul can create the material basis for independence. The *Whole Earth Catalog* tells you where the tools are and how they should be used. The weapons which I have been discussing in these last six chapters are also tools. Bombs, missiles, airplanes, submarines, slingshots, suckerfish, ABM systems, shelters, all are tools. They may be used as tools of survival or as tools of terror and domination. I find in all these examples a general pattern. The weapons of survival offer us a road to a hopeful future, while the weapons of terror offer only a road to damnation. Sadly I have to report that the *Whole Earth Catalog,* true to the American cultural tradition, has a section on guns but no section on shelters.

PART III

PEOPLE

War is waged by men; not by beasts, or by gods. It is a peculiarly human activity. To call it a crime against mankind is to miss at least half of its significance; it is also the punishment of a crime. That raises a moral question, the kind of problem with which this age is disinclined to deal. Perhaps some future attempt to provide a solution for it may prove to be even more astonishing than the last.

FREDERIC MANNING, 1930

9

Amateurs at War

9th Yorkshire Regiment
British Expeditionary Force
September 23, 1915

Dear Father,

. . . We are leading a trench life, not in the comfortable front line, but in a hastily sketched-out reserve line where we have everything to make and not much material to make it with. . . . Alas our field kitchen was destroyed, and the cooks were seen decamping in great haste from the farm where it was housed, a very comic sight which cheered the men up no end. We've had really topping weather, a very good thing considering that we are practically bivouacking in the open. . . . The men in the firing line do a lot of machine-gun and rapid fire at night, and whenever an aeroplane is up about a dozen anti-aircraft let loose at it. So that one continually has to break off in the middle of a sentence—a most irritating thing.

I believe we move out of here shortly into the firing line, which will be much more comfortable and perhaps less randomly dangerous, i.e., anybody hit will have the comfort of knowing he was aimed at. But as a matter of fact I think the whole business as things are going at present (no attacks across the open) is about as safe as riding a motor-bike in London.

Please tell Muff that I want very badly hanks, puttees, socks, pyjamas, winter drawers against the change in the weather.

Your loving son,
Freeman

No. 14 General Hospital
Boulogne
February 1916

Dear Father,

    . . . My arm is going on splendidly. I have already discarded
the sling and taken to dry dressings. . . . Two men here interest me
somewhat. (1) a fellow called James . . . by trade and education a
metallurgical chemist; studied at Zurich, knows Germany very well,
has been to Constantinople and shot bears in Bulgaria, then to
U.S.A. to study at Cornell University in New York Province and
to do work for several big factories over there. As I was dozing off
to sleep last night (I share a room with him) he was telling me of
a thrilling chase of German incendiarists in which he took part as
chauffeur at the beginning of the war. The Germans were trying to
burn down a large aeroplane factory, they were disturbed and escaped in a car, he and the others went in pursuit, one man sitting
in the front of his car and potting at the fugitive car with an automatic pistol with view to puncture tyres. This finally proved successful and the fugitives pulled up in a lonely gorge. James was
knocked on the head, one of the Germans shot through stomach,
one of loyalists hit with heavy revolver bullet in arm which was
shattered. He told me various other interesting adventures since
outbreak of war over there—how he disguised himself and attended
the Deutsche Verein and took down verbatim the speech of a Professor Faust of Cornell University who urged rebellion against
U.S.A. should latter espouse English cause. . . .

    Hope you are keeping fit and not disturbed by fears of
Zeppelins.

Your loving son,
Freeman

July 2, 1916

Dear Father,

    We are in bivouacs pretty near behind the line hearing a
tremendous tow-row but not experiencing any of the dangers of a
battle. We are sleeping entirely in the open, last night in a field, the
night before in a wood, as it has been lovely weather it has been very

jolly and we have done our marching at night when it is cool.
. . . Hope you are all fit. Parcels will probably reach all right.

Your loving son,

Freeman

[Telegram]   Buckingham Palace
July 16, 1916

The King and Queen deeply regret the loss you and the
army have sustained by the death of your son in the service of his
country. Their majesties truly sympathize with you in your sorrow.

Captain Freeman Atkey of the 9th Yorkshire Regiment was thirty-
three years old when he died. Until World War I began he had been
a schoolmaster, teaching classical Greek and history to boys in the
upper forms of the famous English public (i.e., private) schools,
Merchant Taylors' and Marlborough. He was a serious scholar.
Under modern conditions a man of his attainments would be an
assistant professor at a university. In Europe before 1914, the elite
high schools were centers of intellectual life comparable with the
provincial universities of today. Freeman fitted the traditional role
of a dedicated schoolmaster. "His rooms," one of his Marlborough
colleagues wrote after his death, "were constantly the meeting-place
of both boys and masters, where discussions took place on every
imaginable subject—literary, artistic, musical, political, and educational." He loved his Greek, his teaching, and his boys. He never
married. His closest friend was his sister Mildred (Muff), who
shared his intellectual interests and traveled around Europe with
him during school vacations.

And yet the peaceful life of a schoolmaster left Freeman rest-
less and unfulfilled. When war broke out in 1914 he at once en-
listed in the army as a volunteer. He was, by all accounts, a brave
and good-humored soldier. "He loved No-Man's-Land," his Marlborough colleague reported, "and constantly crawled out there at
night. On one occasion a star-shell revealed his tall figure, not
lying down but standing erect in the open. Whereupon, instead of
throwing himself flat, he flung out his arms. 'Tell me if I look like
a tree,' he shouted back to the British trenches." When he came
home from France on leave, he talked freely to his sister about his
life in the army. In spite of the horror and tragedy, he was deeply

happy as a soldier. He told Mildred that he had never really been
alive before. As a schoolmaster he had enjoyed watching over the
minds of gifted boys; as an officer in the front lines he had the
greater joy of caring for both bodies and minds of the men under
his command. In school his friendships with the boys were intellectual, limited by the formalities of his position; in the front lines
the friendships were deeper and closer; the shared dangers and
hardships brought men together as comrades and brothers. The
war gave him at the age of thirty-one his first taste of passionate
involvement in a great enterprise. It made everything he had done
before seem unreal.

Freeman's friend George Dyson had also been a schoolmaster at
Marlborough. Freeman and George were exactly the same age, and
shared a passion for motorbikes. They had once ridden together on
their motorbikes over the Alps to Italy. Otherwise they were as
unlike as two young men could be. Freeman was a dreamer, George
an organizer. Freeman grew up in a prosperous middle-class family
and rowed for his college at Cambridge University. George was the
son of a blacksmith, a self-made man with radical opinions and
abrasive manners. The writer Beverley Nichols gives us in his au-
tobiographical memoir, *Father Figure,* a glimpse of George in his
Marlborough days.

> At last I had a music master—a real music master. He was a young
> man called George Dyson. . . . On the first occasion that I played
> to him, things began badly. . . . I was almost entirely self-taught;
> I had never had a proper music-lesson in my life; I had seldom even
> played on a proper piano. . . . Besides, what should I play?—At
> family tea-parties when I was bidden to perform to our few respect-
> able friends, I would play "The Rustle of Spring" to Lady Opherts
> and the Misses Oldfield and Sir St. Vincent Hammick, who would
> keep time with their feet and heave sighs when it was over and tell
> me that I had a beautiful touch. With "The Rustle of Spring," at
> least, I would be safe.
> I played it.
> But Dyson did not tell me that I had a beautiful touch.
> Instead he said, abruptly, "Do you like that stuff?"
> "Not very much, sir."
> "Then why do you play it?" He laughed and answered the ques-
> tion for me; he was a kindly man. "Family tea-parties?"

The explanation was so poignantly accurate that my cheeks began to burn.

"What would you really like to play, if you chose for yourself?"

"I don't know, sir."

"Chopin?"

"Of course, sir."

"Such as?"

"Could I get to know the piano for a minute, sir?"

"Fire away."

He strolled over to the window and looked out on to the court-yard. In the distance one of the eternal school bells was tolling—the bell that gave warning that the gates would shortly close. It was pitched to the note of E and it had a sad but pleasing after-echo that trembled into E flat. I struck the chord of E minor and began to play, taking the tempo from the bell and allowing the melody to dictate itself. This was better, for now the piano was singing. The tune had a clear shape and fell naturally into a framework of thirty-two bars. I hoped that I would be able to remember it.

"What was that?"

Dyson had turned round from the window and was staring at me intently.

"Nothing, sir. I was making it up."

He seemed about to speak. Then he strode over to the piano, pushed me aside, sat down and replayed the piece that I had just invented.

This was, I think, one of the few supreme moments of my long life. In it I lived more intensely than in any ecstatic climax of passion or of prayer. For a few fleeting seconds I was living as I had been born to live. . . . A great musician had taken this melody of mine that had drifted so fortuitously through the window with the bell, and was developing it with all the resources of his technique and his art. And I knew, and he knew, that it was beautiful.

The last chord died away.

"Was that what you wanted?"

"Yes, sir."

"Then write it down."

"I don't think I could, sir."

It was lucky that Dyson was an impatient man; I was near to tears, and if he had been sympathetic instead of brusque I might have lost control of myself. "What d'you mean, you don't think you could?

You know what a crochet is, don't you? You know what a quaver is, don't you? You can find C on the stave, can't you, and turn it into C sharp or C flat? Damn it all, man, don't you realize you're a composer?"

George was such an outstanding success as music master at Marlborough that he was invited to move to Rugby at double the salary. He arrived at Rugby early in 1914 and within a few months got into a violent quarrel with the headmaster. One of the assistant masters denounced George to the headmaster for allegedly having an affair with his wife. As a result, George found himself in July 1914 out on the street, without a job, publicly disgraced, his career in ruins. The standards of middle-class morality at that time made it unlikely that he would ever be readmitted to the genteel world of the public school. He was not a gentleman. He had no capital and no income, no cushion of family connections to save him from disaster. His thoughts turned to suicide.

Then, in the nick of time, came deliverance. At the beginning of August, suddenly and unexpectedly, Europe plunged into war. Recruiting posters went up all over England: "Your King and Country Need You." With heartfelt relief, at the same time as Freeman but for very different reasons, George volunteered for active service. In return for his services to King and Country he would at least be fed and housed. He was put into the 99th Infantry Brigade and sent to Tidworth on Salisbury Plain for basic training. With luck, after the shindy was over, the wrath of the headmaster of Rugby might have subsided.

What does an army do with a musician? It finds him a job that nobody else particularly wants to do. The 99th Infantry Brigade received an order from the War Office to instruct the troops in the use of hand grenades before they embarked for France. The regular officers of the brigade considered a hand grenade to be a new-fangled and unsporting weapon. They had no wish to become involved with it. So they appointed George brigade grenadier officer with the rank of lieutenant, and left it to him to figure out what to do. George had never seen a hand grenade. He quickly discovered that none were available to the brigade for training purposes. He decided to go to the War Office for help.

The War Office informed him that he could learn about hand grenades at a special officers' training course which was instituted for this purpose at Newcastle in the north of England. The course would last two weeks. George obtained permission from his brigade to enroll in the course and took the train to Newcastle. In Newcastle he appeared at the appointed time and place. The people in Newcastle gave him a friendly welcome, but they had never heard of any hand grenade training course. He spent three days visiting all the army units he could find in the neighborhood of Newcastle. Then he took the train back to Tidworth. He never discovered whether the hand grenade training course had actually existed. He concluded that it had probably got lost, somewhere between the plan and the execution, in the labyrinthine corridors of the War Office.

After returning to Tidworth, George found that his standing among the officers had risen. He was now a specialist. He had taken a special training course. He was the man who knew everything there was to know about hand grenades.

George was a practical fellow. He understood from the beginning that the hand grenade business must be taken seriously. He talked with soldiers who had come back on leave from France, and he learned from them what trench warfare was like. Their accounts made it clear that when it came to hand-to-hand fighting in trenches, a well-aimed hand grenade was a far more effective weapon than a bayonet. If the 99th Infantry Brigade was to be adequately prepared for the fighting that awaited it in France, George had a job to do. He still had not seen a hand grenade. He was unable to find any official source of supplies. So he decided the time had come to be creative. He would invent a hand grenade and manufacture it himself.

As a boy, watching his father at work in his blacksmith's forge, George had learned what could be done with a piece of iron. His left thumb had been permanently flattened by one of his father's hammers. He knew how to design a grenade which the local blacksmith in Tidworth could produce in quantities sufficient for his needs. The grenade was a hollow shell of three-eighth-inch-thick iron. Length three inches, diameter two inches, weight one and one-quarter pounds. Open at one end. He mimeographed some instructions for his men, telling them how to use it:

"This dummy can be used as a live bomb by inserting a small charge of gunpowder, properly enclosed and tamped with earth, with safety fuse attached. The charge should be so small as merely to drive the contents of the shell out of the open end. The shell suffers no damage and can be used repeatedly."

Once he had his grenades, George was ready to go ahead with a vigorous training program. He understood two essential facts about the army. First, the average army recruit would need an enormous amount of practice before he could master the skill of throwing live grenades quickly and accurately from one underground trench into another. Second, if the necessary practice could be organized as a competitive sporting event, it would rapidly become popular. So he began with a platoon of soldiers who had nothing else to do, and put them to work digging two lines of trenches with traverses and listening posts and machine gun emplacements.

> The provision of a suitable training ground is most important. Throwing pitches with distances accurately and plainly marked must be provided, and a scheme of trenches must be designed and made giving opportunities for throwing practice at varying distances, and containing traverses and communication trenches such as can be used in the various stages of training. Clear indications of distance are essential. Only by this means can men be taught to judge distances accurately when observing or throwing. . . . Instructors will keep written scores, and encourage competition. Only those bombs which fall clean into the objective will be allowed to score.

When the digging was finished, he divided the platoon into teams and handed out the dummy grenades. After a week of digging, throwing grenades was fun. The teams competed against each other and their performance improved rapidly. After they had mastered the basic skills of throwing, George organized more elaborate tactical exercises.

> Practice 1. Storming a line of fire trenches from the flank. . . .
> Practice 2. As in Practice 1, but including communication trenches. . . .
> Practice 3. The whole grenadier company will charge a line of trenches in extended order, organize themselves, and advance on one or both flanks as in Practice 2.

Throughout these practices instructors will impress on their men the extreme usefulness of throwing frequently into the more distant sections of the trench. This will render effective reply by the enemy very difficult.

In addition to the training notes for his grenadiers, George also wrote a more lyrical description of their activities for the edification of the British public. The lyrical version was published in October 1915 in *The Spectator*. After explaining the rules of the grenade-throwing game, George went on to discuss the introduction of technical improvements:

> Our greatest trouble is that we cannot throw far enough. At thirty or forty yards we are deadly, but no man can bowl a weight of nearly two pounds much further. Then some grenadier finds a piece of disused gaspipe. Three-inch iron pipe—just the thing! Close one end and put a small charge in. The jam-tin fits it nicely. Fire away. A hundred, a hundred and fifty, two hundred yards! We are almost artillery. Another genius, in whose veins the ancient blood is strong, finds some stout rubber bands, makes a forked wooden frame, and a canvas sling. Trench catapult he calls it; an excellent name. We have seen many devices for hurling jam-tins, but we like this the best. It is simple, it is accurate, and, above all, it is noiseless. It completely deceives the enemy, and we are jubilant. We try every kind of missile at every kind of range. We are delighted and fascinated, and never tire of fighting and experimenting with this latest weapon. This, we feel, is new, exhilarating, scientific. It gives us something to do, something to watch. It is effective, too, as the enemy well knows. We are inventive, ingenious, above all, scientific, we men of this modern age. There is nothing we cannot do when we set our minds to it. There is no situation to which we cannot adapt ourselves. We fight with our brains, and we shall win.

The author of this impassioned piece of prose unfortunately neglected to mention the location of his experiments. The readers of *The Spectator* might easily have gained a misleading impression that the piece was written from the trenches in France. George was in fact still at Tidworth when he wrote it. Freeman was by that time in France, observing George's activities with amusement from the perspective of the front lines. Freeman wrote to his sister: "Yesterday on arrival in first line trenches was delighted to find a note from you, also one from Dyson who is still at Tidworth, a great authority on bombs. . . . Very grateful for the parcel and letters, also Dyson's letter in Spectator—most characteristic. Thanks for the rat-poison but I expect they are drowned by now." Freeman had to deal with problems more mundane than the technology of trench catapults. The real war in France was different from the war which George imagined at Tidworth. George was not the first, nor the last, military inventor who failed to make a clear distinction between simulated battles and real battles.

Meanwhile, back at Tidworth, the noise and gusto of George's training exercises had attracted some official attention. The commander of his brigade came over to see what was going on. He was favorably impressed. A few days later he brought the division commander to have a look. The division commander asked if he could have some copies of George's mimeographed notes to give to his other brigade. The other brigade soon had its training ground and dummy grenades too. Then the corps commander came to visit, and more copies of the mimeographed notes were handed out. So it went on, until finally the news of George's activities reached the War Office. The War Office decided to publish George's notes as an official training manual for the entire British army. A little blue book, small enough to fit into a soldier's pocket, "Grenade Warfare. Notes on the Training and Organization of Grenadiers. By Lieutenant G. Dyson, Price sixpence net," was published in 1915. It was reprinted in massive quantities as the war went on. Best of all, the publisher paid royalties to the author. The royalties on hundreds of thousands of sixpences trickled into George's bank account, and he found himself for the first time in his life free of financial worries. In 1917, when the United States entered the war, the United States War Department needed a manual for the training of American grenadiers, and George's book was republished in New York, this time in hard covers, with a price tag of fifty cents. By that time the author had arrived in France and had seen some real hand grenades in action, but whatever he may have learned in France was not recorded in the later editions of his book.

George's stay in France was briefer than Freeman's. He was promoted to captain and served at the front for a few months. One day, for some reason which he could never afterward remember, he was riding a horse during an artillery bombardment. A shell landed immediately underneath the horse. George woke up to find himself uninjured, lying in a pool of blood and minced horseflesh. After that he was no longer much good as a soldier. He began to have frequent fainting fits. The army doctors diagnosed his condition as shell-shock, which meant that he was sent back to England and given an honorable discharge from the army. He emerged from the army hospital exhausted and bewildered. Having nowhere else to turn, he got in touch with Freeman's sister. She told him the news of Freeman's death.

Mildred Atkey was totally shattered by the death of her brother, the only male friend and companion she had ever had. George consoled her in her grief while she nursed him back to health. Mildred's father found a job for George in the office of a barrister colleague. Before the war was over, Mildred and George were married. Three years later they produced a daughter. Another three years later, when they were both over forty years old, they produced a new Freeman to take the place of the one they had lost. So the moral of the story is that my sister and I owe our lives to a sniper's bullet. If our uncle Freeman had kept his head down, we would never have existed.

Paul Fussell's book *The Great War and Modern Memory* describes with a wealth of literary illustrations the dominating influence of World War I upon the thought and language of postwar England and America. World War I was the turning point of European culture, the point at which the dominant mood changed from liberal idealism to skepticism and black humor. My sister and I, growing up as children amid the ruins, were exposed to the heritage of World War I in full force. Listening to our parents talking about the past, we formed an image of the years before 1914 as a golden age irrecoverably lost, of the war itself as an incomprehensible whirlpool of mud and blood, of the post-war world as a broken-spirited remnant of departed glory. These images of paradise lost, of unspeakable massacre, and of impoverished survival were deeply ingrained in our minds almost as soon as we could talk. We became aware of the death of Uncle Freeman as the central tragic event in our family history, an event on a par with the crucifixion of Jesus, to be spoken about only in tones of hushed reverence. The words which were spoken so often in church, "He died that we might live," could be applied equally well to Jesus and to Uncle Freeman. As children, we thought of the war as an overwhelming natural catastrophe, not as a human action for which our parents' generation might be held responsible. We thought of Uncle Freeman, and of our father too, as innocent victims of the war. We never thought of them as willing participants, as warriors going enthusiastically into battle. Least of all did we think of them as taking delight in the apparatus of killing. Freeman's letters from the front and George's grenade-fighting book were sitting somewhere on a high shelf, out of reach of children's inquisitive hands.

Only much later, as we grew up, my sister and I began to see the realities of World War I behind the myths of our childhood. I remember one crucial event in my awakening to the truth. This happened when I was fifteen years old, on September 3, 1939, the day Prime Minister Chamberlain declared war on Hitler and announced on the radio the beginning of World War II. I was then thinking of this new war in terms of the image I had formed of World War I, as a purposeless and hopeless slaughter with no tolerable end in sight. I felt depressed and scared. I expected that my father, himself one of the victims of World War I, would be at least as depressed and scared as I was. To my great surprise and annoyance, he was not at all depressed. He was disgustingly cheerful. He told us how happy he was that somebody had finally had the courage to stand up and say no to Hitler. He talked about the big new airplane factories where we were building the bombers which would teach Hitler how to behave. I was horrified to hear my humane and peace-loving father expressing these bellicose sentiments, just as if World War I had never happened. What I heard for the first time that day was the old grenade fighter coming back to life.

10

Education of a Warrior

November 1937

In England in November it gets dark early. I walked home as usual after my music lesson, groping my way through the War Cloister. I was thirteen and already I could understand why people said our cloister was the finest war memorial in Europe. It is a square colonnade, built of white stone, enclosing a plot of grass with a plain white cross in the center. The outside wall is unbroken except for three gates for people to pass through. All round the outside wall the names are carved, the names of six hundred boys from our school who were killed in the 1914–1918 war, the war which for us was simply The War. Architecturally, the War Cloister is a masterpiece. Although we walked through it every day, its atmosphere of quietness, dignity, and tragedy never weakened.

That evening as I came through the War Cloister alone, I saw a soldier kneeling. I saw him clearly, a young man in the familiar uniform of The War. Then I looked again, and he wasn't there. I found this not particularly surprising. Later I told my friends about it and we agreed that it was not surprising. We were agnostics, not quite believing in ghosts and not quite disbelieving. Maybe I had had an ordinary hallucination, induced by the solemnity of the War Cloister. Or maybe I had actually seen one of the six hundred, paying his respects there to the living as we did to the dead. If one of the six hundred were still restlessly haunting the earth, it would be a natural thing for him to come to find peace in the War Cloister.

The older generation had fought The War and built the War

Cloister. They were determined that we should constantly be reminded of their tragedy. And indeed our whole lives were overshadowed by it. Every year on November 11 there was the official day of mourning. But much heavier on our souls weighed the daily reminders that the best and the brightest of a whole generation had fallen. English life had sunk into sloth and mediocrity, we were told, because none were left of those who should have been our leaders. The missing generation was conspicuous by its absence in the government and in the professions. Everywhere tired men of sixty-five were doing the work that vigorous men of forty-five should have done. The arithmetic was simple. Our school put out each year a graduating class of eighty boys. Our six hundred dead were more than seven complete years. The classes of 1914, 1915, 1916 were wiped out. Few survived from the eight years 1910–1917.

We of the class of 1941 were no fools. We saw clearly enough in 1937 that another bloodbath was approaching. We knew how to figure the odds. We saw no reason to expect that the next round would be less bloody than the one before. We expected the fighting to start in 1939 or 1940, and we observed that our chances of coming through it alive were about the same as if we had belonged to the class of 1915 or 1916. We calculated the odds to be about ten to one that we would be dead in five years.

Feeling ourselves doomed, we were comforted by the thought that the whole society in which we lived was doomed equally. The coming war would certainly bring massive bombing of civilian populations. We expected bombing, not with old-fashioned high explosives, but with poison gas such as the Italians had recently been using in Ethiopia, or with the anthrax bombs that Aldous Huxley described in *Brave New World*. We expected biological weapons to be used more and more recklessly, until some new Black Death would get out of control and destroy half the population of Europe. Gas had been used recklessly by both sides in World War I, and there was no reason to hope that germ warfare would lend itself to any greater restraint. We then expected World War II to end with man-made plagues destroying our civilization, just as inevitably as forty-five years later we are expecting thermonuclear weapons to do the job in World War III.

In 1937, we of the younger generation had absorbed from our elders this profoundly tragic view of life, and we had not yet asserted our independence. We read and reread the play *The Ascent of F6*, by Auden and Isherwood, which appeared in 1936 and marvelously expressed the mood of the time. I used to know long stretches of this play by heart. Especially one of the hero's opening speeches:

> O, happy the foetus that miscarries and the frozen idiot that cannot cry "Mama"! Happy those run over in the street today or drowned at sea, or sure of death from incurable diseases! They cannot be made a party to the general fiasco. For of that growth which in maturity had seemed eternal it is now no tint of thought or feeling that has tarnished, but the great ordered flower itself is withering; its life-blood dwindled to an unimportant trickle, it stands under heaven now a fright and ruin, only to crows and larvae a gracious refuge.

September 1938

We all enjoyed digging the air raid shelter. This was in the days of crisis before the Munich agreement. Sporting activities were suspended and the boys were put to work with shovels, digging a long trench. It was obvious, as we said, to anybody of the meanest intelligence that the thing would never be of the slightest use. It was a quarter of a mile away from the nearest school building, across an open field. It was in a low-lying spot where any lethal gas was most likely to collect. And after the first good rain it would be full of water anyway. So we set to work with a will, digging this hole in the ground and enjoying the autumn sunshine. The enterprise was so demonstrably useless that we could take part in it without compromising our pacifist principles. We looked with satisfaction at the completed trench, regarding it as a monument to the total bankruptcy of the military mind.

By that time we had made our break with the establishment and we were fierce pacifists. We saw no hope that any acceptable future would emerge from the coming war. We had made up our minds that we would at least not be led like sheep to the slaughter as the class of 1915 had been. Our mood was no longer tragic resignation, but anger and contempt for the older generation which had brought us into this mess. We raged against the hypocrisy and stupidity of our elders, just as the young rebels raged in the 1960s in America, and for similar reasons.

We were not so naive as to blame our predicament upon Hitler. We saw Hitler only as a symptom of the decay of our civilization, not as the cause of it. To us the Germans were not enemies but fellow victims of the general insanity. The first book I read in German was Remarque's *All Quiet on the Western Front,* describing the German class of 1914 torn to pieces by The War in the same way as their English contemporaries. Remarque's book is as powerful a memorial to them as our War Cloister is to our six hundred. My tears stained the pages of my German dictionary as I came to the end of the story. We did not bother to read *Mein Kampf.*

We looked around us and saw nothing but idiocy. The great British Empire visibly crumbling, and the sooner it fell apart the better so far as we were concerned. Millions of men unemployed, and millions of children growing up undernourished in dilapidated slums. A king mouthing patriotic platitudes which none of us believed. A government which had no answer to any of its problems except to rearm as rapidly as possible. A military establishment which believed in bombing the German civilian economy as the only feasible strategy. A clique of old men in positions of power, blindly repeating the mistakes of 1914, having learned nothing and forgotten nothing in the intervening twenty-four years. A population of middle-aged nonentities, caring only for money and status, too stupid even to flee from the wrath to come.

We looked for one honest man among the political leaders of the world. Chamberlain, our prime minister, we despised as a hypocrite. Hitler was no hypocrite, but he was insane. Nobody had any use for Stalin or Mussolini. Winston Churchill was our archenemy, the man personally responsible for the Gallipoli campaign, in which so many of our six hundred died. He was the incorrigible warmonger, already planning the campaigns in which we were to die. We hated Churchill as our American successors in the 1960s hated Johnson and Nixon. But we were lucky in 1938 to find one man whom we could follow and admire, Mahatma Gandhi. We loved him for three things. First, he was against the empire. Second, he was against wealth and privilege. Third, his gospel of nonviolent resistance gave us hope. We seized upon nonviolence as the alternative to never-ending bombs and death. We were not sure whether Hitler could be successfully opposed with nonviolence and turned from his evil ways, but at least there was a chance. With bombs and guns, we were convinced that there was no chance. If the worst came to the worst, if we opposed Hitler nonviolently and he killed us, we should be dying for a good cause. That would be better than dying for Mr. Churchill and the empire.

Brian was our leader. He was sixteen, and Welsh. He had the eloquence of a Welsh preacher and we loved to listen to him talk. He claimed that he could make even the stupidest and stubbornest person believe in nonviolence, if only he could talk to him for six hours. "Talking to them for six hours" was Brian's answer to all problems. His ultimate purpose was to talk to Hitler for six hours, or die in the attempt.

The school had an OTC, corresponding in function to the American ROTC. Brian decided that we should nonviolently resist taking part in the OTC. The school authorities amiably put us to work growing cabbages instead. Some time later the colonel in charge of the OTC shot himself. We greeted his death without sympathy, seeing it as a vindication of our moral superiority.

We subscribed to *Peace News,* the organ of the Peace Pledge Union, and spent our small savings on quantities of propaganda leaflets which the Union supplied. We soon found that leaflets did not make converts to our cause. Nothing short of a six-hour session with Brian seemed to be effective. It was uphill work. In the end Brian had about ten wholehearted disciples, in a school of four hundred boys. The worst of it was that nobody bothered to oppose us. We were just ignored. The rotten society around us blundered along to its inevitable doom, heedless of our warnings.

We had grand visions of the redemption of Europe by nonviolence. The goose-stepping soldiers, marching from country to country, meeting no resistance, finding only sullen noncooperation and six-hour lectures. The leaders of the nonviolence being shot, and others coming forward fearlessly to take their places. The goose-stepping soldiers, sickened by the cold-blooded slaughter, one day refusing to carry out the order to shoot. The massive disobedience of the soldiers disrupting the machinery of military occupation. The soldiers, converted to nonviolence, returning to their own country to use on their government the tactics that we had taught them. The final impotence of Hitler confronted with the refusal of his own soldiers to hate their enemies. The collapse of military institutions everywhere, leading to an era of worldwide peace and sanity.

These visions were for us very real. We knew that we faced a long struggle to make them real even to a minority of our countrymen. But we were not discouraged. After all, Gandhi had struggled for thirty years to make such visions real in India, and he had succeeded. Our self-confidence was sustained by the knowledge that, if our program did not make sense in terms of immediate practical politics, the idea of fighting World War II in order to save the Czechs or the Poles or the European Jews made sense even less. We could see clearly that however badly we might suffer in the coming war, the Czechs and the Poles and the Jews would suffer worse. In this, as in many of our judgments of that time, history has proved us right.

Above all, we were strengthened by the certainty that our program was moral and the society around us was immoral. Whether or not we had a chance of succeeding, we must stand up for the right as we saw it. In 1938 we were no longer responsive to the oriental fatalism of Auden and Isherwood's *F6*. In that year Cecil Day Lewis published a new volume of poems called *Overtures to Death*. His robust pessimism suited our new mood much better:

> So take a happy view—
> This lawn graced with the candle-flames of crocus,
> Frail-handed girls under the flowering chestnut,
>   Or anything will do
> That time takes back before it seems untrue.
>
>   And, if the truth were told,
> You'd count it luck, perceiving in what shallow
> Crevices and few crumbling grains of comfort
>   Man's joy will seed, his cold
> And hardy fingers find an eagle's hold.

September 1940

My father had built a small house on a swampy piece of land, a mile from the nearest village. We came home one fine day after spending a night in London. We found our road barricaded, with a big sign saying: "Danger. Unexploded Bomb." A number of serious men in tin hats were inspecting the property. They had discovered on our lot eight neatly drilled holes, exactly straddling the house. Each hole was round, and so deep that one could not see the bottom. We were informed that in each hole there was sitting a hundred-kilogram time bomb, ready to explode at any moment. It was out of the question for us to live in the house until the bombs had been disarmed. The bomb disposal squads had plenty of pressing business to attend to in London and elsewhere, before they could be expected to come to our help. And in fact it was unreasonable to ask anybody to risk his life digging these bombs out, since they inconvenienced nobody except us.

The bombs had been dropped during the night by some bewildered Germans who had failed to find their way to London. Perhaps they had mistaken the Solent for the Thames. The Solent is two miles wide and from twenty thousand feet it would be much easier to see.

While we were still wondering what to do, a bomb disposal expert drove up to our lot and asked to be shown the holes. As soon as he saw the first hole he knelt down and sniffed into it. Then he laughed. He rapidly went round to the other seven and took a good sniff at each. "You can take down the sign," he said as he drove away. The bombs had all exploded when they landed. Our ground was so soft and sticky that they exploded deep underneath, without even making a crater. When we went into the house we found not a plate broken.

So this was the war against which we had raged with the fury of righteous adolescence. It was all very different from what we had expected. Our gas masks, issued to the civilian population before the war began, were gathering dust in closets. Nobody spoke of anthrax bombs anymore. London was being bombed, but our streets were not choked with maimed and fear-crazed refugees. All our talk about the collapse of civilization began to seem a little irrelevant.

Mr. Churchill had now been in power for five months, and he had carried through the socialist reforms which the Labour party had failed to achieve in twenty years. War profiteers were unmercifully taxed, unemployment disappeared, and the children of the slums were for the first time adequately fed. It began to be difficult to despise Mr. Churchill as much as our principles demanded.

Our little band of pacifists was dwindling. Brian had left the school in 1939, and without him we made no new converts. Those of us who were still faithful continued to grow cabbages and boycott the OTC, but we felt less and less sure of our moral superiority. For me the final stumbling block was the establishment of the Pétain-Laval government in France. This was in some sense a pacifist government. It had abandoned violent resistance to Hitler and chosen the path of reconciliation. Many of the Frenchmen who supported Pétain were sincere pacifists, sharing my faith in nonviolent resistance to evil. Unfortunately, many were not. The worst of it was that there was no way to distinguish the sincere pacifists from the opportunists and collaborators. Pacifism was destroyed as a moral force as soon as Laval touched it.

Gradually it became clear to me that what had happened in France would also happen in England, if ever our pacifist principles were put into practice. Suppose that we succeeded in converting Mr. Churchill and a majority of the British public to the gospel of nonviolence. What then? We would nobly lay down our arms and impress our moral superiority upon the German invaders by silent noncooperation. But the English equivalent of Laval would soon appear, to make a deal with the Germans and make us contemptible in their eyes. Quite soon a few of us would forget our pacifism and begin an armed resistance in the Scottish highlands. After that, Englishmen would have to choose between a collaborationist government in London and a heroic fight in the Cairngorm mountains. Any honest pacifist would choose the Cairngorms.

By the end of 1940, the only members of our group whose faith remained alive were the religious pacifists, boys who believed in nonviolence as a matter of individual conscience independent of political considerations. Sadly I parted company from them. For me pacifism had been not a religion but a political program, and Laval had tarnished it irretrievably.

Those of us who abandoned Gandhi and reenlisted in the OTC did not do so with any enthusiasm. We still did not imagine that a country could fight and win a world war without destroying its soul in the process. If anybody had told us in 1940 that England would survive six years of war against Hitler, achieve most of the political objectives for which the war had been fought, suffer only one third of the casualties we had in World War I, and finally emerge into a world in which our moral and humane values were largely intact, we would have said, "No, we do not believe in fairy tales."

Having been brought up to take a tragic view of life, we were pleasantly surprised by every small rebirth of hope. The ludicrous incompetence with which the Germans conducted their bombing campaign made the war almost enjoyable. We did not need Churchill's oratory to tell us that we could take it. We liked much better the quiet rhythms of T. S. Eliot, whose *East Coker* appeared in September 1940 and sold out five editions by February 1941.

> There is only the fight to recover what has been lost
> And found and lost again and again: and now, under conditions
> That seem unpropitious. But perhaps neither gain nor loss.
> For us, there is only the trying. The rest is not our business.
>
> Home is where one starts from. As we grow older
> The world becomes stranger, the pattern more complicated
> Of dead and living.

July 1943

I arrived at the headquarters of the Royal Air Force Bomber Command just in time for the big raids against Hamburg. On the night of July 24 we killed forty thousand people and lost only twelve bombers, by far the best we had ever done. For the first time in history we created a fire storm, which killed people even inside shelters. The casualties were about ten times as numerous as in a normal attack of the same size without a fire storm.

Nobody understands to this day why or how fire storms begin. In every big raid we tried to raise a fire storm, but we succeeded only twice, once in Hamburg and once two years later in Dresden. Probably the thing happens only when the bombing releases a preexisting instability in the local meteorology. The big slaughter in Hamburg and Dresden was not the result of a political decision to attack those places in any special way. It was a technological accident. Berlin and the Ruhr cities received many more attacks of the same size as Dresden's, but never had a fire storm.

The Americans later had the same experience in Japan. They raised two fire storms, in Tokyo and Hiroshima, each of which killed about a hundred thousand people. Their other raids, including the nuclear attack on Nagasaki, were less destructive.

My office at Bomber Command was in a low wooden building in the middle of a forest. Thick beech trees were growing right up to the windows, so that the room was dark summer and winter. The idea was to make it invisible from the air. I do not know whether it was in fact invisible; the Germans never disturbed us.

I had come to this place after an interview with the novelist C. P. Snow, who was at that time responsible for putting technically trained people into appropriate jobs. I was nineteen and had finished two years at the university, so that I counted as a trained mathematician. Snow explained to me that my job, which was called Operational Research, would require little mathematics but a lot of common sense and political tact. I went to it willingly.

In a short time I became the Bomber Command expert on collisions. Since we bombed at night and did not fly in formation, collisions occurred from time to time. The crews who returned had many experiences of narrowly avoided collisions. They also frequently reported seeing fatal collisions over Germany, but it was impossible to trust these reports, because a single bomber hit by a shell and falling in two pieces would look like a collision. The crews were understandably resentful. They were willing to risk being shot down by German fighters, feeling that they had at least a chance to shoot back, but to die in collisions seemed utterly pointless.

The Command had a difficult decision to make. On the one hand, we disliked to lose bombers in collisions. On the other hand, we knew that the preponderant cause of bomber losses, then running at the almost unendurable rate of 4 percent per operation, was the German night fighters. By bunching the bombers closer together we reduced the losses to fighters, using the same principle that made convoying of ships a good tactic against submarines. Each time we ordered the bombers to fly closer, we cut down the total losses and increased the anxiety of the crews about collisions. The Command had to decide how far we could go in concentrating the bomber stream before we would begin to lose more to collisions than we should save from fighters. The first essential in making a sound decision was to know how many bombers were colliding.

I collected whatever information I could find about collisions. About the collisions we were ultimately interested in, lethal collisions over Germany, I found no information that I could trust. But I had good information about nonlethal collisions over Germany, since all damage to returning bombers was regularly reported to us in detail. With more difficulty I collected evidence concerning nonlethal and lethal collisions in night flying over England. The numbers of each kind were small but reliable. The ratio of lethal to nonlethal collisions over England was about three to one. In this ratio I had already allowed for the fact that some nonlethal collisions over England would have been lethal if they had occurred over

Germany. So I told the Command that our best guess at the number of lethal collisions over Germany was to multiply the number of nonlethal collisions by three. That was all the mathematics I had to do.

In practical terms, my information meant that we were losing only about one bomber to collisions in a thousand sorties. We told the commander in chief that this was not nearly enough. We advised him to increase fivefold the density of the bomber force, so that the collision losses would come up to one-half percent. We told him that he would save much more than one-half percent in losses to fighters. The Command followed our advice, and the crews reluctantly obeyed. This decision confirmed the crews' belief that their commander in chief, familiarly known as Bert Harris or Butcher Harris, was as callous toward them as he was toward the Germans.

Bert Harris was a man of the same stamp as his American contemporary Curtis LeMay, who organized the strategic bombardment of Japan. Strategic bomber forces seem to require such men to command them. Secure in his personal relationship with Churchill, Harris ran his show as he saw fit, frequently ignoring or overriding his nominal superiors at the Air Ministry. At one time I had on my desk a lengthy memorandum addressed to Harris by Air Chief Marshal Sir Norman Bottomley, Deputy Chief of the Air Staff, entitled "On the Proper Use of a Bomber Force." Underneath the title was penciled in Harris's neat hand: "A lesson for Grandma on how to suck eggs. A.T.H." Unfortunately, we had in those days no Xerox machines to preserve such indiscretions for the enjoyment of future historians.

I was in a highly privileged position at Bomber Command. I knew much more than most of the operational officers about the general course of the campaign. I knew much more than the cabinet ministers in London about the details of our operations. I was one of very few people who knew what were the objectives of the campaign, how miserably we were failing to meet these objectives, and how expensive this was for us in money and lives. The bombing campaign represented roughly one quarter of the total British war effort. It was costing the Germans less than this to defend themselves and to repair the industrial damage. Their defenses were so effective that the Americans had to give up daylight bombing over most of Germany from the fall of 1943 until the summer of 1944. We stubbornly refused to give up when the Americans did, but the defenses made it impossible for us to bomb accurately. We stopped trying to hit precise military objectives. Burning down cities was all we could do, and so we did that. Even in killing the civilian population we were inefficient. The Germans had killed one person for every ton of bombs that they dropped on England. To kill a German, we dropped on the average three tons.

I felt deeply my responsibility, being in possession of all this information which was so carefully concealed from the British public. I was sickened by what I knew. Many times I decided I had a moral obligation to run out into the streets and tell the British people what stupidities were being done in their name. But I never had the courage to do it. I sat in my office until the end, carefully calculating how to murder most economically another hundred thousand people.

After the war ended, I read reports of the trials of men who had been high up in the Eichmann organization. They had sat in their offices, writing memoranda and calculating how to murder people efficiently, just like me. The main difference was that they were sent to jail or hanged as war criminals, while I went free. I felt a certain sympathy for these men. Probably many of them loathed the SS as much as I loathed Bomber Command, but they, too, had not had the courage to speak out. Probably many of them, like me, lived through the whole six years of the war without ever seeing a dead human being.

Already by 1943 the war had made us all insensitive. Poetry did not heighten our feelings then as it had done earlier. In 1943 Cecil Day Lewis spoke for us in a short poem entitled "Where Are the War Poets?"

> They who in folly or mere greed
> Enslaved religion, markets, laws,
> Borrow our language now and bid
> Us to speak up in freedom's cause.
>
> It is the logic of our times,
> No subject for immortal verse—
> That we who lived by honest dreams
> Defend the bad against the worse.

August 1945

I was all set to fly to Okinawa. We had defeated the Germans, but Mr. Churchill had still not had enough. He persuaded President Truman to let him join in the bombing of Japan with a fleet of three hundred bombers which he called Tiger Force. We were to be based in Okinawa and, since the Japanese had almost no air defenses, we were to bomb, like the Americans, in daylight.

I found this continuing slaughter of defenseless Japanese even more sickening than the slaughter of well-defended Germans. But still I did not quit. By that time I had been at war so long that I could hardly remember peace. No living poet had words to describe that emptiness of the soul which allowed me to go on killing without hatred and without remorse. But Shakespeare understood it, and he gave Macbeth the words:

> . . . I am in blood
> Stepp'd in so far that, should I wade no more,
> Returning were as tedious as go o'er.

I was sitting at home, eating a quiet breakfast with my mother, when the morning paper arrived with the news of Hiroshima. I understood at once what it meant. "Thank God for that," I said. I knew that Tiger Force would not fly, and I would never have to kill anybody again.

11

Scientists and Poets

Technology, in the impressions of World War I which I absorbed as a child, was a malevolent monster broken loose from human control. This view of technology was widespread in England at that time, not only among the poets and literary intellectuals whose writings Paul Fussell quotes in *The Great War and Modern Memory*, but also among scientists. The most memorable description of the war which I read as a scientifically inclined teen-ager came from the biologist J. B. S. Haldane:

> I can see before me two scenes from my experience of the late war. The first is a glimpse of a forgotten battle of 1915. It has a curious suggestion of a rather bad cinema film. Through a blur of dust and fumes there appear, quite suddenly, great black and yellow masses of smoke which seem to be tearing up the surface of the earth and disintegrating the works of man with an almost visible hatred. These form the chief parts of the picture, but somewhere in the middle distance one can see a few irrelevant-looking human figures, and soon there are fewer. It is hard to believe that these are the protagonists in the battle. One would rather choose those huge substantive oily black masses which are so much more conspicuous, and suppose that the men are in reality their servants, and playing an inglorious, subordinate and fatal part in the combat. It is possible, after all, that this view is correct.

Haldane published this vignette in 1924 in a little book with the title *Daedalus, or Science and the Future*, which I found in my high school science library. It sold well and was widely read in scientific circles. Haldane had been an outstandingly brave and conscientious soldier. His friends in the trenches had given him the nickname Bombo because of his attachment to a noisy experimental trench mortar which he liked to carry around in the front lines and blast off unexpectedly from time to time. Besides experimenting with trench mortars, he also served as guinea pig in experiments on the effectiveness of various types of war gases and gas masks. In spite of all these extracurricular volunteer activities, he survived the war. His cold and clinical view of the battles of 1915 extended also to the future:

> The prospect of the next world-war has at least this satisfactory element. In the late war the most rabid nationalists were to be found well behind the front line. In the next war no one will be behind the front line. It will be brought home to all concerned that war is a very dirty business.

The literature of disgust was louder in England than elsewhere. This may have had something to do with a fact noted by Paul Fussell:

> There were national styles in trenches as in other things. The French trenches were nasty, cynical, efficient and temporary. Kipling remembered the smell of delicious cooking emanating from some in Alsace. The English were amateur, vague, ad hoc and temporary. The Germans were efficient, clean, pedantic and permanent. Their occupants proposed to stay where they were.

My uncle, writing from France in 1915, confirms Fussell's impression:

> The line we are now in is different from our previous lot, very much more ramshackle, evidently constructed in a great hurry under heavy shell fire. It has never really been taken in hand and bits of old houses, old clothes, tin pots, sacks, etc. etc. make up the core of the defences. You must not imagine a fire trench as dug *down*, it is dug up, nowadays, more of a breast-work than a trench, and the original builders used any old thing to do it with. . . . We are plagued with rats and mice, and if you can discover a poison which makes them die out in the open and not in their holes, please send it.

The soldiers of all nationalities carried home from the war memories of pain, death, and waste. But in British memories there remained a uniquely pervasive background of physical squalor. The lasting image of war was men sharing a mud-filled ditch with corpse-fed rats. The degradation of the living left in men's minds a deeper revulsion than the sacrifice of the dead. During the years leading up to the outbreak of World War II, when my school friends and I looked ahead to the future, we were not sure whether being killed would be worse than surviving. Wilfred Owen's poem "Mental Cases," in which Owen is describing survivors of the battles of 1917, gave us a picture of what might await us if we were unlucky enough to survive:

> Who are these? Why sit they here in twilight?
> —These are men whose minds the Dead have ravished.
> Memory fingers in their hair of murders,
> Multitudinous murders they once witnessed.
> Wading sloughs of flesh these helpless wander,
> Treading blood from lungs that had loved laughter.
> Always they must see these things and hear them,
> Batter of guns and shatter of flying muscles,
> Carnage incomparable, and human squander,
> Rucked too thick for these men's extrication.

Owen himself was not one of the survivors. He was killed leading an attack on November 4, 1918, seven days before the armistice.

Thirty years later, the invention and use of nuclear weapons carried the technology of death a giant step further. The nuclear bombs with their mushroom clouds make Haldane's vision of war, the black explosions attended by doomed and puny human servants, look even more plausible. How could this have happened? How could supposedly sane people, with the stink of the trenches still fresh in their memory, bring themselves to create a new technology of death a thousand times more powerful than the guns of World War I? To answer these questions, it is necessary once again to examine the career of Robert Oppenheimer, the man who, both as actor and as symbol, played the central role in the history of nuclear weapons.

Many books, and a couple of plays, have been written about Oppenheimer. Some of them contain more fantasy than fact. I, too, have been guilty of writing an Oppenheimer fantasy, in a recent book where I identified him with MF, the fictional hero of *The Ascent of F6*. If I venture now to return to the discussion of Oppenheimer's life and character, it is because a rich new source of historical facts has recently become available. These facts throw a fresh light on Oppenheimer and on the mental climate out of which nuclear weapons grew.

The new source is the volume of *Letters and Recollections* of Robert Oppenheimer, edited by Alice Smith and Charles Weiner. It gives us a far more authentic and many-sided picture of Oppenheimer than we had before. In 1981 I met Robert's brother Frank at a meeting in Toronto and thanked him for allowing Smith and Weiner to publish Robert's letters to him, which are in many ways the best and the most revealing in the whole collection. "Yes," said Frank. "At one time I had thought of publishing his letters to me in a separate book. But it is much better to have the five or six characters Robert showed to his various friends all together in one place."

In 1932, when Robert was twenty-seven and Frank was nineteen, Robert wrote a letter to Frank on the subject of discipline. "But because I believe that the reward of discipline is greater than its immediate objective, I would not have you think that discipline without objective is possible: in its nature discipline involves the subjection of the soul to some perhaps minor end; and that end must be real, if the discipline is not to be factitious. Therefore I think that all things which evoke discipline: study, and our duties to men and to the commonwealth, war, and personal hardship, and even the need for subsistence, ought to be greeted by us with profound gratitude; for only through them can we attain to the least detachment; and only so can we know peace." I have pulled these sentences out of their context. It is true, as Frank said, that Robert's letters to him show only one face of a six-faced mountain. But still I believe that these two sentences contain a key to the central core of Robert's nature, to the sudden transformation which changed him eleven years later from bohemian professor to driving force of the bomb project at Los Alamos. Perhaps it also contains a key to the dilemmas we face today in trying to deal wisely with the problems of nuclear weapons and nuclear war.

How could it have happened that a sensitive and intelligent young man in the year 1932 put war on his short list of things for which we should be profoundly grateful? This little word "war" appears in his letter untouched by any trace of irony. Oppenheimer's gratitude for it is as sincere as the gratitude of the poet

Rupert Brooke, who greeted the international catastrophe of 1914 with the famous words: "Now God be thanked who has matched us with His Hour." But Brooke died in 1915, and his reputation as a poet was irretrievably smashed in the years of muddy slaughter which followed. The poets whose works survived the war and were read by the literary intellectuals of Oppenheimer's generation were the poets of plain-speaking disillusionment, Owen and Sassoon, describing war as seen by the victims:

> If you could hear, at every jolt, the blood
> Come gargling from the froth-corrupted lungs . . .

To their voices was added a little later the unheroic portrait of demobilized soldiers and their wives in Eliot's "Waste Land." Finally, there appeared in Berlin in 1928 the most famous of all the literary descriptions of World War I, Remarque's *All Quiet on the Western Front.* My copy of Remarque's book was bought in Austria in June 1929, by which time 450,000 copies had been printed. Oppenheimer was then in Switzerland, studying physics at the Federal Institute of Technology in Zurich. There is no evidence in his letters from Zurich that he read Remarque, or that he was even aware of the rising tide of militarism in Germany, against which Remarque's book was the last despairing protest.

The hero of Remarque's book is Paul Bäumer, a young soldier who sees each of his friends and comrades killed one by one, most of them gruesomely and to no military purpose. The villain is the schoolmaster Kantorek, who preaches the glories of military service and persuades the whole of Paul's high school class to enlist in the army even before they are drafted. After the first slow and pointless death, Paul reflects:

> Of course this has nothing to do with Kantorek. What would the world come to if we said it was his fault? There were thousands of Kantoreks, all convinced that they were acting for the best while keeping themselves safe and comfortable. And that was for us the proof of their bankruptcy. . . . While they were still writing and talking, we watched our friends dying in field-hospitals. While they proclaimed patriotic duty to be the greatest thing on earth, we knew that the fear of death is stronger. That does not mean that we were mutineers, deserters, cowards, all those words which they used so freely—we loved our country just as they did, and we went bravely

forward every time we were told to attack. But now we understood. We had finally learned to see. And we saw that nothing was left of their world. We were suddenly and fearfully alone, and we had to find our way through, alone.

Recently I lent my copy of Remarque's book to a German friend, an old lady who lived through the two wars in Germany. She was surprised. "But this is beautifully written," she said, "and it rings true. I wonder why they wouldn't let us read it. We were always told that respectable people shouldn't read it." She had the misfortune to be a daughter of a respectable upper-class German family, and so she read Remarque fifty years too late. Perhaps Oppenheimer, growing up in the rarefied literary atmosphere of Ethical Culture and Harvard, suffered from a similar disadvantage. Even so, it comes as a shock to find him in 1932 writing about war in the manner of Rupert Brooke and Kantorek.

There were other voices in the 1920s than Haldane and Owen and Eliot and Remarque. I do not know whether Oppenheimer read *The Seven Pillars of Wisdom* by T. E. Lawrence, a man whose many-sided strengths and weaknesses curiously paralleled Oppenheimer's own. I recently learned, from Charles Osborne's biography of Auden, that T. E. Lawrence was the original model for the character of MF in *The Ascent of F6*. When the play was originally performed in London in 1937, the critics greeted it without enthusiasm. They complained that the authors never made it clear whether MF was intended to be a hero or an impostor, a genius or a charlatan. The authors knew very well what they were about. This ambiguity was an essential part of the legend of T. E. Lawrence. And similar ambiguities surround the character of Oppenheimer. Lawrence was, like Oppenheimer, a scholar who came to greatness through war, a charismatic leader and a gifted writer, who was accused with some justice of occasional untruthfulness. *The Seven Pillars* is a vivid and subtly romanticized history of the Arab revolt against Turkish rule, a revolt which Lawrence orchestrated with an extraordinary mixture of diplomacy, showmanship, and military skill. The book describes war at its most attractive, a war of individuals fighting for their freedom, a war of small groups without professional bureaucracy, a war in a desert with few civilian casualties. The war which Lawrence sang was a war of brains and bravery, the exact opposite of the war of mud and stupidity in which Remarque fought on the

Western Front. *The Seven Pillars* begins with a dedicatory poem, with words which perhaps tell us something about the force that drove Robert Oppenheimer to be the man he became in Los Alamos:

> I loved you, so I drew these tides of men into my hands,
>   And wrote my will across the sky in stars
> To earn you Freedom, the seven pillared worthy house,
>   That your eyes might be shining for me
>   When we came

and with words which tell of the bitterness which came to him afterward:

> Men prayed that I set our work, the inviolate house,
>   As a memory of you.
> But for fit monument I shattered it, unfinished: and now
> The little things creep out to patch themselves hovels
>   In the marred shadow
>   Of your gift.

And there was Joe Dallet. Dallet was the first husband of Robert Oppenheimer's wife Kitty. Born into a wealthy family, he rebelled against his background, became a Communist, and organized a steel-workers' union in Pennsylvania. In 1937 he went to Spain to fight on the losing side in the Spanish civil war. Kitty tried to follow him to Spain, but only got as far as Paris when she heard that he had been killed in action. Three years later she married Robert. Robert and Kitty were well suited to each other; they settled down and raised a family and supported each other in sickness and in health, through all Robert's triumphs and tribulations, until his death. But I often felt that it must have been hard for Robert, at least in the early years, to be living in a silent ménage à trois with the ghost of a dead hero.

The Spanish war captured Robert's imagination and caused him to become politically engaged. He gave substantial amounts of money to war relief funds and attended numerous meetings. Seventeen years later, in his letter of March 4, 1954, to General Nichols, general manager of the United States Atomic Energy Commission, replying formally to the allegations which had been made against his veracity and loyalty, Robert wrote: "The matter which most engaged my sympathies and interest was the war in Spain. This was not a matter of understanding and informed convictions. I had never been to Spain; I knew a little of its literature; I knew nothing of its history or politics or contemporary problems. But like a great many other Americans I was emotionally committed to the Loyalist cause." It was easy for Robert and his left-wing friends, viewing the war from a distance of six thousand miles through a screen of righteous indignation, to romanticize and oversimplify. They looked on the war as a simple fight for freedom, a heroic struggle of right against wrong. They did not read George Orwell's *Homage to Catalonia,* the best eyewitness record of the war, written by a man who fought in it as a private soldier and faithfully set down on paper the heroism and the sordidness, the tragedy and the folly. Orwell's book sold poorly in England and was not published in the United States. The right wing disliked Orwell because he was a socialist, and the left wing disliked him because he told the truth. The truth was too complicated to fit into the ideological categories of left and right. To a man who kept his eyes open and was not afraid to say what he saw, the disasters of the war could not be blamed on one side alone.

Looking back on these events some years afterward, Orwell said: "The thing that, to me, was truly frightening about the war in Spain was not such violence as I witnessed, nor even the party feuds behind the lines, but the immediate reappearance in left-wing circles of the mental atmosphere of the Great War. The very people who for twenty years had sniggered over their own superiority to war hysteria were the ones who rushed straight back into the mental slum of 1915." These are strong words, coming from a man who had stormed a Fascist strongpoint in the first wave of a bungled infantry attack. "Such violence as I witnessed" included several months of service in a front-line trench, several days of interparty street fighting in Barcelona, and a bullet through the neck which probably saved Orwell's life by making him unfit for further military activities. For Orwell these hardships were trivial compared with the mental anguish of seeing brave comrades betrayed by incompetent leaders and slandered by lying propaganda. He saw his intellectual friends, willfully blind to realities, as no better than the patriotic journalists of 1915: "All the familiar war-time idiocies, spy-hunting, orthodoxy-sniffing (Sniff, sniff. Are you a good Anti-Fascist?), the retailing of incredible atrocity stories, came back into vogue as though the intervening years had never happened." One of the minor side effects of the war in Spain was that it erased from the minds of left-wing intellectuals the hard-earned lessons of

World War I. They saw the Loyalist cause in the Spanish war as clean, heroic, and virtuous. They forgot what Wilfred Owen and the veterans of Passchendaele could have told them, that the conditions of twentieth-century warfare tend to make heroism irrelevant. In the romanticized view of the Spanish war which Robert Oppenheimer absorbed from his friends in Berkeley in the late 1930s, the legend of Joe Dallet, the rich man's son who fought on the side of the workers and laid down his life for their cause, fitted naturally into place. Robert encountered the legend as soon as he encountered Kitty, as he wrote in his letter of 1954 to General Nichols: "When I met her I found in her a deep loyalty to her former husband."

Recently I learned from the historian Richard Polenberg at Cornell University some facts about Joe Dallet's life and death. Dallet was unlike the majority of the left-wing intellectuals who flocked to Spain to fight for the republic. Dallet took soldiering seriously. He believed, like Robert, in discipline. He quickly became an expert on the repair, maintenance, and use of machine guns. He drilled his troops with old-fashioned thoroughness, making sure that they knew how to take care of their weapons and how to use them effectively. In an anarchic situation, his unit was conspicuously well-organized. His men caught from him the habit of competence, the pride of a steelworker who knows how to handle machinery. At moments of relaxation, when he sat down with his friends over a bottle of wine, he talked mostly about his beloved machine guns. This was the image of Joe which Joe's friends brought to Kitty in Paris when they came to see her after his death. This was the image which Kitty brought to Robert when she married him.

From Joe's guns it was a short step to Robert's bombs. When Robert accepted in 1942 the job of organizing the bomb laboratory at Los Alamos, it seemed to him natural and appropriate that he should work under the direct command of General Groves of the United States Army. Other leading scientists wanted to keep the laboratory under civilian control. Professor Isidor Rabi of Columbia University was one of those most strongly opposed to working for the army. Robert wrote to Rabi in February 1943, explaining why he was willing to go with General Groves: "I think if I believed with you that this project was 'the culmination of three centuries of physics,' I should take a different stand. To me it is primarily the development in time of war of a military weapon of some consequence. I do not think that the Nazis allow us the option of [not] carrying out that development." Rabi did not join the laboratory.

Late in 1944, as the Los Alamos project moved toward success, tensions developed between civilian and military participants. Captain Parsons of the U.S. Navy, serving as associate director under Oppenheimer, complained to him in a written memorandum that some of the civilian scientists were more interested in scientific experiments than in weaponry. Oppenheimer forwarded the memorandum to General Groves, with a covering letter to show which side he himself was on: "I agree completely with all the comments of Captain Parsons' memorandum on the fallacy of regarding a controlled test as the culmination of the work of this laboratory. The laboratory is operating under a directive to produce weapons; this directive has been and will be rigorously adhered to." So vanished the possibility that there might have been a pause for reflection between the Trinity test and Hiroshima. Captain Parsons, acting in the best tradition of old-fashioned military leadership, armed the Hiroshima bomb himself and flew with it to Japan.

Some of the people who worked under Oppenheimer at Los Alamos asked themselves afterward: "Why did we not stop when the Germans surrendered?" For many of them, and for Oppenheimer in particular, the principal motivation for joining the project at the beginning had been the fear that Hitler might get the bomb first. The Germans had a large number of competent scientists, including the original discoverers of nuclear fission, and a secret German uranium project was known to exist. The danger that Hitler might acquire nuclear weapons and use them to conquer the world seemed real and urgent. But that danger had disappeared by the end of 1944. Nobody imagined that Japan was in a position to develop nuclear weapons. So the primary argument which persuaded British and American scientists to go to Los Alamos had ceased to be valid long before the Trinity test. It would have been possible for them to stop. They might at least have paused to ask the question, whether in the new circumstances it was wise to go ahead to the actual production of weapons. Only one man paused. The one who paused was Joseph Rotblat from Liverpool, who, to his everlasting credit, resigned his position at Los Alamos and left the laboratory in December 1944 when it became known that the German uranium project had not progressed far enough to make the manufacture of bombs a serious possibility. Twelve years later Rotblat helped Bertrand Russell to launch the Pugwash movement, an

informal international association of scientists dedicated to the cause
of peace. From that time until today, Rotblat has remained one of
the moving spirits of Pugwash. The reason why the others did not
pause is to be seen clearly in Oppenheimer's assurance to General
Groves, written on October 4, 1944: "The laboratory is acting
under a directive to produce weapons; this directive has been and
will be rigorously adhered to." Oppenheimer had accepted on behalf of himself and his colleagues the subordination of personal
judgment to military authority. The war against Japan was still
raging. To step aside from the production of a decisive weapon,
while soldiers were dying every day in the Pacific islands, would
have seemed like an act of treason. It was wartime, and in wartime
the ethic of the soldier, "Theirs not to reason why," prevails.

Fighting for freedom. That was the ideal which pulled young
men to die in Spain, to take up armed resistance against Hitler in
the mountains of Yugoslavia, and to go to work with Oppenheimer
in Los Alamos. Fighting for freedom, the traditional and almost
instinctive human response to oppression and injustice. Fighting for
freedom, the theme song of the Spanish war and of World War II
from beginning to end. Cecil Day Lewis wrote in 1937 a war poem
called "The Nabara," a long poem, perhaps the only poem which
adequately describes the spirit of those who went to fight against
hopeless odds in the early battles of the Second World War, even
though the poem was written before that war started. "The Nabara"
is a dirge for fifty-two Spanish fishermen, the crew of an armed
trawler which lost a battle against one of Franco's warships. It is also
perhaps a dirge for all of us who have chosen to fight for freedom
with the technologies of death. I quote here a few of the concluding
stanzas:

> Of her officers all but one were dead. Of her engineers
> All but one were dead. Of the fifty-two that had sailed
> In her, all were dead but fourteen—and each of these half-killed
> With wounds. And the night-dew fell in a hush of ashen tears,
> And *Nabara's* tongue was stilled.
>
> . . . .
>
> *Canarias* lowered a launch that swept in a greyhound's curve
> Pitiless to pursue
> And cut them off. But that bloodless and all-but-phantom crew
> Still gave no soft concessions to fate: they strung their nerve

For one last fling of defiance, they shipped their oars and threw
Hand-grenades at the launch as it circled about to board them.
But the strength of the hands that had carved them a hold on
        history
Failed them at last: the grenades fell short of the enemy,
Who grappled and overpowered them,
While *Nabara* sank by the stern in the hushed Cantabrian sea.

They bore not a charmed life. They went into battle foreseeing
Probable loss, and they lost. The tides of Biscay flow
Over the obstinate bones of many, the winds are sighing
Round prison walls where the rest are doomed like their ship to
        rust—
Men of the Basque country, the Mar Cantabrico.

. . . .

For these I have told of, freedom was flesh and blood—a mortal
Body, the gun-breech hot to its touch: yet the battle's height
Raised it to love's meridian and held it awhile immortal;
And its light through time still flashes like a star's that has turned
        to ashes,
Long after *Nabara's* passion was quenched in the sea's heart.

This poem appeared in Day Lewis's *Overtures to Death*. It
resonated strongly with the tragic mood of those days, when the
Spanish war was slowly drawing to its bitter end and the Second
World War was inexorably approaching. When I was in high
school in 1938, our chemistry teacher Eric James, who was the
best teacher in the school, put aside chemistry for an hour and
read "The Nabara" aloud. He subsequently became famous as a
university vice-chancellor and is now sitting in the House of
Lords. I can still hear his passionate voice reading "The Nabara,"
with the boys listening spellbound. That was perhaps the last occasion on which it was possible to recite an epic poem in all sincerity to honor the heroes of a military action. At Hiroshima, the
new technology of death made military heroism suddenly old-
fashioned and impotent. After Hiroshima, Day Lewis's lofty sentiments no longer resonated. The generation which grew up after
Hiroshima found its voice in 1956 in the character of Jimmy Porter, the young man at center stage in John Osborne's play *Look
Back in Anger*. Here is Jimmy Porter, griping as usual, and inci-

dentally telling us important truths about the effect of nuclear weapons on public morality:

> I suppose people of our generation aren't able to die for good causes any longer. We had all that done for us, in the thirties and the forties, when we were still kids. There aren't any good, brave causes left. If the big bang does come, and we all get killed off, it won't be in aid of the old-fashioned, grand design. It'll just be for the Brave New nothing-very-much-I-thank-you. About as pointless and inglorious as stepping in front of a bus.

Jimmy Porter brings us back to where Haldane left us in 1924. The two world wars seemed totally different to the people who fought in them and lived through them from day to day, but they begin to look more and more alike as they recede into history. The first war began with the trumpet blowing of Rupert Brooke and ended with the nightmares of Wilfred Owen. The second war began with the mourning of Day Lewis and ended with the anger of Jimmy Porter. In both wars, the beginning was young men going out to fight for freedom in a mood of noble self-sacrifice, and the end was a technological bloodbath which seemed in retrospect meaningless. In the first war, the idealism of my uncle perished and the hand grenades of my father survived; in the second war, the idealism of Joe Dallet perished and the nuclear weapons of Robert Oppenheimer survived. In both wars, history proved that those who fight for freedom with the technologies of death end by living in fear of their own technology.

12

The Scholar-Soldier

Oppenheimer's activities as a scholar-soldier did not cease with the end of World War II. After the first Soviet nuclear test explosion in 1949, he took the lead in pushing for a vigorous development of tactical nuclear weapons to be used by the United States Army for the defense of Western Europe. Here is the testimony of his friend Walt Whitman (the chemist, not the poet of that name), speaking as a character witness on Oppenheimer's behalf during the security hearings of 1954:

> I should say that always Dr. Oppenheimer was trying to point out the wide variety of military uses for the bomb, the small bomb as well as the large bomb. He was doing it in a climate where many folks felt that only strategic bombing was a field for the atomic weapon. I should say that he more than any other man served to educate the military to the potentialities of the atomic weapon for other than strategic bombing purposes; its use possibly in tactical situations or in bombing 500 miles back. He was constantly emphasizing that the bomb would be more available and that one of the greatest problems was going to be its deliverability, meaning that the smaller you could make your bomb in size perhaps you would not have to have a great big strategic bomber to carry it, you could carry it in a medium bomber or you could carry it even in a fighter plane. In my judgment his advice and his arguments for a gamut of atomic weapons, extending even over to the use of the atomic weapon in air defense of the United States, has been more productive than any other one individual. You see, he had the opportunity

to not only advise in the Atomic Energy Commission, but advise in the military services in the Department of Defense. The idea of a range of atomic weapons suitable for a multiplicity of military purposes was a key to the campaign which he felt should be pressed and with which I agreed.

As a consequence of his interest in tactical nuclear weapons, Oppenheimer traveled to Paris in November 1951 to talk with General Eisenhower, who was then in command of American forces in Europe. Eisenhower was quickly persuaded that tactical nuclear weapons would help his armies to carry out their mission of defense. The results of these discussions were incorporated in an official report called *Vista*, to which Oppenheimer made substantial contributions. In his own testimony at the security hearings, he said:

I believe my contribution, apart from incidentals, to the writing of this report was a notion that occurred very early and I believe has remained in all drafts, and that is still basic to my own views, and that is that this is not a very fully known subject—what atomic weapons will do, either tactically or strategically, that as you go into battle, you will learn a great deal, and the primary preparation must be of two kinds. First that you have capabilities which allow you a lot of options, which give you choices that you can make at the time, and second, that you be so set up that if your guesses have been wrong, your technical preparations are such that you can change quickly in the course of the battle. If you are wrong about the effect of a bomb on an airfield, if you are not getting away with it, that you can make the proper reassignment of fissionable material and hardware and aircraft to do what is effective. These were the two guiding ideas that I believe I brought into the organization of the report. . . .

We said that we were in a coalition with the Europeans and that one of the things which we must be alert to is how the Europeans would view the destruction of their own cities by the enemy. Therefore, we needed to envisage the situation that would occur if we used our strategic air as a deterrent to the destruction of Europe's cities, as well as our own, and in that circumstance there was still a great deal that could and should be done with atomic weapons, and that we should be prepared for that contingency. Europe was not easy to defend, and the point that we wished to make was that there was more than one way in which the atom could be used in what might be a very critical campaign. . . . It was to call very prominently to the attention of the services that there might be considerations against the then present air plan, and that nevertheless there were very important things to do with the atom.

Oppenheimer's efforts to sell tactical nuclear weapons to the army succeeded all too well. The recommendations of the *Vista* report were accepted and have been the basis of NATO strategy ever since. The six thousand NATO tactical warheads now in Europe are an enduring monument to Oppenheimer's powers of persuasion. I once asked him, long after he had lost his security clearance, whether he regretted having fought so hard for tactical nuclear weapons. He said, "No. But to understand what I did then, you would have to see the air force war plan as it existed in 1951. That was the goddamnedest thing I ever saw. Anything, even the war plans we have now, is better than that." The 1951 war plan was, in short, a mindless obliteration of Soviet cities. I could sympathize with Oppenheimer's hatred of the Strategic Air Command mentality, having myself seen the same mentality at work in the British Bomber Command. I recalled an evening which I spent at the bar of the Bomber Command officers' mess, at a time in 1944 when our bombers were still suffering heavy losses in their nightly attacks on German cities. I listened then to a group of drunken headquarters staff officers discussing the routes they would order their planes to take to Leningrad and Moscow in the war with Russia which they were looking forward to after this little business in Germany was over. Oppenheimer had heard similar talk in his encounters with the American air force. Compared with that, even a nuclearized army seemed to him to be a lesser evil.

Under the circumstances existing in 1951, the idea of tactical nuclear weapons made sense both militarily and politically. The circumstances included a substantial margin of superiority of American over Soviet nuclear forces, both in quantity of weapons and in means of delivery. The circumstances also included a war in Korea, with United States troops fighting hard to defend South Korea against a North Korean invasion supported by the Soviet Union. At that moment of history, Oppenheimer was facing a triple nightmare. He was afraid, first, that the Korean War would spread to Europe; second, that a local invasion of West Berlin or West Germany would be answered by the United States Air Force's 1951 war plan, which meant the nuclear annihilation of Moscow and Leningrad; third, that the surviving Soviet nuclear forces, unable to touch the United States, would take their revenge on Paris and London. It was reasonable to think that the worst part of this nightmare could be avoided if the United States could respond to local invasions with local use of nuclear weapons on the battlefield. So long as United States nuclear forces were quantitatively and qualitatively superior, there was a good chance that a Korean-style invasion of Western Europe could be stopped by a few judiciously placed bombs and that the invaders could be persuaded to withdraw without destruction of cities on either side. Oppenheimer argued, as he reports in his 1954 testimony, that the possibility of a restrained and local use of nuclear weapons would strengthen the resolve of Western European governments and enable them to stand firm against Soviet demands. The same arguments for tactical nuclear weapons are still heard today, long after the disappearance of the American superiority which made them realistic.

Oppenheimer had another reason for pushing tactical nuclear weapons. During the months which followed the 1949 Soviet test explosion, he was fighting to dissuade the United States government from embarking on a crash program to produce hydrogen bombs. One of the arguments against the hydrogen bomb program was that it would divert scarce resources and manpower from the development of small and flexible fission weapons. Oppenheimer came to regard the tactical weapons as a substitute for the hydrogen bomb, and he hoped that a vigorous development of tactical weapons would make a postponement of the hydrogen bomb program politically acceptable. His hopes were, in the event, illusory. The government accepted his advice to go full steam ahead with tactical weapons, and rejected his advice to go slow with the hydrogen bomb. In the end, both the army and the Strategic Air Command got all the weapons they wanted.

When he tried to take nuclear weapons away from the air force and give them to the army, Oppenheimer was hoping to harness in the cause of sanity the potent force of interservice rivalry. Interservice rivalry is one of the dominant political forces in almost all societies, in war as well as in peace. I wish some historian would supplement Admiral Mahan's classic work *The Influence of Sea Power upon History* with a new study entitled "The Influence of Interservice Rivalry upon History." All too often, it is interservice rather than international rivalries which dictate strategies and drive arms races. Oppenheimer discovered, when he tried to use the army–air force rivalry for his own purposes, that interservice rivalry is less easy to control than nuclear fission. The air force easily brushed aside Oppenheimer's opposition, and the air force's allies in the government took revenge by instigating the loyalty hearings which brought his political career to an end.

The military doctrine of the NATO alliance is still based upon the possibility of first use of nuclear weapons by the allied armies to counter a Soviet non-nuclear invasion. How far this doctrine departs from sanity can be vividly seen in an old army field manual, FM–101–31–1, on nuclear weapons employment. This field manual is an unclassified document, used for the training of United States officers and readily available to foreign intelligence services. It describes how the well-educated staff officer should make his plans during tactical nuclear operations. Various examples are presented of fictitious nuclear engagements, each of them conducted in a style appropriate to an ROTC field day. Here is "an example of a corps commander's initial guidance to his staff":

Aggressor has organized the area between our current positions and the BLUE River for a determined defense. The decisive battle during the coming operation will be fought west of the BLUE River. Although we have a limited number of nuclear weapons for this operation, I am willing to expend 30 to 40 percent of our allocation in penetrating the Aggressor main and second defense belts, and advancing to the BLUE River. Corps fires will be used to engage Aggressor nuclear delivery means and those reserve maneuver forces which have the capability of adversely affecting the outcome of the battle. These fires will be delivered as soon as the targets are located. These fires, together with the nuclear weapons allocated to the subordinate units, will insure that we inflict maximum casualties and damage to Aggressor units west of the BLUE River and will insure our successful attack to secure crossings over the BLUE River.

Once we are across the BLUE River, we must be ready to exploit our crossings and move rapidly through the passes of the SILVER Mountains and seize the communications center of FOXVILLE. Be extremely cautious in planning the employment of nuclear weapons in the SILVER Mountains, as I want no obstacles to our advance created in these critical areas.

Retain one-fourth to one-third of our nuclear weapons in reserve
for the attack to seize FOXVILLE, since I anticipate a stubborn enemy
defense there, and for the defense against the Aggressor counterat-
tacks which are sure to follow when we seize FOXVILLE.

Weapons over 50 KT yield will not be allocated to divisions.

The problems of securing adequate intelligence concerning pro-
spective nuclear targets are also discussed:

Delay of nuclear attacks until detailed intelligence is developed may
impede the effectiveness of the attack. On the other hand, engage-
ment of a target without some indication of its characteristics may
cause an unwarranted waste of combat power.

So the staff officer receiving ambiguous reports of major enemy
units moving through populated friendly territory must take upon
himself the responsibility of deciding whether to risk "an unwarranted waste of combat power." Fortunately, his task will be made
easier by a well-designed system of nuclear bookkeeping. "Suggested forms or methods by which needed information can be kept
at various staff agencies are discussed below." Samples are provided
of forms to be filled out from time to time, summarizing the numbers of nuclear weapons of various kinds expended and unexpended.
Very little is said about the possible disruption of these arrangements by enemy nuclear bombardment. But at least the well-pre-
pared staff officer knows what to do in one possible contingency.
Section 4.17.c on Nuclear Safety reads in its entirety: "Enemy duds
are reported to the next higher headquarters."

I ought to apologize to the authors of FM–101–31–1 for holding
up their work to ridicule. Their handbook is no more absurd than
my father's 1915 handbook on grenade fighting. They lack practical
experience of nuclear warfare, just as my father lacked experience
of grenade fighting. When experience is lacking, the handbook
writer does the best he can, using a mixture of common sense and
imagination to fill the gaps in his knowledge. The military doctrines
summarized in FM–101–31–1 were valid for a certain period of
history, roughly from 1951 to 1960, when tactical nuclear wars
might have been small-scale and truly limited. The handbook represents a sincere attempt to put Oppenheimer's philosophy of local
nuclear defense into practice. I have taken my quotations from the
1963 edition of FM–101–31–1, the latest edition that I have seen.

Later editions have no doubt been brought up to date, with tactical exercises and procedures more appropriate to modern conditions. But when all due allowances are made for the historical context out of which FM–101–31–1 arose, it is still a profoundly disquieting document.

No matter how FM–101–31–1 may have been revised since 1963, it remains true that the doctrines governing the use and deployment of our tactical nuclear weapons are basically out of touch with reality. The doctrines are based on the idea that a tactical nuclear operation can be commanded and controlled like an ordinary non-nuclear campaign. This idea may have made sense in the 1950s, but it makes no sense in the 1980s. I have seen the results of computer simulations of tactical nuclear wars under modern conditions, with thousands of warheads deployed on both sides. The computer wars uniformly end in chaos. High-yield weapons are used on a massive scale because nobody knows accurately where the moving targets are. Civilian casualties, if the war is fought in a populated area, exceed military casualties by a large factor. If even the computers are not able to fight a tactical nuclear war without destroying Europe, what hope is there that real soldiers in the fog and flames of a real battlefield could do better?

The doctrines displayed in FM–101–31–1 are doubly dangerous. First, these doctrines may deceive our own political leaders, giving them the false impression that tactical nuclear war is a feasible way to defend a country. Second, these doctrines spread around the world, and give the military staffs of countries large and small the impression that every army wanting to stay ahead in the modern world should have its own tactical nuclear weapons too. If FM–101–31–1 had been stamped "Top Secret," it would not have been so harmful. In that case I would not have been writing about it here. But since our military authorities published it unclassified in order to give it a wide distribution, there is no point in trying to keep its existence a secret. The best thing to do in these circumstances is to call attention to its errors and inadequacies, so that people in military intelligence services around the world may not take it too seriously.

In recent years, leaders of government in the United States and in Europe have come to understand that the purpose of the deployment of tactical nuclear weapons is primarily political rather than military. That is to say, the weapons are deployed as a demonstration of the American political commitment to the NATO alliance, not as a system of military hardware which could actually provide a meaningful defense of Europe. But this separation between political and military purposes of weapons is necessarily hedged about with ambiguities. On the one hand, the political sensitivities of NATO have imposed on the administration of tactical nuclear forces a command structure of unique complexity to ensure that the weapons will not be used irresponsibly. On the other hand, the troops in the field have to be trained and indoctrinated using manuals like FM–101–31–1, which make the firing of nuclear weapons into a standard operating procedure. The whole apparatus for handling tactical nuclear weapons is schizophrenic, trying in vain to accommodate the incompatible requirements of multinational political control and military credibility.

Tactical nuclear weapons deployed in forward positions overseas are fundamentally more dangerous to world peace than strategic weapons deployed in silos and in submarines. Tactical weapons are more dangerous for two reasons. First, tactical weapons are in places where local wars and revolutions may occur, with unpredictable consequences. Second, tactical weapons are deployed, as strategic weapons are not, with a doctrine which allows United States forces to use them first in case of emergency. Many of the tactical weapons are so vulnerable and so exposed that it would make no sense to deploy them in their present positions if the option of first use were renounced. The combination of local political instability with vulnerable weapons and the option of first use is a recipe for disaster. In many ways, it is a situation reminiscent of the Europe of 1914, when the instability of the Hapsburg Empire was combined with vulnerable frontiers and rigid mobilization schedules. Compared with the immediate danger that a local conflict in an area of tactical weapons deployment might escalate into nuclear chaos, the instabilities of the strategic arms race are remote and theoretical.

The United States already made one important unilateral move to mitigate the danger of tactical weapons. The most dangerous of all tactical weapons was the Davy Crockett, a nuclear trench mortar with a low-yield warhead which was supposed to be carried by small mobile units. FM–101–31–1 says (p. 38): "Allocate some Davy Crockett weapons to the cavalry squadron." A nuclear-armed cavalry squadron is a fine example of military euphemism. In reality it meant that Davy Crocketts were deployed in jeeps which were theoretically free to roam around the countryside. The army decided that this was carrying nuclear dispersal too far. It was impossible to guarantee the physical security of the Davy Crocketts if they were allocated to small units as originally intended. Dispersal in small units also increased the risk of unauthorized firing in case of local hostilities or breakdown of communications. So the army wisely withdrew the Davy Crocketts from service and shipped them home, achieving thereby a real diminution in the risk of war at no political cost.

The same logic which got rid of the Davy Crocketts would dictate a continued withdrawal, unilateral or bilateral, of other tactical weapons, starting with those which because of their short range have to be deployed closest to the front line. Nuclear artillery shells would be a good candidate for the next round of withdrawals. The chief virtue of nuclear artillery was its high accuracy compared with the rockets of twenty years ago. Now the accuracy of rocket guidance is comparable with the accuracy of artillery. Guns are considerably more cumbersome and more vulnerable than rockets. Nuclear guns have to be placed in forward positions to be effective, they are hard to move quickly, and they are in danger of being overrun whenever there is a local breakthrough of enemy forces. If nuclear shells were not already deployed in our armies overseas, nobody would now dream of introducing them. Their military value is marginal, and they increase the risk that small-scale battles may involve us in unintended nuclear hostilities. They could be withdrawn, like the Davy Crocketts, with a substantial net gain to our security.

It is a strange paradox of history that the greatest present danger of nuclear war arises from these tactical weapons which Oppenheimer promoted with such good intentions during his period of political ascendancy. Oppenheimer considered tactical weapons to be relatively benign because they could be used in local fighting without immediately destroying civilization. Today this same property of the tactical weapons makes them the most dangerous. They are dangerous because they are apparently benign, because they can be used in ways which are not immediately suicidal, because they allow the world to slide gradually from local squabbles into holocaust. The weapons themselves have not changed much between 1951 and today. What has changed is the balance of forces. In 1951 the Soviet nuclear forces were absolutely and relatively small, so that Oppenheimer could reasonably think of using a few nuclear weapons to stop a Soviet land army while keeping enough in reserve to deter any Soviet nuclear response. Today the Soviet nuclear forces are enormous and evenly matched to ours, and the Soviet authorities have said clearly on numerous occasions that their response to any first use of nuclear weapons by NATO would be massive and devastating. Today the Soviet forces deter us from using nuclear weapons, just as much as our forces deter the Soviet Union, and the chief danger of outbreak of nuclear war arises from the fact that our doctrines for first use of tactical nuclear weapons do not recognize the existence of that deterrence.

Oppenheimer's enthusiasm for tactical nuclear weapons resulted from a narrowing of his horizons in both time and space. Immediately after the end of World War II, while the revolutionary impact of Hiroshima was still fresh, he had striven with all his strength to achieve an international control of nuclear weaponry under the auspices of the United Nations. He had played a major role in drafting the United States plan for an international atomic energy authority with effective power to regulate and operate nuclear facilities in all countries. The plan was imaginative, bold, and generous. It failed to win Soviet acceptance. It was not Oppenheimer's fault that the American negotiators did not seriously try to reach a compromise acceptable to the Soviet Union. Probably no plan subordinating national armaments to international control could have overcome the fear and suspicion with which the Soviet government regarded any outside intrusion into its territory. Oppenheimer could not have done more than he did, using all the eloquence and influence at his command, to preach the necessity of international control to all who would listen. During those years from 1945 to 1948, he transcended his role as an American weaponeer and became for a while an international statesman, a spokesman for the world scientific community. Then, after the Soviet test in 1949, his horizons began to narrow. The failure of the United Nations negotiations had made a nuclear arms race inevitable. Oppenheimer became once again an American weaponeer. His horizon shrank in space from the world to the United States, in time from the grand march of history to the day-to-day problems of government.

Oppenheimer pushed tactical nuclear weapons because they offered a counterweight to the Strategic Air Command in the interservice rivalries of the Truman administration, and because they offered a counterweight to Soviet tank armies in case of a war in

Western Europe. These motivations are clear from his testimony at the 1954 security hearings. His actions were dominated by short-term considerations. There is no evidence that he ever considered the long-term consequences of tactical nuclear weapons, the inevitable Soviet response and the permanently increased risk of nuclear war arising by accident or miscalculation.

After the Korean War broke out in 1950, we see Oppenheimer's horizons closing in even further. He became again, as in the Los Alamos days, a good soldier committed to the service of his country's military strength. The result of that commitment was a rebirth of the old delight in the technicalities of nuclear weapons. "There was still a great deal that could and should be done with atomic weapons," he said in his 1954 testimony. When I read the testimony today, I cannot escape the impression that Robert Oppenheimer was still dazzled by the power and the brilliance of the technology which he had pioneered. In 1951, just as in 1943, he was ready to march with the soldiers in "the development in time of war of a military weapon of some consequence."

What are we to learn from this melancholy story? The main lesson is that if we want to save the world from the horrors of nuclear war, we must begin by winning over the soldiers to our side. It is not enough to organize scientists against nuclear war, or physicians against nuclear war, or clergymen against nuclear war, or even mothers against nuclear war. We need captains and generals against nuclear war. We need to persuade the soldiers in all countries, and especially the young men who will be the next generation of military leaders, that they cannot decently fight with nuclear weapons. The elimination of nuclear weapons must be presented to the public as a response to the demands of military honor and self-respect, not as a response to fear.

It is good to make people afraid of nuclear war. But fear is not enough. The generation which grew up after World War I was well indoctrinated in the horrors of trench warfare. Whether or not they read Wilfred Owen or Erich Remarque, they met every day the widows and orphans and crippled survivors of the war. They looked back to the slaughters of Verdun and Passchendaele as we look back to the slaughter of Hiroshima, and they were properly afraid. Pacifist movements flourished in the 1920s and 1930s, and disarmament programs enjoyed wide public support. The fear of a repetition of World War I was almost universal. But human beings, for better or for worse, are so constituted that they are not willing to let their lives be ruled for very long by fear. Pride, anger, impatience, and even curiosity are stronger passions than fear. Thousands of men, including my uncle Freeman, lost their lives in World War I because their curiosity got the better of their fear. They could not resist the urge to stick their heads up out of the trench to see what was happening. Thousands more, including Joe Dallet, lost their lives in a hopeless cause in Spain because their fear was weaker than their anger. There is a deep force in the human spirit which drives us to fight for our freedoms and hang the consequences. Even the fear of nuclear holocaust is not strong enough to prevail against this force. When the trumpets sound and the cause is perceived to be just, young men of spirit, whether they are revolutionaries like Dallet or scholars like Oppenheimer, will lay aside their fears and their misgivings to join the parade, joyfully submitting themselves to the necessities of military discipline; for as Oppenheimer wrote to his brother, "only through them can we attain to the least detachment; and only so can we know peace."

We cannot defeat with fear alone the forces of misguided patriotism and self-sacrifice. We need above all to have sound and realistic military doctrines, doctrines which make clear that the actual use of nuclear weapons cannot either defend our country or defend our allies, that the actual use of nuclear weapons in a world of great powers armed with thousands of warheads cannot serve any sane military purpose whatever. If our military doctrines and plans once recognize these facts, then our military leaders may be able to agree with those of our allies and our adversaries upon practical measures to make the world safer for all of us. If our soldiers once understand that they cannot defend us with nuclear weapons, they may contribute their great moral and political influence to help us create a world in which non-nuclear defense is possible. If the soldiers can be turned against nuclear weapons, then ordinary civilians and politicians will be able to campaign for nuclear disarmament without being considered cowardly or unpatriotic. The road of discipline and patriotic self-sacrifice need no longer be the road to nuclear holocaust.

The human situation, sitting naked under the threat of nuclear war, is desperate but not hopeless. One hopeful feature of our situation is the demonstrable unreality of the military plans and deployments typified by Army Field Manual FM–101–31–1. There is a real hope that the soldiers in various countries may rebel against such unrealities and demand a world in which they can fulfill their honorable mission of national defense. The scholar-soldier Robert Oppenheimer persuaded General Eisenhower in 1951 that the American army needed tactical nuclear weapons. Oppenheimer's arguments may have had some merit in the circumstances of 1951. The circumstances of 1983 are totally different. The world is now waiting for another scholar-soldier, or for a soldier who is not a scholar, to help us move back along the long road from the illusory world of FM–101–31–1 to a world of sanity.

13

Generals

At 2:30 P.M. on August 31, 1946, the former chief of the Operations Staff of the German armed forces, Colonel-General Alfred Jodl, made his final statement to the Nuremberg War Crimes Tribunal:

> Mr. President and Justices of the court. It is my unshakable belief that history will later pronounce an objective and fair judgment on the senior military commanders and their subordinates. They, and with them the German armed forces as a whole, faced an insoluble problem, namely, to wage a war which they had not wanted, under a supreme commander who did not trust them and whom they only partially trusted, with methods which often contradicted their doctrines and their traditional beliefs, with troops and police forces not fully subject to their command, and with an intelligence service which was partly working for the enemy. And all this with the clear knowledge that the war would decide the existence or non-existence of the beloved fatherland. They were not servants of Hell or of a criminal. They served their people and their fatherland.
>
> For myself, I believe that no man can do better than to struggle for the highest goal which he is in a position to achieve. That and nothing else was the guiding principle of my actions all along. And that is why, no matter what verdict you may pass on me, I shall leave this court with my head held as high as when I entered it many months ago. If anyone calls me a traitor to the honorable tradition of the German army, or if anyone says that I stayed at my post for reasons of personal ambition, I say he is a traitor to the truth.

In this war, hundreds of thousands of women and children were destroyed by carpet-bombing, and partisans used without scruple whatever methods they found effective. In such a war, severe measures, even if they are questionable according to international law, are not crimes against morality and conscience. For I believe and profess: duty toward people and fatherland stands above every other. To do that duty was my honor and highest law. I am proud to have done it. May that duty be replaced in a happier future by an even higher one: duty toward humanity.

On October 10 he wrote a final letter to his friends in the German army.

Dear friends and comrades. In the months of the Nuremberg trial I have borne witness for Germany, for her soldiers, and for history. The dead and the living crowded around me, giving me strength and courage. The verdict of the court went against me. That came as no surprise. The words which I heard from you were for me the true verdict. I was never proud in my life until now. Today I can and I will be proud. I thank you, and one day Germany will thank you, because you did not run away from one of her truest sons in his hour of need and death. Your future lives must not be filled with sadness and hate. Think of me only with respect and pride, just as you think of all the soldiers who died on the battlefields of this cruel war as they were required to do by law. Their lives were sacrificed to make Germany more powerful, but you should believe that they died to make Germany better. Hold fast to this belief and work for it all your lives.

On October 15 he wrote his last letter to his wife:

And so I tell you at the end, you must live and overcome your grief. You must spread love around you and give help to those who need it. You must not make more of me than I was, or than I wanted to be. You must believe and make it known that I worked and fought for Germany and not for her politicians. Oh, I could go on writing like this forever, but now in my ears I hear the bugles playing taps, and the old familiar song—do you hear it, my love?—Soldiers must go home.

At 2 A.M. the next morning he was hanged.
Alfred Jodl was a Bavarian, not a Prussian. Probably that was

one of the reasons Hitler chose him as chief of staff and kept him at his side throughout the war. Jodl nevertheless embodied the old Prussian tradition of military professionalism, with all its virtues and vices. Albert Speer, who sat with him in the dock at Nuremberg, wrote of him afterward: "Jodl's precise and sober defense was rather imposing. He seemed to be one of the few men who stood above the situation." For six years Jodl had worked, day after day and night after night, planning and organizing the campaigns in which millions died. He begged Hitler many times to relieve him of this responsibility, to give him a subordinate command at one of the fighting fronts. Hitler refused, and Jodl obeyed, steadfast up to the end. Jodl had sworn an oath, on his honor as a soldier, to obey Hitler as supreme commander. This oath of soldierly loyalty was for Jodl the unbreakable bond, holier than the Catholic faith in which he had been raised, stronger than his obligation to the welfare of the German people which he believed himself to be serving. On the day that he came to Berlin to take up his duties as chief of staff, a week before the German armies marched into Poland, he said to his wife: "This time I am afraid it looks like the real thing. I don't yet know for sure. But thank God, that is a problem for the politicians and not for us soldiers. I know only one thing; if we once get on board this boat there won't be any climbing out of it."

Jodl's personal religion and code of ethics were summed up in one word, *Soldatentum,* a German word which fortunately cannot be translated into English. The literal equivalent in English is "soldierliness," but the English word altogether misses the tone of solemnity which belongs to the German, and thereby misses the greater part of the meaning. The English word "militarism" means something else entirely. An accurate translation of *Soldatentum* would have to be a paraphrase: the profession of soldiering considered as a quasi-religious vocation. The emotional flavor of it is well conveyed in the writings of Jodl which I have quoted. In English, the word "chivalry" had once a similar aroma, but it became archaic and metaphorical after knights ceased to fight on horseback.

We are fortunate to have a biography of Jodl written by his widow, Luise. Luise Jodl was a career woman, working with the same dedication as her husband in the bureaucracy of the general staff of the German armed forces. She shared her husband's code of honor and his professional pride. During the Nuremberg trial she helped the lawyers to prepare his defense. After he died, she wrote his biography while the events were still fresh in her mind. The book is valuable, not only for its authentic portrait of Alfred Jodl but also for its portrait of Luise. She, too, was a person of strong character and intelligence, driven to disaster by the ideal of *Soldatentum*. At the beginning of her book she placed a quotation from T. S. Eliot's poem "Little Gidding":

> And what you thought you came for
> Is only a shell, a husk of meaning
> From which the purpose breaks only when it is fulfilled
> If at all. Either you had no purpose
> Or the purpose is beyond the end you figured
> And is altered in fulfilment.

For the title of her book she took Eliot's words: *Beyond the End*. Eliot wrote these words in the quietness of wartime England, in the early years of the war, when no end was in sight. The passage continues with lines which Luise Jodl must have known but did not choose to quote:

> There are other places
> Which also are the world's end, some at the sea jaws,
> Or over a dark lake, in a desert or a city—

One of those other places was Nuremberg, where Luise found herself in October 1946, alone among the ruins, faced with the tasks of piecing together the fragments of her husband's life and distilling some meaning from the dishonor of his death.

Perhaps the most brilliant field commander on either side in World War II was Hermann Balck. He commanded the motorized infantry regiment which led the decisive German breakthrough into France in 1940. Fighting later on the Eastern Front, he constantly surprised the Russians with unexpected moves and tactics. In the spring of 1945 he led the last German offensive of the war, holding off the Russian armies in Hungary long enough so that he could retreat in good order into Austria and finally surrender his troops to the Americans. He was, unlike Jodl, a real Prussian. He fought as Jodl was not permitted to fight, in the front lines with his soldiers. He was accused of no war crimes. In 1979, at the age of eighty-five, he entertained an American interviewer with his reminiscences.

On Prussia: "You need to see Prussia's situation in Europe, first of all. Prussia was a small country surrounded by superior forces.

Therefore, we had to be more skillful and more swift than our enemies. That started perhaps with Frederick the Great at the battle of Leuthen where he defeated, and defeated thoroughly, a force of Austrians about twice as big as his own. In addition to being more clever than our opponents, we Prussians also needed to be able to mobilize much more quickly than our enemies."

On the breakthrough across the Meuse River in 1940: "We knew in advance that we had to execute the crossing and I had already rehearsed it on the Moselle with my people. During this practice I had a couple of good ideas. First, every machine gun not occupied in the ground action was employed for air defense. Second, every man in the regiment was trained in the use of rubber boats. When we got to the Meuse, the engineers were supposed to be there, to put us across. They never arrived, but the rubber boats were there. So you see, if I hadn't trained my people, the Meuse crossing would have never happened. Which once again leads to the conclusion that the training of the infantryman can never be too many-sided. . . .

"The operation lay under intense French artillery fire. I had thrust forward to the Meuse with one battalion after some brief fights with the French outposts, and I had set up my regimental command post up front there on the Meuse, along with the forward battalion. I went along with them to make sure that some ass wouldn't suddenly decide to stop on the way. You know, the essence of the forward command idea is for the leader to be personally present at the critical place. Without that presence, it doesn't work."

On a tank battle in Russia in 1942: "I was heavily engaged in an attack with the 11th Panzer Division. Corps Headquarters called up at 7 o'clock in the evening and said that there had been a serious breakthrough 20 kilometers to my left, and that I should hurry over and take care of the breakthrough. I said, 'Well, let me clean up the situation here and then I'll take care of the breakthrough.' They said, 'No, the situation on your left is terrible, and you've got to cease your attack immediately and clean up the breakthrough as fast as possible.' I immediately gave the verbal order extricating us from the attack and directing the division to move and prepare for the new counterattack against the breakthrough 20 kilometers away. We launched our counterattack at 5 o'clock the next morning, and achieved such surprise that we bagged 75 Russian tanks without the loss of a single one of our own. Of course, one of the key reasons why we were able to achieve such quick movement was that I marched with the units. After all, the men were dead tired and nearly finished. I rode up and down the columns and asked the troops whether they preferred to march or bleed. To compare our speed with the Russians, I would estimate that a Russian armored division would have required at least 24 hours longer to have achieved the same movement we achieved in 10 hours. I had much less experience against the Americans, so I can only guess that the Americans would have been slightly faster than the Russians."

On attack and defense: "It's quite remarkable that most people believe that attack costs more casualties. Don't even think about it; attack is the less costly operation. . . . The matter is, after all, mainly psychological. In attack, there are only 3 or 4 men in the division who carry the attack; all the others just follow behind. In defense, every man must hold his position alone. He doesn't see his neighbors; he just sees whether something is advancing towards him. He's often not equal to the task. That's why he's easily uprooted. Nothing incurs higher casualties than an unsuccessful defense. Therefore, attack wherever it is possible. Attack has one disadvantage: all troops and staffs are in movement and have to jump. That's quite tiring. In defense you can pick a foxhole and catch some sleep."

On generalship: "There can be no fixed schemes. Every scheme, every pattern is wrong. No two situations are identical. That is why the study of military history can be extremely dangerous. Another principle that follows from this is: never do the same thing twice. Even if something works well for you once, by the second time the enemy will have adapted. So you have to think up something new. No one thinks of becoming a great painter simply by imitating Michelangelo. Similarly, you can't become a great military leader just by imitating so-and-so. It has to come from within. In the last analysis, military command is an art: one man can do it and most will never learn. After all, the world is not full of Raphaels either."

When Balck was a prisoner of war he resolutely refused to cooperate with American officers who asked him to contribute his reminiscences to an American historical project. Thirty years later, he had mellowed sufficiently to allow himself to be interviewed. The constant theme of his military career was learning to do more with less. He was always inventing new tricks to confound the enemy in front of him and the bureaucrats behind him. If I had to choose an epigraph for a biography of Balck, I would not take it from T. S. Eliot but from the old Anglo-Saxon poem commemorating the battle of Maldon:

> Thought shall be harder, heart the keener,
> Courage the greater, as our strength lessens.

Balck, like the Saxons who fought the Danes at Maldon in the year 991, belonged to a tradition of soldiering older than *Soldatentum*, older than chivalry. Balck fought well because he enjoyed fighting well, and because he had a talent for it. As a professional soldier, he took his job seriously but not solemnly.

Jodl and Balck exemplify two styles of military professionalism, the heavy and the light, the tragic and the comic, the bureaucratic and the human. Jodl doggedly sat at his desk, translating Hitler's dreams of conquest into daily balance sheets of men and equipment. Balck gaily jumped out of one tight squeeze into another, taking good care of his soldiers and never losing his sense of humor. For Jodl, Hitler was Germany's fate, a superhuman force transcending right and wrong. Balck saw Hitler as he was, a powerful but not very competent politician. When Jodl disagreed with Hitler's plan to extend the German advance south of the Caucasus Mountains by dropping parachutists, the disagreement was for Jodl a soul-shattering experience. When Balck appealed directly to Hitler to straighten out a confusion in the supply of tanks and trucks, Hitler's failure to deal with the situation came as no surprise to Balck. "As it turned out," reports Balck, "Hitler never was able to gain control over the industry." Jodl went on fighting to the bitter end because he had made Hitler's will his highest law. Balck went on fighting because it never occurred to him to do anything else.

I chose my two examples of military professionalism from Germany because the German side of World War II displays the moral dilemmas of military professionalism with particular clarity. Both Jodl and Balck were good men working for a bad cause. Both of them used their professional skills to conquer and ravage half of Europe. Both of them continued to exercise their skills through the long years of retreat when the only result of their efforts was to prolong Europe's agony. Both of them appeared to be indifferent to the sufferings of the villagers whose homes their tanks were smashing and burning. And yet the judgment of Nuremberg made a distinction between them. Whether or not the Nuremberg tribunal was properly constituted according to international law, its decisions expressed the consensus of mankind at that moment of history. Jodl was hanged; Balck was set free; and the majority of interested bystanders agreed that justice had been done.

Roughly speaking, the distinction which the tribunal established and the public approved was a distinction between strategy and tactics. Balck was forgiven for waging war aggressively at the tactical level. Jodl was condemned for waging war aggressively at the strategic level. In the view of the tribunal, it is a sin for a soldier to plan campaigns for the overthrow and destruction of peaceful neighbors, but it is no sin for a soldier serving in such a campaign to be master of his trade. Rightly or wrongly, the public still approves the old tradition of military professionalism, giving honor and respect to soldiers who fight bravely in a bad cause.

The distinction between strategy and tactics is not the only difference between Jodl and Balck. There is another difference, which is equally important, although it was not used by the Nuremberg judges to justify their condemnation of Jodl, namely the distinction between soldiering and *Soldatentum*, the distinction between soldiering as a trade and soldiering as a cult. Balck was a likable character because he did not take himself too seriously. He went on winning battles, just as Picasso went on painting pictures, without pretentiousness or pious talk. He won battles because the skill came to him naturally. He never said that battle-winning was a particularly noble or virtuous activity; it was simply his trade. Jodl was unlikable and in the end diabolical because he set soldiering above humanity. He made his soldier's oath into a holy sacrament. He believed that he must be true to his ideal of *Soldatentum* even if it meant dragging Germany down to destruction. To be a good soldier was to him more important than to save what was left of Germany. He identified his duty as a soldier with loyalty to Hitler, and so he became infected with Hitler's insanity. The ideal of *Soldatentum* became an obsession, detached from reason, from reality, and from common sense.

Germany was an extreme case of military professionalism run wild, and the judgment at Nuremberg was an exceptional nemesis. But every country which gives an exalted status to its military leaders runs a risk of catching the German madness. There, but for the grace of God, go we. Something of the German madness infected the American South at the time of the Civil War. Like Germany, the states of the Confederacy made a cult of soldiering. It was no accident that the most brilliant generals of the Civil War were all fighting on the Southern side. Long before the war began, the Southern states had established a cultural tradition which encouraged their best minds to become professional soldiers. The tradition of exaggerated respect for military prowess was doubly disastrous for the South. It led to the overconfident enthusiasm and the illusions of military superiority with which the South went to war at the beginning. And it produced the spirit of sacrificial dedication in which the Southerners fought on to the bitter end, when the prolongation of the war was bringing to their country nothing but ruin and destruction. Robert Lee was a great general and a great gentleman, but all his tactical skill and strength of character only made the sufferings of his people heavier. The people of the Southern states, daily enduring death and destruction as a result of his activities, continued until the end to lavish upon him their unbounded love and admiration. When he returned to his home in Richmond after his surrender, he was greeted by an immense throng of cheering citizens. There was much in Lee that was noble and worthy of respect, but the hero-worship which surrounded him during and after the war was altogether disproportionate. The mystique of Lee distorted the Southerners' view of the world for a long time. Robert Lee was a greater general than Hermann Balck and a finer human being than Alfred Jodl, but his role in history was the same as theirs, to lead his beloved people to disaster. Any society which idolizes soldiers is tainted with a collective insanity and is likely in the end to come to grief.

England has been luckier in its choice of heroes. The British navy has been for hundreds of years the senior service, and the popular heroes of England have been admirals rather than generals. As a child in England, I learned to take it for granted that anybody making a career in the army must be intellectually subnormal. Army officers, on the stage or in real life, were figures of fun. Naval officers were also subject to occasional ridicule, but jokes about navy people were friendly rather than contemptuous. The navy commanded a certain respect even from the irreverent young. We were told that our Admiral Jellicoe, commander of the Grand Fleet during World War I, was the only man on either side who could have lost the war in one afternoon. He did not, after all, lose the war. Even though he was not very bright, and his one great battle, Jutland, was not a brilliant success, at least he did better than the generals on the

Western Front. He kept cool and did not waste his ships in fruitless
and unnecessary attacks.

The English language reflects the English bias in favor of sea
captains. We have no word for soldierly virtue corresponding to the
German *Soldatentum*. But we use naturally the word "seamanship,"
which has the same emotional resonance as *Soldatentum*, transferred
from soldiers to sailors. Seamanship means not just technical competence in handling a ship; it includes also steadiness of nerve and
strength of character, the virtues which Alfred Jodl subsumed under
the heading *Soldatentum*. In England these virtues are perceived as
belonging to sailors rather than to soldiers.

The English have not been exempt from the vice of military
idolatry. A hundred years ago, Robert Louis Stevenson wrote an
essay with the title "The English Admirals," eloquently expressing
the feelings of pride and glory which were then driving the worldwide expansion of the British empire:

> Their sayings and doings stir English blood like the sound of a
> trumpet; and if the Indian Empire, the trade of London, and all the
> outward and visible ensigns of our greatness should pass away, we
> should still leave behind us a durable monument of what we were
> in these sayings and doings of the English Admirals. Duncan, lying
> off the Texel with his own flagship, the Venerable, and only one
> other vessel, heard that the whole Dutch fleet was putting to sea.
> He told Captain Hotham to anchor alongside him in the narrowest
> part of the channel, and fight his vessel until she sank. "I have taken
> the depth of the water," added he, "and when the Venerable goes
> down, my flag will still fly." And you observe that this is no naked
> Viking in a prehistoric period; but a Scotch member of Parliament,
> with a smattering of the classics, a telescope, a cocked hat of great
> size, and flannel underclothing. In the same spirit, Nelson went into
> Aboukir with six colours flying; so that even if five were shot away,
> it should not be imagined he had struck. . . . And as our Admirals
> were full of heroic superstitions, and had a strutting and vainglori-
> ous style of fight, so they discovered a startling eagerness for battle,
> and courted war like a mistress. . . .

Trowbridge went ashore with the Culloden, and was able to take
no part in the battle of the Nile. "The merits of that ship and her
gallant captain," wrote Nelson to the Admiralty, "are too well
known to benefit by anything I could say. Her misfortune was great

in getting aground, while her more fortunate companions were in
the full tide of happiness." This is a notable expression, and depicts
the whole great-hearted, big-spoken stock of the English Admirals
to a hair. It was to be "in the full tide of happiness" for Nelson to
destroy five thousand five hundred and twenty-five of his fellow-
creatures, and have his own scalp torn open by a piece of langridge
shot. Hear him again at Copenhagen. A shot through the mainmast
knocked the splinters about; and he observed to one of his officers
with a smile, "It is warm work, and this may be the last to any of
us at any moment," and then, stopping short at the gangway, added
with emotion, "But, mark you, I would not be elsewhere for thousands." . . . The best artist is not the man who fixes his eye on
posterity, but the one who loves the practice of his art. And instead
of having a taste for being successful merchants and retiring at
thirty, some people have a taste for high and what we call heroic
forms of excitement. If the Admirals courted war like a mistress; if,
as the drum beat to quarters, the sailors came gaily out of the
forecastle—it is because a fight is a period of multiplied and intense
experiences, and, by Nelson's computation, worth thousands to any
one who has a heart under his jacket.

This is the stuff on which English children of the 1880s were
raised. It is no better and no worse than the German patriotic
literature of the same period. England and Germany were both in
a mood of exuberant nationalism. Winston Churchill and Adolf
Hitler both grew up under its influence. Churchill and Hitler were
both military romantics; both acted out their private dreams of glory
by becoming great war leaders. And yet the effects of such glorification of the martial spirit in England and in Germany were vastly
different. Churchill, and the English society which he represented,
remained fundamentally sane, while Hitler's military visions led
him and his society to paranoia and destruction. There were many
historical and social reasons for the difference. No single factor by
itself can explain such a profound divergence between neighboring
cultures. But it may be that the most important cause of the difference between English and German destinies was the technical difference between the circumstances of sea and land warfare. War at
sea, throughout the long period of British maritime ascendancy, was
war for limited objectives. The technical limitations of sea power
limited the human consequences of victory and defeat. None of

Nelson's great victories resulted in the ruin of a province or the unconditional surrender of a country. The means of naval warfare determined the ends. Since the means were modest, the ends stopped short of insanity. No similar limitation of the means kept land warfare from escalating into wholesale conquest and genocide.

It is easy to go back into history and find other examples of sound and unsound military professionalism. Particularly illuminating in this respect is the contrast between the careers of Washington and Napoleon. Washington, fighting a war of limited objectives with means which were even more limited, laid the foundations for a durable and stable government in America. Everything which Washington built has lasted for two hundred years. Napoleon, fighting wars of unlimited objectives with armies greater than Europe had seen before, built an empire which crashed in ruins even before he was dead.

What can we learn from this picture gallery of soldiers, beginning with Jodl and Balck and Lee and ending with Washington and Napoleon? Professional soldiers and sailors have a necessary and honorable role to play in human affairs. The traditional respect which nations pay to military valor cannot be denied. As every country has a right to self-defense, every country has a right to give honor to its military leaders. But the honoring of military leaders brings deadly danger to mankind unless both the moral authority granted to them and the technical means at their disposal are strictly limited. Military power should never be confused with moral virtue, and military leaders should never be entrusted with weapons of unlimited destruction.

Nineteenth-century England was lucky to have military heroes who were modest both in their moral pretensions and in their material resources. Robert Louis Stevenson expressed in a nutshell the philosophy which allowed England to acquire an empire without losing a sense of proportion: "Almost everybody in our land, except humanitarians and a few persons whose youth has been depressed by exceptionally aesthetic surroundings, can understand and sympathize with an Admiral or a prize-fighter." This is the limit beyond which the pursuit of military glory should not go. A successful general or admiral should be honored no more and no less than a successful boxer.

The cult of military obedience, and the cult of weapons of mass destruction, are the two great follies of the modern age. The cult of

obedience brought Germany to moral degradation and dismember-
ment. The cult of weapons of mass destruction threatens to bring
us all to annihilation. It was, regrettably, the airmen of England who
led the world into the cult of destruction. The Italian Douhet first
preached the gospel of strategic bombing in the 1920s, but the
British Sir Hugh Trenchard was the first to put Douhet's gospel
into practice. England turned decisively away from the civilized
nineteenth-century tradition of limited-objective warfare when
Trenchard persuaded his government to build a force of heavy
bombers with the deliberate aim of attacking the German civilian
economy. The limited character of naval armament had made the
exercise of British sea power in the nineteenth century peculiarly
benign. The exercise of air power is subject to no such limitations.
A strategy of strategic bombardment ensures that war will be total.
And where England led the way into the era of strategic bombing,
the United States was quick to follow. Already in the 1930s, England and America were set on the path which led to Hiroshima and
Nagasaki. The cult of destruction possessed our bomber generals,
and as a result of their activities we have been living under the threat
of destruction ever since.

The advent of nuclear weapons has brought a new class of
military professionals into existence, men whose careers are based
on specialized knowledge of nuclear technology and nuclear delivery systems. In the Soviet Union, the new class of nuclear warriors
rose to sudden prominence during the Khrushchev regime of the
early 1960s. "These soldier-technicians with their special skills and
higher education," reports John Erickson in his study of the Soviet
armed forces,

> represented at once a challenge to the dominance of the traditional
> officers and a break with the accepted image of the military com-
> mander; it was, therefore, but a short step to question the nature of
> command in modern war and thus to jeopardise the authority of the
> commander, who in an age of computers and nuclear weapons
> could no longer rely upon the simple military values of courage and
> selfless dedication—even intuition was no substitute for technical
> skill and competence. On the other hand, the traditionalists were
> not slow to mount their own counterattack against the encroach-
> ments of the technocrats; they pointed out that undue stress on
> theoretical training could simply turn officers into "shkolasty"—

bookworms—and that the technocrats showed a marked indifference to the political educational work conducted in the Soviet armed forces, insisting that their job was confined to the technological element and ended with ensuring combat readiness.

During the twenty years which have elapsed since Khrushchev's reforms, the technocrats have been peacefully assimilated into the Soviet military hierarchy; they now occupy many of the top positions. In the United States the process of assimilation began earlier and has been even more complete. As a result, there now exists in both countries a formidable array of high-ranking officers and government officials whose lives are dedicated to the management and operation of nuclear weapons systems. In both countries, the nuclear soldiers are supported by an equally formidable array of civilian scientists and technicians. All these people have come to take it for granted that the deployment of nuclear weaponry on a massive scale is essential to the security of their countries. They identify nuclear destructive power with national security, and so they become trapped in the cult of destruction, just as Alfred Jodl, by identifying obedience to Hitler with service to Germany, became trapped in the cult of obedience.

From time to time a lonely voice of a military leader is heard, speaking out against nuclear weaponry. Those who speak out are usually retired officers who have seen war at first hand and know how wide is the gap between strategic theory and reality. One such officer is Lieutenant General Arthur Collins, who commanded troops in World War II and in Vietnam. In a recent essay entitled "Strategy for Disaster" he discusses the American plans for a nuclear defense of Western Europe and argues that, even if one disregards the catastrophic civilian casualties of a nuclear defense and looks at the problem from a narrowly military point of view, the planned use of nuclear weapons makes no sense. If we try to defend Europe with nuclear weapons, says General Collins, we are playing a game which the Soviet Union knows how to win.

From my reading, Soviet nuclear doctrine appears to be more comprehensive, consistent, and realistic than similar US doctrine. The difference between US and Soviet tactical nuclear doctrine, and the difference in yield and range between US and Soviet tactical nuclear weapons, guarantees that US scenarios and theories of controlling tactical nuclear war would lead to NATO's defeat. . . .

Many war games and studies have shown that where the first use of nuclear weapons is careful and discreet, the side that initiated the nuclear attack is overwhelmed by a sudden and massive enemy response. Ask any US commander what he would do if his units were hit by a few small nuclear weapons. The response would be to call urgently for all the nuclear firepower he could get. Are the Russians likely to be more restrained in similar circumstances? Soviet military doctrine gives little evidence of concern for collateral damage, especially on hostile soil. The most likely result of NATO's first use of neutron bombs would be for NATO to lose faster. . . .

Too many tactical nuclear war scenarios deal with NATO, Korea, or some other distant land. . . . The best of all lessons on tactical nuclear war would come from a tactical nuclear war-game of the conflict between the Atlanticans fighting the Pacificans with the Mississippi as the national boundary. Provide the Atlanticans with a stockpile similar to the 7000 nuclear weapons in NATO to be used in accordance with US doctrine, and the Pacificans with a stockpile similar to the Soviet stockpile of about 3500 weapons to be used in accord with Soviet nuclear doctrine. The results would be certain to grab someone's attention.

General Collins does not believe that Western Europe is indefensible. On the contrary, he thinks that a non-nuclear defense of NATO territory is feasible and affordable. Only the addiction of our military and political leaders to nuclear weapons deprived us of all incentive to build a defense system that would really work.

Throughout the history of warfare, two styles of professional soldiering have alternately prevailed, the style of brains and quick reaction and the style of stupor and mass destruction. World War I was the classic example of a war of stupor and mass destruction. After World War I was over, the pioneers of mobile armored warfare, Von Seeckt in Germany and De Gaulle in France and Fuller in England, understood how to avoid a repetition of the mass slaughters of the Western Front. Unfortunately, France did not listen to De Gaulle but built the Maginot Line instead; England did not listen to Fuller but built Bomber Command instead; Germany, however, listened to Von Seeckt and built the panzer divisions which almost won World War II. The panzer divisions did what they were supposed to do. They made possible a war of brains and quick reaction. They made possible the elegant victories of Hermann Balck. The early blitzkrieg campaigns of Hitler were amazingly nondestructive compared with the campaigns of World War I. The mass slaughters of World War II arose from the failure of the blitzkrieg in Russia, from the deliberate barbarities of the German police forces, and from the Allied policy of strategic bombardment. In spite of all these horrors, the basic idea of mobile armored warfare was sound. It enabled small armies to win campaigns with a minimum of slaughter.

As a rule, professional soldiers who take pride in their profession prefer the weaponry of brains and quick reaction to the weaponry of mass destruction. But the advent of nuclear weapons caused military doctrines to take a strong swing backward in the direction of mass destruction. For thirty years, in the United States and in the Soviet Union, the technology of nuclear weaponry has dominated strategic thinking. Wars of stupor and mass destruction were again in fashion. Perhaps the time has now come for the pendulum to swing the other way. Many of the nuclear technocrats who have risen in the military establishment through the exercise of their technical and managerial skills are turning to non-nuclear technology as nuclear technology becomes more and more detached from real military needs. The technological arms race itself is moving away from mass destruction toward weapons which give scope to brains and initiative. To lead the way toward a sane strategy of limited means and limited objectives, we need an alliance of old traditionalists and young technocrats within the armed services, based upon a shared conviction that national security and nuclear weaponry are not synonymous.

Every soldier who commands nuclear forces, and every civilian strategist who theorizes about them, should from time to time imagine himself sitting in the dock at Nuremberg at the end of World War III and preparing his defense. Would his defense be any more convincing to the judges than the defense of Alfred Jodl? Jodl was, according to his own opinion and the opinion of his friends, an honorable man and a good soldier. The nuclear commanders and strategists are, so far as I know them, honorable men and good soldiers too. Jodl was condemned because his cult of obedience led to the death of millions. If the nuclear strategists' cult of destruction should also lead to the death of millions, are they less deserving of condemnation?

14

Diplomats

Generals can make war, but it takes a diplomat to make peace. Great diplomats are rarer than great generals. Throughout human history, the tools of war have been studied too much and the tools of diplomacy too little. In the modern era more than ever before, weaponry commands disproportionate attention and the art of understanding the purposes of foreign governments is neglected.

A historic meeting between a great diplomat and a great general occurred on June 26, 1813. The Austrian Prince Metternich went to Dresden to speak with the Emperor Napoleon. Napoleon was then, after his retreat from Moscow, still at war with Russia and Prussia. Austria was neutral. Metternich was sent by the Austrian Emperor Francis to learn as much as he could about Napoleon's state of mind. Metternich summarized the Dresden conversation in his memoirs sixteen years later. Napoleon is the first to speak:

"So you too want war; well, you shall have it. I have annihilated the Prussian army at Lützen; I have beaten the Russians at Bautzen; now you wish your turn to come. Be it so; the rendezvous shall be in Vienna. Men are incorrigible: experience is lost upon you. Three times I have replaced the Emperor Francis on his throne. I have promised always to live in peace with him; I have married his daughter. At the time I said to myself you are perpetrating a folly; but it was done, and to-day I repent of it." This introduction doubled my feeling of the strength of my position. I felt myself, at this crisis, the representative of all European society. If I may say so—Napoleon seemed to me small!

After some detailed discussion of the Russian campaign, Metternich continued the conversation:

"I have seen your soldiers: they are mere children. Your Majesty has the feeling that you are absolutely necessary to the nation: but is not the nation also necessary to you? And if this juvenile army that you levied but yesterday should be swept away, what then?" When Napoleon heard these words he was overcome with rage, he turned pale, and his features were distorted. "You are no soldier," said he, "and you do not know what goes on in the mind of a soldier. I was brought up in the field, and a man such as I am does not concern himself much about the lives of a million of men." With this exclamation he threw his hat, which he had held in his hand, into the corner of the room. I remained quite quiet, leaning against the edge of a console between the two windows, and said, deeply moved by what I had just heard, "Why have you chosen to say this to me within these four walls? Open the doors, and let your words sound from one end of France to the other. The cause which I represent will not lose thereby."

When Napoleon dismissed me, his tone had become calm and quiet. I could no longer distinguish his features. He accompanied me to the door of the reception-room. Holding the handle of the folding-door, he said to me, "We shall see one another again." "At your pleasure, Sire," was my answer, "but I have no hope of attaining the object of my mission." "Well now," said Napoleon, touching me on the shoulder, "do you know what will happen? You will not make war on me?" "You are lost, Sire," I said, quickly. "I had the presentiment of it when I came; now, in going, I have the certainty."

This conversation was no doubt edited and embellished in Metternich's memory before being recorded. Nevertheless, it stands as a monument of the diplomat's art, a historic triumph of insight and intelligence over pride and passion. Two years later, Napoleon's power was broken, and Metternich was reconstructing the political architecture of Europe at the Congress of Vienna. Napoleon had dominated Europe during the twenty years of war which ended in his defeat at Waterloo; Metternich was to be the dominant figure in the thirty years of European peace which followed.

The era of Metternich's ascendancy lasted from 1815 to 1848, from Napoleon's exile until the year of republican revolutions. Metternich's era has much to teach us. It was a time when diplomacy succeeded in holding war in check, when diplomats controlled the affairs of nations more than at any time since. It was in other respects a time like our own, with economic change and social discontent seething everywhere beneath the surface of political stability. Metternich's successes and failures hold up a mirror to us, showing us what diplomacy can and cannot do.

Metternich's purpose was to maintain an international order in Europe by establishing a permanent alliance of conservative governments with an effective monopoly of military power. He was successful insofar as the governments of Austria, Prussia, Russia, and France did in fact remain at peace with one another and assisted one another in suppressing internal dissent. The Holy Alliance of 1815 was affirmed by all the monarchs of Europe except the Prince Regent of England, the Sultan of Turkey, and the Pope. But as time went on, the divisive force of nationalism proved stronger than the unifying force of international order. First England and then France broke away from the Holy Alliance. Revolutionary republicanism in France and revolutionary nationalism in Hungary finally erupted in violence in 1848 and brought Metternich's era to an end.

Even during the early years of his ascendancy, Metternich did not have things all his own way. He was opposed by another great diplomat, George Canning of England, whom Metternich described as "a malevolent meteor hurled by an angry Providence against Europe." Canning quietly undermined Metternich's international order as Metternich had undermined Napoleon's. Canning's objective was not an international order but a balance of power. He said when he became British foreign secretary in 1822: "Things are getting back to a wholesome state again. Every nation for itself and God for us all." In 1823 he encouraged the American President Monroe to proclaim the Monroe Doctrine, which protected the rebellious republics of Latin America from attempts by the conservative European powers to reestablish Spanish rule. In a debate in the House of Commons in 1826 he explained how his support of the Latin republics fitted into his doctrine of the balance of power in Europe:

Is the balance of power a fixed and unalterable standard? Or is it not a standard perpetually varying, as civilization advances, and as new nations spring up and take their place among established political communities? The balance of power a century and a half ago was to be adjusted between France and Spain, the Netherlands, Austria and England. Some years afterwards, Russia assumed her high station in European politics. Some years after that, Prussia became not only a substantive, but a preponderating monarchy. Thus, while the balance of power continued in principle the same, the means of adjusting it became more varied and enlarged. . . . I say, then, that if we have been for the present dispossessed of anything in our situation as forming part of the balance of power, we have been fully compensated. Was it necessary to blockade Cadiz, I say, to restore the situation of England? No. I look at the possessions of Spain on the other side of the Atlantic; I look at the Indies and I call in the New World to redress the balance of the old.

Canning died one year later, but his death brought no lasting relief to Metternich. Canning's policies were pursued with even greater vigor by Palmerston, who actively supported the European revolutionary nationalist movements in their defiance of Metternich's international order. In 1848 Palmerston was still in power at the British Foreign Office, contemplating Metternich's downfall with unconcealed satisfaction.

Palmerston in his turn got into trouble in 1861, when the American Civil War broke out and his habit of friendly assistance to nationalist insurrections led him into collision with the government of the United States. He was then prime minister of Great Britain. He had always been an active opponent of slavery, but he saw no reason why the principle of the balance of power should not be applied in North America as well as in Europe. Although England was officially neutral, Palmerston welcomed the secession of the Southern states as a balance to the power of the North. His vigorous opposition to the Northern blockade of the South almost brought the British navy into the Civil War on the side of the Confederacy. The cool heads of Prince Albert in Windsor and Abraham Lincoln in Washington kept the quarrel over the blockade from escalating into open warfare. Palmerston was persuaded, for once in his long life, to keep quiet. The Union cause prevailed in the Civil War, and, so far as North America was concerned, the principle of international order prevailed over the principle of balance of power. Metternich, defeated by Palmerston in Europe, took his posthumous revenge in America.

In the diplomacy of our own time we still see, at the heart of all our difficulties, the unresolved conflict between the two great objectives of international order and balance of power. The diplomacy of Roosevelt during World War II, like the diplomacy of Metternich during the Napoleonic Wars, was concentrated upon the setting up of a durable postwar international order. Disagreements among the Allied powers over territory, or over the composition of the Polish government, were not allowed to interfere with Roosevelt's primary purpose, which was to maintain the unity of the wartime alliance. Roosevelt cheerfully agreed to Soviet territorial expansion and hegemony in Eastern Europe, believing that this would encourage the Soviet Union to cooperate with the United States in the organization of the postwar world. He preferred to deal with Stalin in personal summit meetings rather than through diplomatic channels. He thought that his direct contact with Stalin would enable him to overcome the habitual Soviet attitude of suspicion and hostility toward the United States. His overriding objective was to bring Stalin as a full partner into the operation of an international organization to keep the world at peace. As a result of Roosevelt's efforts, the United Nations was established in 1945 as the instrument of international order, just as the Holy Alliance was established for the same purpose in 1815.

While Roosevelt was pursuing his grand design of international order, George Kennan, a diplomat of a more traditional kind, was minister-counselor at the American embassy in Moscow. Roosevelt had little respect for professional diplomats. The people in Washington responsible for negotiating with Soviet emissaries the ground rules of the United Nations Organization did not look to their embassy in Moscow for advice. Nobody asked Kennan for his opinion about what was being done. Kennan nevertheless, in August 1944, wrote down for his own satisfaction the advice which he would have given if he had been asked for it:

Underlying the whole conception of an organization for international security is the simple reasoning that if only the status quo could be rigidly preserved there could be no further wars in Europe, and the European problem, so far as our country is concerned, would be solved. This reasoning, which mistakes the symptoms for the disease, is not new. It underlay the Holy Alliance, the

League of Nations, and numerous other political structures set up by nations which were for the moment satisfied with the international setup and did not wish to see it changed. These structures have always served the purpose for which they were designed just so long as the interests of the great powers gave substance and reality to their existence. The moment this situation changed, the moment it became in the interests of one or another of the great powers to alter the status quo, none of these treaty structures ever stood in the way of such alteration. . . .

Those provisions of our proposals that are designed to prevent a great nation from conquering and dominating a small nation reflect a thinking which is naïve and out of date. We ignore completely the time-honored conception of the puppet state which underlies all political thought in Asia and Russia, and occasionally appears in Eastern and Central Europe as well. This conception alone mocks any legalistic formulas for the regulation of international life. Try asking the head of the Outer Mongolian Republic whether Mongolia has any grievances against Russia. He will pale at the thought. He is personally in the power of the Russian police system, and his people live under the shadow of the Red army. . . .

The conception of law in international life should certainly receive every support and encouragement that our country can give it. But it cannot yet replace power as the vital force for a large part of the world. And the realities of power will soon seep into any legalistic structure which we erect to govern international life. They will permeate it. They will become the content of it; and the structure will remain only the form. International security will depend on *them*, on the realities of power, not on the structure in which they are clothed. We are being almost criminally negligent of the interests of our people if we allow our plans for an international organization to be an excuse for failing to occupy ourselves seriously and minutely with the sheer power relationships of the European peoples.

It did not take long for Kennan's assessment of the United Nations to prove itself correct. The Holy Alliance remained united and harmonious for five years, from 1815 until 1820, before the process of incipient disintegration became visible. The United Nations maintained a superficial unity of purpose for only half as long. By 1947 the United Nations had become what it has been ever since, a forum of national rivalry rather than of international authority.

During the brief period of postwar harmony, while hopes still survived of an international order based on friendly cooperation of the Allied powers, one historic attempt was made to give these hopes substance. The attempt was made in 1946 to establish a truly supranational authority with monopolistic power to own and regulate nuclear weaponry. Nuclear weaponry was then a new and revolutionary factor in human affairs. Here, if anywhere, was a chance to create a new international order before national rivalries in the possession and deployment of nuclear weapons would have time to develop. The initial impetus behind the idea of international ownership of nuclear facilities came from the physicists Niels Bohr and Robert Oppenheimer, who had worried together about the future of nuclear weaponry while they worked on the bomb project at Los Alamos. Bohr had succeeded in talking to Churchill and Roosevelt on this subject during the war, but he had not succeeded in gaining their confidence. After the war, Oppenheimer persuaded Under Secretary of State Acheson and other leading figures in the American government to make a serious effort to achieve international control of nuclear energy. Oppenheimer was not as great a physicist as Bohr, but he was a more skillful diplomat. The result of his diplomacy was the Baruch Plan, the formal American proposal to place all nuclear facilities under international ownership. The Baruch Plan was placed before the United Nations in 1946. If the plan had been accepted by the Soviet Union, it would perhaps have fulfilled Roosevelt's dream of an international order arising from the common interest of mankind in the prevention of war. Conceivably, if the International Atomic Development Authority had been set up with the powers envisaged in the plan, the unprecedented renunciation of national sovereignty in the area of nuclear weaponry might have gradually been extended, as Bohr had originally hoped, to a renunciation of national sovereignty over other kinds of armaments and ultimately to a renunciation of the sovereign right of nations to wage war.

There were many detailed provisions in the Baruch Plan which made it difficult for the Soviet Union to accept. But it soon became clear, when the plan was debated in the United Nations, that the Soviet Union was not interested in negotiating points of detail. The Soviet Union was fundamentally opposed to the renunciation of national sovereignty which the plan demanded. The Soviet Union proposed, instead of a supranational authority with sovereign powers, a simple treaty prohibiting the manufacture and ownership of nuclear weapons. The Soviet Union agreed with George Kennan that national power came first, international order second.

Americans old enough to remember the high hopes engendered by the Baruch Plan frequently lament the great opportunity that was missed when the Soviet Union rejected it. Today, with the wisdom of hindsight, we may equally lament the great opportunity that was missed when the United States rejected the Soviet prohibition treaty. The Soviet proposal, if it had been accepted, would also have been an instrument of international order, more modest than the Baruch Plan but perhaps more practical and more durable. The American government, having made heroic efforts to achieve an internal consensus for the negotiation of the Baruch Plan, was in no mood to examine carefully the merits of the Soviet proposal. So far as American public opinion was concerned, there were only two alternatives: either total international control of nuclear energy through the Baruch Plan, or none at all. After the initial proposals of both sides had been rejected, no serious effort was made to achieve a compromise agreement. The surge of hope for the establishment of an international order had reached its high-water mark, and was ebbing rapidly as the year 1946 came to an end.

A few months later, two years after the end of World War II in Europe, George Kennan was asked by American Secretary of State Marshall to prepare the plan of European economic recovery known to history as the Marshall Plan. The philosophy underlying the Marshall Plan was succinctly stated by Kennan at the time: "I think it may be fairly stated, as a working rule for dealing with the Russians, that only those people are able to get along *with* them who have proven their ability to get along *without* them." In other words, an effective international order in Europe is impossible unless it is based on an effective balance of power. The Marshall Plan was the decisive first step in establishing a political balance of power in Europe. The reinforcement of this balance by the military Atlantic Pact came a year later. Kennan believed in a balance of power based on the economic and political strengthening of Western European governments. He was in favor of a military balance of power provided that it did not become heavily dependent on the rearmament of West Germany. And he was unalterably opposed to making the balance of power dependent on arming Atlantic Pact forces with nuclear weapons.

After 1948, the American government moved rapidly from the exaggerated belief in Soviet-American cooperation which Kennan criticized in 1944 to an even more exaggerated belief in military confrontation. Kennan's period of ascendancy in the State Department coincided with the period when belief in international order and belief in balance of power were briefly held in equilibrium. In 1950, when the Korean War began and the United States announced its intention to develop thermonuclear weapons, the equilibrium tipped decisively toward military confrontation. Kennan thereafter reverted to his role as critic of government policy, criticizing now from the other side. In 1953 he resigned from government service and began a new career as a historian in Princeton. Ever since his retirement from government, he has been preaching, to all who would listen, that the balance of power is to be valued as a foundation for a durable international order, not as an end in itself, that the most effective tools for establishing a balance of power are economic and political rather than military, and that the least appropriate tools of all for this purpose are weapons of mass destruction.

Soviet-American diplomacy since 1953 has been dominated by the continuing nuclear arms race and by the technical details of weaponry. Whenever an attempt is made to negotiate an agreement setting limits to the arms race, the public discussion of the agreement in the United States is concentrated upon fine points of weapon performance and verification technology. During the discussions of a comprehensive test ban treaty in the late 1950s and early 1960s, the argument centered almost exclusively on the technical capability of seismic detection systems to discriminate underground bomb tests from earthquakes. The senators who conducted public hearings on the test ban became almost as expert in seismology as the scientists who came to testify. This overemphasis on technical details made the problem of verifying the test ban seem more and more formidable. The negotiation of a comprehensive test ban was abandoned in 1963 because the verification system demanded by the seismologically expert American politicians was too intrusive to be acceptable to the Soviet Union. A similar overemphasis on technical details obstructed the ratification of the SALT II treaty by the American Senate in 1979. The text of the treaty was excessively complicated, with elaborate definitions and rules for counting numbers of weapons in various categories. It was difficult for the advocates of the treaty to defend it against opponents who claimed that the Soviet Backfire bombers were incorrectly counted or that the number of SS-18 missiles allowed by the treaty gave the Soviet Union an unfair advantage. Once again, a reasonable treaty was nibbled to death by people raising small technical objections. This has been the tragedy of nuclear diplomacy for the last thirty years: Just as, according to Gresham's law of economics, bad money drives good money out of circulation, so, in the public perception of arms control agreements, unimportant technical issues drive broader political objectives out of sight.

When President Kennedy sent his Under Secretary of State Averell Harriman to Moscow in 1963 to negotiate the atmospheric test ban treaty, Harriman was careful to exclude technical specialists from his team of negotiators. Technical advisers went with Harriman to Moscow but did not participate directly in negotiations. Harriman believed that this separation of the roles of expert adviser and decisionmaker was one of the main reasons for the success of his mission. Ten years later he said in testimony before the Senate Committee on Foreign Relations:

> These matters have got to be left to the political leaders of our nation. The expert is out to point out all the difficulties and dangers . . . but it is for the political leaders to decide whether the political, psychological and other advantages offset such risks as there may be.

Two other factors were essential to the success of the 1963 negotiation: the character of the atmospheric test ban treaty and the character of Averell Harriman himself. The treaty was deliberately kept short and simple and free from technical jargon. The entire text fills three printed pages. The substantive part of it fills only half a page. The only numbers in it are paragraph numbers and dates and a single reference to Article 102 of the Charter of the United Nations. The treaty leaves no openings for opponents to attack it on points of technical detail. The credentials of Harriman as negotiator were also difficult to attack. He was wise in the ways of American politics. He had been ambassador in Moscow when Kennan was minister-counselor, he had long experience of dealing with the Soviet government, and he was personally acquainted with Khrushchev. Above all, he understood the importance of timing in negotiations. He knew that the momentum of progress toward a treaty could easily be lost if the negotiations were prolonged. He went after the treaty at top speed, like Hermann Balck getting his soldiers across the Meuse. Harriman afterward described to his friend Glenn Seaborg how he set the pace of the negotiations:

> When we arrived at the [Moscow] airport, the press people rushed up and asked all sorts of questions, one of which was, "How long do you think you'll be here?" I felt that if we said that it was a very complicated proposition that would take a long time, the Soviets would have felt a need to string it out a long time or else it would look as if they were giving in to our side. So I said, "Well, now, if Chairman Khrushchev is as interested in having a test-ban treaty as President Kennedy and Prime Minister Macmillan are, we ought to be out of here in two weeks!" They *got* us out in *less* than two weeks—they were pressing us to get out. One cannot be sure, but I feel that after reading my remarks Khrushchev may have taken it on himself to prove that he was just as keen for a test-ban as the President and Macmillan. A lot of these people who talk so glibly about the Russians don't realize what these men are. They're human beings. They react. If you understand them and know how they react it's much easier to deal with them.

The atmospheric test ban treaty was successful because Harriman did not allow arguments about the technical specification of forbidden explosions or about the technical problems of verification to distract attention from the treaty's primary purpose. During the weeks before Harriman went to Moscow, I happened to be at the Arms Control and Disarmament Agency in Washington, helping the scientists there to study these technical problems which Harriman wisely excluded from the negotiations. At that time the Agency still hoped to achieve a comprehensive test ban, and the main subject of our study was the effectiveness of various arrangements of seismic detectors for identifying underground bomb tests. In the course of these studies we made an interesting discovery. As the detection systems became technically better, they became politically worse. The reason for this paradox was simple. The detection system had a double task—to identify bomb tests as artificial and to identify earthquakes as natural. The system could fail in two ways—either by missing a real bomb test or by giving a false-alarm reaction to an earthquake. The designers of the instruments were constantly improving them by making them more sensitive, so that fewer real bomb tests should be missed. But every increase in sensitivity resulted in a large increase in the expected number of false alarms. The designers did not understand that in the monitoring of a test ban treaty, a high false-alarm rate would be far more troublesome politically than a low detection rate. While they were making the system technically better by raising the detection rate of underground explosions, they were at the same time making the system politically unworkable by raising the frequency of false alarms. After we saw what was happening, we suggested to our superiors in the Agency that if they wanted to achieve a comprehensive test ban, they should try to make the monitoring seismic instruments as insensitive as possible. Averell Harriman might have recognized the merits of this suggestion, but the administrators of the Disarmament Agency did not. The seismic detection networks continued to become more sensitive, the false-alarm rates continued to rise, and the chance of negotiating a comprehensive test ban treaty in 1963 was missed.

The paradox of verifiability arises not only in connection with test ban treaties but in the monitoring of arms control agreements of all kinds. According to the official doctrine of the United States, all arms control agreements to which the United States is a party must be verifiable. But too much verification gives rise to incessant false alarms and destroys whatever political benefits the agreement was intended to achieve. This is the paradox: too much verification may be as bad as too little. The avoidance of false alarms is particularly important if the verification system is public. False alarms are less damaging if verification is done in secret—for example, by satellite photography. But the United States has only a limited ability to keep undigested intelligence reports secret; even if false alarms can be kept out of the newspapers, a verification apparatus had better not be too sensitive. It is easy for a technical surveillance system to collect more information than it is capable of evaluating. The careful evaluation of a single ambiguous event can absorb the attention of intelligence experts for several weeks. If ambiguous events are detected too frequently, careful evaluation is impossible, and the random output of an oversensitive verification system can easily be misinterpreted as a systematic pattern of violations of a treaty.

Verification of treaties is important, just as military strength is important. But verification, like military strength, must be pursued as a means to an end and not as an end in itself. The end which verification is supposed to serve is to discourage the parties to a treaty from serious and deliberate violations. A limited and unobtrusive verification system is usually adequate for this purpose. When verification becomes an end in itself, it stands in the way of arms control, just as it stood in the way of the comprehensive test ban in 1963. "The trouble with you is you want to spy. That's your purpose," said Khrushchev to Harriman in 1963. Khrushchev's accusation was unjust insofar as it was addressed to Harriman personally. It was a just criticism of the American technical experts and politicians who have made the details of verification systems seem more important than the substance of the agreements which are to be verified.

Official American doctrine holds that unverifiable agreements are worthless. This doctrine may or may not be true, depending on circumstances. An extreme example of an unverifiable agreement is the 1975 convention on biological weapons, signed by the United States, Britain, and the Soviet Union. The convention prohibits production and possession of biological weapons, disease agents, toxins, and delivery systems. Since disease agents are small and easily manufactured in inconspicuous bacteriological laboratories, verification of the convention by technical means is impossible. The chief purpose of the convention is to strengthen the traditional consensus of mankind that biological warfare is in some sense peculiarly evil and dishonorable. The value of the convention for this purpose remains largely intact, whether or not it is verified and whether or not it is violated. There is evidence indicating that the convention has been violated by the Soviet Union. Biological toxins are said to have been supplied by the Soviet Union to Vietnam and used by Vietnamese forces in terror attacks on villages in Laos. But the convention remains in force and remains useful. The Soviet government officially denies any involvement with whatever may have happened in Laos. And the American government wisely refrains from using the events in Laos as a pretext for abrogating the convention. If the reports of toxin attacks in Laos are true, the use of toxins appears to have been clandestine, and the signature of Secretary Brezhnev on the biological weapons convention imposes an important constraint on further exercises of the same kind. Without the convention, the friends of the victims would not even have legal grounds for protest and inquiry.

The biological weapons convention illustrates the general thesis that arms control agreements do not have to be perfect in order to be useful. Our choice is not between imperfect and perfect arms control agreements; it is between imperfect agreements and none at all. An agreement does not automatically lose its value as soon as it is violated. Verifiability is only one desirable quality, and not the most essential, of a satisfactory agreement. If we subject our diplomacy to arbitrary rules, for example to the rule that all agreements must be verifiable, we are subordinating human judgment to technology and making arms control subservient to the gathering of intelligence. It is, in the end, only a diplomat like George Kennan or Averell Harriman, with personal knowledge of Soviet society and an understanding of the political forces at work under the surface of Soviet power, who can judge when the time is ripe to enter into an agreement. The value of an agreement depends less on its technical verifiability than on its political robustness. A useful agreement is one which not only helps to maintain a stable balance of power but also helps to build a frame for a new international order.

For thirty years we have seen arms control negotiations making intermittent progress, sometimes succeeding, sometimes failing, sometimes ending in treaties, sometimes ending in frustration, while the nuclear arms race goes on. The negotiations deal laboriously and in detail with particular weapons and verification procedures. The political compulsions which drive the arms race remain untouched. George Kennan already understood in 1950 the nature of these political compulsions, and he understood what had to be done in order to overcome them. Having come to the end of his term of office as director of the Policy Planning Staff in the State Department, he wrote a memorandum to the secretary of state summarizing his understanding of nuclear weapons and nuclear policies:

The real problem at issue, in determining what we should do at this juncture with respect to international control, is the problem of our attitude towards weapons of mass destruction in general, and the role which we allot to these weapons in our own military planning. Here, the crucial question is: Are we to rely on weapons of mass destruction as an integral and vitally important component of our military strength, which we would expect to employ deliberately, immediately, and unhesitatingly in the event that we become in-

volved in a military conflict with the Soviet Union? Or are we to
retain such weapons in our national arsenal only as a deterrent to
the use of similar weapons against ourselves or our allies and as a
possible means of retaliation in case they are used? According to the
way this question is answered, a whole series of decisions are influenced, of which the decision as to what to do about the international control of atomic energy and the prohibition of the weapon
is only one. . . .

We may regard [nuclear weapons] as something vital to our conduct of a future war—as something without which our war plans
would be emasculated and ineffective—as something which we
have resolved, in the face of all the moral and other factors concerned, to employ forthwith and unhesitatingly at the outset of any
great military conflict. In this case, we should take the consequences
of that decision now, and we should obviously keep away from any
program of international dealings which would bring us closer to
the possibility of agreement on international control and prohibition of the atomic weapon.

Or we may regard them as something superfluous to our basic
military posture—as something which we are compelled to hold
against the possibility that they might be used by our opponents.
In this case, of course, we take care not to build up a reliance upon
them in our military planning. Since they then represent only a
burdensome expenditure of funds and effort, we hold only the
minimum required for the deterrent-retaliatory purpose. And we
are at liberty, if we so desire, to make it our objective to divest
ourselves of this minimum at the earliest moment by achieving a
scheme of international control.

This memorandum of 1950 goes to the heart of the matter, and
explains why the subsequent thirty years of arms control negotiations were sterile and frustrating. It is unreasonable to expect negotiation to result in nuclear disarmament if the negotiating parties do
not really wish to disarm. Already in 1950, Kennan took the position which he has steadily maintained ever since, saying that the
decision of the American government to rely upon the first use of
nuclear weapons as a defense against non-nuclear attack was a fundamental mistake. He predicted accurately that the first-use policy
would stand in the way of any serious effort to bring the nuclear
arms race under control, would prevent any military disengagement

of Soviet and American forces in Europe, and would in the end deprive us of any possibility of using military strength to achieve reasonable political purposes. For many years he was a voice crying in the wilderness, alone in his consistent opposition to the first-use policy. Recently a number of public figures have joined him. Both in America and in Europe, more and more people are coming to understand that the first-use policy is incompatible with any coherent strategy of national defense. It may be a long time before the policy is officially abandoned. Whatever progress we are making in that direction is largely due to Kennan's leadership. Kennan is hopeful that the Soviet Union would be willing to go far in nuclear disarmament if the United States were sincerely committed to this course of action. Both in the official pronouncements of the Soviet government and in the private conversations of Soviet citizens we find reiterated a desire for the complete abolition of nuclear weapons. Only if we negotiate seriously and in good faith can we find out whether this desire is genuine.

Kennan has no hope that much of value can emerge from arms control negotiations conducted in the style of the recent SALT talks, with each side striving only to retain a maximum of weaponry for itself while putting the other side to maximum disadvantage. As he says, such negotiations

> are not a way of escape from the arms-race; they are an integral part of it. Whoever does not understand that when it comes to nuclear weapons the whole concept of relative advantage is illusory—whoever does not understand that when you are talking about absurd and preposterous quantities of overkill the relative sizes of arsenals have no serious meaning—whoever does not understand that the danger lies, not in the possibility that someone else might have more missiles and warheads than we do, but in the very existence of these unconscionable quantities of highly poisonous explosives, and their existence, above all, in hands as weak and shaky and undependable as those of ourselves or our adversaries or any other mere human beings: whoever does not understand these things is never going to guide us out of this increasingly dark and menacing forest of bewilderments into which we have all wandered.

Underneath the melody of Kennan's flowing prose we hear from time to time a deep organ tone of moral indignation, that moral indignation which is in the end the only human force strong enough to save us from our follies. For thirty years he has been telling us that our readiness to use nuclear weapons against other human beings is not merely a military miscalculation and a political mistake but an insult to mankind and to God. Now, at long last, the world is beginning to listen.

15

Russians

Iosip Shklovsky is a Soviet astronomer of unusual brilliance, with several major discoveries to his credit. He is known to the Soviet public as a writer of books and magazine articles describing the astronomical universe in a lively popular style. At scientific meetings he spices his technical arguments with jokes and paradoxes. He has wide interests outside astronomy and can talk amusingly on almost any subject. He enjoys unorthodox ideas, and he took a leading part in encouraging international efforts to listen for radio signals which might reveal the existence of intelligence in remote parts of the universe. In his professional life he projects an image of a happy, active, and successful man of the world. In private, like many Soviet intellectuals, he is melancholic. He told me once that he has lived with a feeling of inner loneliness since he discovered, at the end of World War II, that he was the only one of his high school graduating class to have survived. He was the scientist in the class, and the authorities kept him out of the army to work on technical projects. The others went to the front and died. Soviet citizens of Shklovsky's generation still bear the scars of war. Those who are younger grew up hearing tales of war told by their parents and grandparents. All alike carry deep in their consciousness a collective memory of suffering and irreparable loss. This is the central fact conditioning the Soviet view of war. Russians, when they think of war, think of themselves not as warriors but as victims.

Another vignette of Soviet life illustrates the same theme. It was a cold Sunday in late November, and I had the day free after a week of astronomical meetings in Moscow. The radio astronomer Nikolai

Kardashev took me on a sightseeing trip to the ancient cities of Vladimir and Suzdal, halfway between Moscow and Gorky. We started before dawn and drove two hundred kilometers in darkness in order to arrive before the crowds. As we approached Suzdal we saw old monasteries shining golden in the light of the rising sun. Vladimir and Suzdal were places of refuge for monks and artists during the bitter centuries when Mongols and Tartars ruled in Russia. Both cities were taken and destroyed by the Mongols in 1238. They lay directly in the path of the army of Subutai, which swept across half of Europe in a merciless campaign of conquest. The inhabitants later rebuilt the cities, raised churches and filled them with religious paintings. Vladimir and Suzdal lie far enough to the North-East so that they escaped the invasions which ravaged Kiev and Moscow in later centuries. Andrei Rublov, the greatest painter of old Russia, worked at Vladimir in the fifteenth century. Buildings and paintings survive from the thirteenth century onward. Kardashev and I spent the day wandering from church to church among busloads of schoolchildren from Moscow and Gorky. The last stop on our tour was the city museum of Vladimir. Here we found the densest concentration of schoolchildren. The museum is in a tower over one of the ancient gates of the city. Its emphasis is historical rather than artistic. The main exhibit is an enormous diorama of the city as it was at the moment of its destruction in 1238, with every detail faithfully modeled in wood and clay. Across the plains come riding endless lines of Mongol horsemen, slashing arms, legs, and heads off defenseless Russians whom they meet outside the city walls. The armed defenders of the city are on top of the walls, but the flaming arrows of the Mongols have set fire to the buildings behind them. Already a party of horsemen has broken into the city through a side gate and is beginning a general slaughter of the inhabitants. Blood is running in the streets and flames are rising from the churches. On the wall above this scene of horror there is a large notice for schoolchildren and other visitors to read. It says: "The heroic people of Vladimir chose to die rather than submit to the invader. By their self-sacrifice they saved Western Europe from suffering the same fate, and saved European civilization from extinction."

The diorama of Vladimir gives visible form to the dreams and fears which have molded the Russian people's perception of themselves and their place in history. Central to their dreams is the

Mongol horde slicing through their country, swift and implacable. It is difficult for English-speaking people to share such dreams. The Russian experience of the Mongol invasions is so foreign to us that we gave the word "horde" a new and inappropriate meaning when we borrowed it into our language. English-speaking people came to Asia as traders and conquerors protected by a superior technology. Our view of Asia is mirrored in the image which the word "horde" conveys to an English-speaking mind. A horde in our language is a sprawling, undisciplined mob. In Russian and in the original Turkish, a horde is a camp or a tribe organized for war. The organization of the Mongol horde in the thirteenth century was technically far in advance of any other military system in the world. The Mongols could travel and maintain communications over vast distances; they could maneuver their armies with a speed and precision which no other power could match. It took the Russians a hundred and fifty years to learn to fight them on equal terms, and three hundred years to defeat them decisively. The horde in the folk memory of Russia means an alien presence moving through the homeland, ravaging and consuming the substance of the people, subverting the loyalty of their leaders with blackmail and bribes. This is the image of Asia which three centuries of suffering implanted in the Russian mind. It is easy for us in the strategically inviolate West to dismiss Russian fears of China as "paranoid." If we had lived for three centuries at the mercy of the alien horsemen, we would be paranoid too.

British prime ministers, soon after they come into office, customarily visit Washington and Moscow to get acquainted with American and Soviet leaders. When Prime Minister Thatcher made her state visit to Moscow she had two amicable meetings with Chairman Brezhnev. At the end of the second day she remarked (this was before the Afghanistan invasion and the Polish crisis) that she was happy to discover that there were no urgent problems threatening to bring the United Kingdom and the Soviet Union into conflict. Brezhnev then replied with some emphatic words in Russian. Thatcher's interpreter hesitated, and instead of translating Brezhnev's remark asked him to repeat it. Brezhnev repeated it and the interpreter translated: "Madam, there is only one important question facing us, and that is the question whether the white race will survive." Thatcher was so taken aback that she did not venture either to agree or to disagree with this sentiment. She made her exit without further comment. What she had heard was a distant echo of the Mongol hoofbeat still reverberating in Russian memory.

After the Mongols, invaders came to Russia from the West— from Poland, from Sweden, from France, and from Germany. Each of the invading armies was a horde in the Russian sense of the word, a disciplined force of warriors superior to the Russians in technology, in mobility, and in generalship. Especially the German horde invading Russia in 1941 conformed to the ancient pattern. But the Russians had made some progress in military organization between 1238 and 1941. It took them three hundred years to drive out the Mongols but only four years to drive out the Germans. During the intervening centuries the Russians, while still thinking of themselves as victims, had become in fact a nation of warriors. In order to survive in a territory perennially exposed to invasion, they maintained great armies and gave serious study to the art of war. They imposed upon themselves a regime of rigid political unity and military discipline. They gave high honor and prestige to their soldiers, and devoted a large fraction of their resources to the production of weapons. Within a few years after 1941, the Russians who survived the German invasion had organized themselves into the most formidable army on earth. The more they think of themselves as victims, the more formidable they become.

The Russian warriors are now armed with nuclear weapons on a massive scale. The strategic rocket forces of the Soviet Union are comparable in size and quality with those of the United States. The Soviet rocket commanders could, if they were ordered to do so, obliterate within thirty minutes the cities of the United States. It therefore becomes a matter of some importance for us to understand what may be in the Soviet commanders' minds. If we can read their intentions correctly, we may improve our chances of avoiding fatal misunderstanding at moments of crisis. Nobody outside the Soviet government can know with certainty the purposes of Soviet deployments. The American experts who study Soviet armed forces and analyze the Soviet literature devoted to military questions have reached diverse conclusions concerning Soviet strategy. Some say that Soviet intentions are predominantly defensive, others that they are aggressive. But the disagreements among the experts concern words more than substance. To a large extent, the disagreements arise from attempts to define Soviet policies in a language derived from American experience. The language of American strategic analysis is alien and inappropriate to the Russian experience of war. If we make the intellectual effort to understand Russian strategy in their terms rather than ours, as a product of Russian history and military tradition, we shall find that it is usually possible to reconcile the conflicting conclusions of the experts. An awareness of Russian historical experience leads us to a consistent picture of Soviet policies, stripped of the distorting jargon of American strategic theory.

The two experts on whom I mostly rely for information about Soviet strategy are George Kennan and Richard Pipes. Their views of the Soviet Union are generally supposed to be sharply divergent. Kennan has a reputation for diplomatic moderation; Pipes has a reputation for belligerence. Kennan recently summarized his impressions of the Soviet leadership as follows:

> This is an aging, highly experienced, and very steady leadership, itself not given to rash or adventuristic policies. It commands, and is deeply involved with, a structure of power, and particularly a higher bureaucracy, that would not easily lend itself to policies of that nature. It faces serious internal problems, which constitute its main preoccupation. As this leadership looks abroad, it sees more dangers than inviting opportunities. Its reactions and purposes are therefore much more defensive than aggressive. It has no desire for any major war, least of all for a nuclear one. It fears and respects American military power even as it tries to match it, and hopes to avoid a conflict with it. Plotting an attack on Western Europe would be, in the circumstances, the last thing that would come into its head.

Pipes is a Harvard professor who has been on the staff of the National Security Council in the Reagan administration in Washington. He stated his view of Soviet strategy in a recent article with a provocative title: "Why the Soviet Union Thinks It Could Fight and Win a Nuclear War." Here are a couple of salient passages:

> The classic dictum of Clausewitz, that war is politics pursued by other means, is widely believed in the United States to have lost its validity after Hiroshima and Nagasaki. Soviet doctrine, by contrast, emphatically asserts that while an all-out nuclear war would indeed prove extremely destructive to both parties, its outcome would not be mutual suicide: the country better prepared for it and in possession of a superior strategy could win and

emerge a viable society. . . . Clausewitz, buried in the United
States, seems to be alive and prospering in the Soviet
Union. . . .

For Soviet generals the decisive influence in the formulation of
nuclear doctrine were the lessons of World War 2, with which, for
understandable reasons, they are virtually obsessed. This experience they seem to have supplemented with knowledge gained from
professional scrutiny of the record of Nazi and Japanese offensive
operations, as well as the balance-sheet of British and American
strategic-bombing campaigns. More recently, the lessons of the
Israeli-Arab wars of 1967 and 1973 in which they indirectly par-
ticipated seem also to have impressed Soviet strategists, reinforcing
previously held convictions. They also follow the Western literature, tending to side with the critics of mutual deterrence. The
result of all these diverse influences is a nuclear doctrine which
assimilates into the main body of the Soviet military tradition the
technical implications of nuclear warfare without surrendering any
of the fundamentals of this tradition. The strategic doctrine adopted
by the USSR over the past two decades calls for a policy diametri-
cally opposite to that adopted in the United States by the predomi-
nant community of civilian strategists: not deterrence but victory,
not sufficiency in weapons but superiority, not retaliation but offensive action.

These remarks of Pipes were intended to be frightening,
whereas Kennan's remarks were intended to be soothing. And yet,
if one looks at the substance of the remarks rather than at the
intentions of the writers, there is no incompatibility between them.
I have myself little doubt that both Kennan's and Pipes's statements
are substantially true. Kennan is describing the state of mind of
political leaders who have to deal with the day-to-day problems of
managing a large and unwieldy empire. Pipes is describing the state
of mind of professional soldiers who have accepted responsibility for
defending their country against nuclear-armed enemies. It is perhaps a virtue of the Soviet system that the problems of everyday
politics and the problems of preparation for a supreme military crisis
are kept apart and are handled by separate groups of specialists. The
Soviet military authorities themselves insist vehemently on the necessity of this separation of powers. They know that Stalin's min-
gling of the two powers in 1941, when for political reasons he

forbade his generals to mobilize the army in preparation for Hitler's attack, caused enormous and unnecessary Soviet losses and almost resulted in total defeat. Kennan's picture of the Soviet political power structure is quite consistent with the central conclusion of Pipes's analysis, that Soviet military doctrines are based on the assumption that the war for which the Soviet Union must be prepared is a nuclear version of World War II. We should be relieved rather than frightened when we hear that Soviet generals are still obsessed with World War II. World War II was from the Soviet point of view no lighthearted adventure. One thing of which we can be quite sure is that nobody in the Soviet Union looks forward with enthusiasm to fighting World War II over again, with or without nuclear weapons.

The words with which Pipes intends to scare us, "victory . . . superiority . . . offensive action," are precisely the goals which the Russians achieved, after immense efforts and sacrifices, at the end of World War II. If, as Pipes correctly states, Soviet strategy is still dominated by the lessons learned in World War II, it is difficult to see what other goals than these the Soviet armed forces should be expected to pursue. Pipes makes these goals sound frightening by placing them in a misleading juxtaposition with American strategic concepts taken from a different context: "not deterrence but victory, not sufficiency in weapons but superiority, not retaliation but offensive action." The American strategy of deterrence, sufficiency, and retaliation is a purely nuclear strategy having nothing to do with war as it has been waged in the past. The Soviet strategy of victory, superiority, and offensive action is a continuation of the historical process by which Russia over the centuries repelled invaders from her territory. Both strategies have advantages and disadvantages. Neither is aggressive in intention. Both are to me equally frightening, because both make the survival of civilization depend on people behaving reasonably.

The central problem for the Soviet military leadership is to preserve the heritage of World War II against oblivion, to transmit that heritage intact to future generations of soldiers who never saw the invader's boot tramping over Russian soil. Soviet strategists know well what nuclear weapons can do. They are familiar with the American style of nuclear strategic calculus, which treats nuclear war as a mathematical exercise with the result depending only on the numbers and capabilities of weapons on each side. Soviet generals can do such calculations as well as we can. But they do not believe the answers. The heritage of World War II tells them that wars are fought by people, not by weapons, that morale is in the end more important than equipment, that it is easy to calculate how a war will begin but impossible to calculate how it will end. The primary concern of all Soviet strategic writing that I have seen is to make sure that the lessons of World War II are well learned and never forgotten by the rising generation of Soviet citizens. These lessons which the agonies of World War II stamped indelibly into Russian minds were confirmed by the later experience of the United States in Vietnam. A Russian acquaintance once asked me how it happened that American nuclear strategists appeared to have learned nothing from the lessons of Vietnam. I had to reply that the reason they learned nothing was probably because they did not fight in Vietnam themselves. If they had fought in Vietnam, they would have learned to distrust any strategic theory which counts only weapons and discounts human courage and tenacity.

Tolstoy's *War and Peace* is the classic statement of the Russian view of war. Tolstoy understood, perhaps more deeply than anyone else, the nature of war as Russia experienced it. He fought with the Russian army at Sevastopol. He spent some of his happiest years as an artillery cadet on garrison duty in the Caucasus. In *War and Peace* he honored the courage and steadfastness of the ordinary Russian soldiers who defeated Napoleon in spite of the squabbles and blunders of their commanders. He drew from the campaign of 1812 the same lessons which a later generation of soldiers drew from the campaigns of World War II. He saw war as a desperate improvisation, in which nothing goes according to plan and the historical causes of victory and defeat remain incalculable.

Tolstoy's thoughts about war and victory are expressed by his hero Prince Andrei on the eve of the battle of Borodino. Andrei is talking to his friend Pierre.

"To my mind what is before us to-morrow is this: a hundred thousand Russian and a hundred thousand French troops have met to fight, and the fact is that these two hundred thousand men will fight, and the side that fights most desperately and spares itself least will conquer. And if you like, I'll tell you that whatever happens, and whatever mess they make up yonder, we shall win the battle to-morrow; whatever happens we shall win the victory." "So you think the battle to-morrow will be a victory," said Pierre. "Yes, yes," said Prince Andrei absently. "There's one thing I would do, if I were in power," he began again, "I wouldn't take prisoners. What sense is there in taking prisoners? That's chivalry. The French have destroyed my home and are coming to destroy Moscow; they have outraged and are outraging me at every second. They are my enemies, they are all criminals to my way of thinking. . . . They must be put to death. . . . War is not a polite recreation, but the vilest thing in life, and we ought to understand that and not play at war. We ought to accept it sternly and solemnly as a fearful necessity."

The battle was duly fought, and Prince Andrei was mortally wounded. The Russians lost, according to the generally accepted meaning of the word "lose": half of the Russian army was destroyed; after the battle the Russians retreated and the French advanced. And yet, in the long view, Prince Andrei was right. Russia's defeat at Borodino was a strategic victory. Napoleon's army was so mauled that it had no stomach for another such battle. Napoleon advanced to Moscow, stayed there for five weeks waiting for the Czar to sue for peace, and then fled with his disintegrating army in its disastrous stampede to the West. "Napoleon," concludes Tolstoy, "is represented to us as the leader in all this movement, just as the figurehead in the prow of a ship to the savage seems the force that guides the ship on its course. Napoleon in his activity all this time was like a child, sitting in a carriage, pulling the straps within it, and fancying he is moving it along."

The fundamental divergence between American and Soviet strategic concepts lies in the fact that American strategy demands certainty while Soviet strategy accepts uncertainty as inherent in the nature of war. The American objectives—deterrence, sufficiency, and retaliation—are supposed to be guaranteed by the deployment of a suitable variety of invulnerable weapons. The name of the American nuclear strategy is "assured destruction," with emphasis upon the word "assured." Any hint of doubt concerning the assurance of retaliation creates consternation in the minds of American strategists and even in the minds of ordinary American citizens. This demand for absolute assurance of retaliation is the main driving force on the American side of the nuclear arms race. Soviet strategists, on the other hand, consider the quest for certainty in war to be a childish delusion. The Soviet strategic objectives—victory, superiority, and offensive action—are goals to be striven for, not conditions to be guaranteed. These objectives cannot be assured by any fixed quantity of weapons, and they remain valid even when they are not assured. Soviet strategy sees war as essentially unpredictable, and the objectives as dimly visible through chaos and fog.

Richard Pipes's statement, "The Soviet Union thinks it could fight and win a nuclear war," while literally true, does not have the dire implications which Americans are inclined to impute to it. It does not mean that the Soviet high command has a plan for attacking the United States with a calculable assurance of victory. It means that the Soviet leaders have an intuitive confidence, based on their historical experience, in the ability of the Soviet armed forces and population to withstand whatever devastation may be inflicted upon them and ultimately to defeat and destroy whoever attacks them. This confidence of the Soviet leaders in the superior endurance and discipline of their own people is not based upon calculation. It is not a threat to American security. Hard as it may be for Americans to accept, the confidence of the Russian people in their ability to survive the worst that we can do to them is a stabilizing influence which it is to our advantage to preserve. The demand for survival is the main driving force on the Soviet side of the arms race. Insofar as we undermine the confidence of the Soviet leaders in the ability of their people to endure and survive, we are forcing them to drive their side of the arms race harder.

Because of the divergent views of American and Soviet strategists concerning the nature of nuclear war and the possibility of technical assurance, American and Soviet strategic objectives are strictly incommensurable. It is natural for Americans to believe that the American objective of deterrence is more reasonable or more modest than the Soviet objective of victory. But the objective of deterrence comes with a demand for absolute assurance, while the objective of victory comes, if at all, only at the end of a long road of incalculable chances and immense suffering. From a Soviet viewpoint, the objective of victory may be considered the more modest, since it is based only on hope and faith while the objective of deterrence is based on calculated threats. It is futile to expect that we can convert the Soviet military leaders to our way of thinking or that they can convert us to theirs. Our different ways of thinking are deeply rooted in our different historical experiences. We do not need to think alike in order to survive together on this planet. We need only to understand that it is possible to think differently and to respect each other's points of view.

The necessity of respecting the Russian point of view concerning nuclear strategy does not imply that we need to approve the activities of the Soviet government in other areas. We may, and we should, disapprove strongly of the means by which Russian rulers through the centuries have fortified themselves against external and internal enemies, the steady territorial expansion, the subjugation and oppression of neighboring peoples, the wholesale uprooting of populations, the extermination of political opponents, the disregard for human rights, and the denial of historical truth. Everybody who has once set foot in the Soviet Union knows what it means to live under the shadow of a secretive and unscrupulous government. Everybody I know who has crossed a Soviet border in the outward direction experiences a feeling of relief at the moment of crossing. All of us who live at a safe distance from the territory of the KGB have good reason to consider ourselves lucky. We cannot expect Poles or Crim Tartars or Jews, or members of other national groups which have been oppressed for centuries by Russia, to excuse these oppressions as an unfortunate consequence of the Russians' legitimate need for self-defense. Just because the Russians have frequently been victims of aggression, it does not follow that they deserve our sympathy when they become aggressors. Richard Pipes, coming himself from a Polish background, observes with a cold eye the transition of the Russians from the role of victim to the role of tyrant:

The Communist revolution of 1917, by removing from positions of influence what there was of a Russian bourgeoisie, a class Lenin was prone to define as much by cultural as by socioeconomic criteria, in effect installed in power the muzhik, the Russian peasant. And the muzhik had been taught by long historical experience that cunning and coercion alone ensured survival: one employed cunning when weak, and cunning coupled with coercion when strong. Not to use force when one had it indicated some inner weakness. Marxism, with its stress on class war as a natural condition of mankind so long as the means of production were privately owned, has merely served to reinforce these ingrained convictions.

This bleak diagnosis of the Russian soul contains a large element of truth. But it does us no good to continue bewailing the fact that Russian political traditions are less humane and more violent than ours. Our task is not to recreate the Russians in our own image but to deal with them as they are. If we are to deal with them successfully, we need to listen carefully to the disagreeable message of Richard Pipes, but we need even more to listen to the practical wisdom of George Kennan.

Kennan's view of Soviet society is based on long and intimate contact with Soviet bureaucracy as well as with ordinary Soviet citizens. He sees the individual human beings behind the facade of ideology. He is constantly fighting against the tendency of Americans to oversimplify and dehumanize their adversaries. For Kennan the Soviet Union is, first of all, a great and complicated assemblage of peoples burdened with a harsh historical heritage. Like other societies, it is more deeply concerned with its own internal problems than with the problems of the world outside. Like other societies, it sees itself as more threatened than threatening. Like other societies, it is struggling unsuccessfully to deal with the problems of alienated youth and rigid bureaucracy in a time of rapid economic change.

Kennan is well aware of the unpleasant characteristics of the Soviet state, the paranoid secretiveness, the intolerance of dissent, the self-righteous rhetoric, the casual cruelty, the glorification of military strength. Yet he bids us look behind these harsh realities and understand the human circumstances from which they arise. He sees the Soviet leaders as a group of elderly and conservative men, whose chief ambition is to push the Soviet Union along the path of economic progress which the Communist ideology promises to bring about. To accomplish this task, the leaders have only three tools: the authoritarian party apparatus, the overcentralized bureaucracy, and the armed forces. The party apparatus and the bureaucracy are clearly inadequate for the direction of a modern industrial economy. Of all the institutions of the Soviet state, the armed forces stand highest in technical competence, in morale, and in genuine contact with the masses of the population. The army in the Soviet Union is, as the French army was in the time of Napoleon, the poor man's university. In the eyes of the ordinary Soviet citizen as well as in the secret corridors of the Kremlin, the armed forces command a disproportionate share of authority and prestige. The massive accumulation of Soviet weaponry arises from this internal ascendancy of the armed forces, not from any deliberate plan of world conquest.

Kennan sees Soviet society as conservative but very far from static. He sees great historical changes occurring beneath the rigid surface of the system. A few months ago he said to me in the course of a casual conversation, "It is odd that I have been worrying for fifty years, for all of my professional life, about the strength of Soviet society. And now I am worrying about its weakness. I begin now seriously to worry that the whole thing may disintegrate." He takes seriously the recent evidence of social decay in the Soviet Union, the rise in drunkenness and infant mortality, the prevalence of bribery and corruption, the loss of a sense of purpose among the children of the elite. He sees great and possibly disastrous changes ahead if the processes of decay continue. He looks back at the events of 1917, when the American people joyfully welcomed the collapse of the Czarist empire and were surprised to see it replaced by the far more vicious tyranny of Lenin. He sees the American government now ignorantly harassing the present Soviet regime, careless of the possibility that this comparatively benign group of leaders will in their turn be replaced by something more malignant. He likes to quote in this connection Hilaire Belloc's cautionary tale for children, "Jim, Who ran away from his Nurse, and was eaten by a Lion":

> His father, who was self-controlled,
> Bade all the children round attend
> To James's miserable end,
> And always keep a-hold of Nurse
> For fear of finding something worse.

Kennan sees Soviet power, with all its faults, as an essential component in any foreseeable system of international order. He is appalled when he contemplates the chaos that would descend upon much of Europe and Asia if Soviet power should suddenly collapse. And he is appalled by the irresponsibility of Americans who talk of weakening or destroying Soviet power and do not give any serious thought to the consequences. He deplores the excessive attention paid in America to Soviet exiles and dissidents. It was the Russian exiles who inflamed American opinion against the Czar's government in the years leading up to 1917. The recent wave of exiles is

having a similar effect on Soviet-American relations today. Kennan
does not blame the exiles for their bitter feelings toward the Soviet
regime, but he blames Americans who try to outdo them in hatred
of the regime without considering what kind of alternative political
authority could possibly replace it.

Kennan's fate, throughout his long double career as government
servant and independent scholar, is to be a teller of complicated
truths to people who prefer simple illusions. Sometimes he has been
driven close to despair by the inability of the American political
system to pay attention to people with expert knowledge of the
world outside. In 1944, when he was a member of the American
embassy staff in Moscow, deeply troubled by the gap between
American perception and Soviet realities, he wrote a thirty-five-
page essay summarizing his firsthand view of Russia, for the benefit
of his superiors in Washington. Kennan afterward described the
concluding sentences of this essay as "a melancholy, but for me
personally most prophetic, passage":

> There will be much talk about the necessity for "understanding
> Russia"; but there will be no place for the American who is really
> willing to undertake this disturbing task. The apprehension of what
> is valid in the Russian world is unsettling and displeasing to the
> American mind. He who would undertake this apprehension will
> not find his satisfaction in the achievement of anything practical for
> his people, still less in any official or public appreciation for his
> efforts. The best he can look forward to is the lonely pleasure of one
> who stands at long last on a chilly and inhospitable mountaintop
> where few have been before, where few can follow, and where few
> will consent to believe that he has been.

For thirty-nine years since these words were written, Kennan
has continued, as diplomat and historian, to bring us his reports
from the mountaintop. He knows now that his efforts have not
always been unappreciated.

My own view of the mountaintop has been derived partly from
conversations with Kennan, partly from brief scientific visits to the
Soviet Union, and partly from readings in Russian literature. The
readings in Russian literature began earliest and have left the deepest
impression. As a teen-ager I worked my way through the *Oxford
Book of Russian Verse,* guided by Maurice Baring's magnificent introduction. I found there, among other things, the poem "On the

Field of Kulikovo" by Alexander Blok, which tells more about the Russian view of war than a whole library of strategic analysis. The battle of Kulikovo was fought a century and a half after the destruction of Vladimir, but Blok's poem carries the same haunting message as the diorama in the Vladimir museum. Blok is riding over the steppe with the Russian horsemen the night before the battle:

> I am not the first, nor the last, warrior,
> Many years more will my country suffer.

At Kulikovo the Russians for the first time defeated a Tartar horde. The battle was a turning point in the centuries-long struggle of Russians against Tartars, not the end of the struggle but a new beginning. Blok wrote his poem in the year 1908, at a time of peace and prosperity, but he felt already the shadow of approaching storms:

> I perceive you now, beginning
> Of high turbulent days. Once more
> Over the enemy camp the winging
> Of swans is heard, swans trumpeting War.

Ten years later, in January 1918, three months after the Bolshevik seizure of power, amid the chaos and cold of revolutionary Petrograd, Blok wrote his greatest poem, "The Twelve," which tells more about the nature of Soviet power than a whole library of Kremlinology. The twelve are a group of young soldiers of the Red Guard, marching through the city in a snowstorm, rough and tough and profane and trigger-happy:

> "Grip your gun like a man, brother.
> We'll pump some lead into Holy Russia,
> Ancient, peasant-ridden, fat-arsed Mother Russia.
> Freedom, Freedom! Down with the cross!"
> "Open your cellars: quick, run down!
> The scum of the earth are hitting the town!"
> Abusing God's name as they go,
> The twelve march onward through the snow,
> Prepared for anything,
> Regretting nothing.

In the final scene of the poem, the twelve are chasing a shadowy figure who lurks in a snowdrifted alleyway. They shout at the figure

to surrender, then open fire. The echoes of their gunshots die away.
The howling of the storm continues.

> So they march with sovereign tread.
> Behind them limps the hungry dog,
> Ahead of them, carrying the blood-red flag,
> Unseen in the blizzard,
> Untouched by the bullets,
> Stepping soft-footed over the snow
> In a swirl of pearly snowflakes,
> Crowned with a wreath of white roses,
> Ahead of them goes Jesus Christ.

Blok remained in Russia until his death in 1921. Shortly before
he died, he reaffirmed the vision which "The Twelve" had recorded:

> I do not go back on what I wrote then, because it was written in
> harmony with the elemental: for instance, during and after the
> writing of "The Twelve," for some days I physically felt and heard
> a great roar surrounding me, a continuous roar, probably the roar
> of the collapse of the old world. . . . The poem was written in that
> exceptional and always very brief period when the passing revolu-
> tionary cyclone raises a storm in every sea. . . . The seas of nature,
> life and art were raging and the foam rose up in a rainbow over
> them. I was looking at that rainbow when I wrote "The Twelve."

My own personal encounter with the armed forces of the Soviet
revolution occurred in a later and more tranquil time. It was in May
1956, when the Russians organized the first postwar international
meeting of high-energy physicists in Moscow. Russian experimental work in high-energy physics had previously been kept secret, for
reasons which had little to do with military security. The last years
of Stalin's life had been years of terror and silence for Soviet intellectuals; even in the nonpolitical domain of physical science, publication had been severely restricted and contacts with foreign scientists
almost nonexistent. When Stalin died, the icy grip of secrecy slowly
weakened. In 1954 Ilya Ehrenburg was allowed to publish his novel
The Thaw, which described the fresh stirrings of Soviet life after the
long winter. By 1956 the physicists were ready to celebrate the
return of spring with a big conference to which colleagues from all
over the world were invited. The conference was a joyful occasion

for the Russians and for us too. Old friendships were renewed and new friendships established. The Russian newspapers gave us front-page coverage, and proudly described how the great leaders of international science were now coming to Moscow to learn about the great achievements of Soviet scientists.

After the Moscow meeting ended, I went with a group of foreign scientists to Leningrad. Accompanied by two Intourist guides, we went sightseeing along the shore to the west of the city. We walked by mistake into a coastguard station, evidently a restricted military area. An ordinary Russian seaman came out to shoo us away, shouting, *"Nelzya,"* which means "Forbidden." At that moment we noticed that our guides, afraid of being held responsible for our error, were walking rapidly away in the opposite direction. So we stayed and had a friendly chat with the seaman in our broken Russian. When I said we were foreign scientists, he broke out into a broad smile and said, "Oh, I know who you are. You are the people who came to the meeting in Moscow, and you know all about pi-mesons and mu-mesons." He pulled out of his pocket a crumpled copy of *Pravda* which contained a report of our proceedings. After that, he invited us into the station and proudly introduced us to his comrades. We sat with them for some minutes and did our best to explain to them what we had learned in Moscow about pi-mesons and mu-mesons. When we said good-bye, our host shook our hands warmly and said, "Why do you not come to our country more often? Be sure to tell the people in your countries, and your wives and children, that we would like to see more of them." As I walked back into Leningrad and reflected upon this encounter, I found myself sadly wondering whether an average American coastguard sentry, confronted unexpectedly with a group of Russian physicists speaking broken English, would have greeted them with equal friendliness and understanding.

16

Pacifists

Thoughtlessly I said to the Russian sailor in the coastguard station, "You should also come and see us in America." He looked at me, laughing, with his broad young face. "How could we come to America? That's impossible. We are warriors." It was strange to hear him use that word, *voyenniye*— "warriors." He looked so unwarlike, sitting with his friends around the table and chatting with us about pi-mesons and mu-mesons. And yet the word spoke truth. His trade was war. He belonged to that ancient brotherhood of warriors which Blok described in his poems, the horsemen riding by night over the field of Kulikovo, the twelve marching in the snowstorm through the desolate streets of Petrograd. All his friendliness, his intellectual curiosity, his boyish humor, could not alter the fact that he was a willing tool of Soviet power. A warrior he was, and a warrior he would remain, even after he finished his term of military service and found his niche in civilian society. All his life, he would be proud to have been a part of the Soviet navy. If ever he was called to sail into battle and die for his country, he would hesitate no more than those who sailed with Nelson at Trafalgar. If ever he was called to launch the missile that would obliterate a city, he would hesitate no more than those who aimed the bombs at Hiroshima and Nagasaki. When I imagine nuclear war, the nightmare begins with that young Russian sailor pressing the button which blows us all to smithereens, and as he presses it, he says, "We are warriors," with that same laughing voice of murderous innocence which I heard in Leningrad long ago.

Is there no other way? Is there no other tradition for our young men to follow than the tradition of warriors marching into battle to defend the honor of their tribe? Indeed there is another tradition, the tradition of pacifism, which also has a long and honorable history. For hundreds of years there have been religious sects which held warfare to be contrary to the will of God. Anabaptists and Quakers were preaching the gospel of nonviolence in the seventeenth century, and suffering persecution for their beliefs. This old tradition of nonviolence was personal rather than political. The Quakers allowed no authority to come between the individual conscience and God. They refused, as individuals, to bear arms or to take any part in the waging of wars. They did not seek political power for themselves or attempt to control the actions of governments. They simply declared that they would not take any action forbidden by their consciences. The tradition of personal pacifism which they established has proved durable. It has lasted for three hundred years and has taken root in many countries. Pacifism as a code of personal ethics has proved itself able to weather the storms of war and political change.

Pacifism as a political program is a more recent development. A political pacifist is one who advocates the ethic of nonviolence as a program for a political movement or for a government. Theorists of pacifism make a sharp distinction between personal and political pacifism. In the real world, this distinction is useful but never sharp. There is a continuum of pacifism, extending all the way from the private faith of the traditional conscientious objector to the modern rituals of nonviolent demonstration staged by political action groups in front of television cameras. Pacifism may be a matter of individual conscience or a matter of tactical calculation. Most commonly it is a mixture of both. If pacifism is ever to prevail in the modern world, it must be both personal and political, cherishing the deep roots of the religious pacifist tradition and at the same time exploiting the opportunities provided by modern communications to mobilize public protest. Gandhi, the first and greatest of modern political pacifists, showed us how it can be done.

The Quakers stand in the middle of the pacifist continuum, not so fully engaged in politics as Gandhi, not so detached as the Amish of Pennsylvania, who try to withdraw altogether from the violence and evil of the world. Quakers live in the world of anger and power and seek to mitigate its evils. The Quaker ethic has always encouraged its adherents to concern themselves with other people's sufferings. "Concern" in the Quaker vocabulary means more than sympathy; it means practical help for people in need and practical intervention against injustice. Large numbers of Quakers, following the example of their founder, George Fox, express their concern by campaigning in the political arena for humanitarian and pacifist ideals. But they act as individuals, not as an organized movement. Perhaps the main reason for the durability of the Quakers' influence is the fact that they are tied to no government and no party. Their pacifism is a private commitment based on conscience, not a political tactic dependent on success or popularity. They are not, like the followers of Gandhi, liable to defect from their pacifist principles when the political winds change.

The great and permanent achievement of the Quakers was the abolition of slavery. This social revolution, with the accompanying profound changes in public morality, took centuries to complete and was not the work of Quakers alone. But the earliest agitators against slavery were mostly Quakers. All through the eighteenth century, in England and in America, Quakers were prime movers in the uphill struggle, first to put an end to the profitable trade in fresh slaves from Africa, and later to put an end to the profitable exploitation of slaves wherever they happened to be. My great-great-great-uncle Robert Haynes was a prominent citizen of the island of Barbados, owner of several sugar plantations and several hundred slaves. In his diary for the year 1804 he complained bitterly of the public agitation against slavery which was then gathering strength in England. He knew who his enemies were. "I am likewise minded," he wrote, "to attribute a fair share of the blame to the underhand activities of a sect known as Quakers. These, from the very beginnings of the settlement of our island having played a very subtle—and in these days all too little heeded—part in the instigation of others to rebellion, at the same time openly avowing their detestation to any form of violence! Not scrupling, withall, to avail themselves fully of the safety and protection afforded them by the laws and defenses of this country. All this savouring of cant and hypocrisy such as I, for one, find hard to stomach."

The next item in Robert Haynes's diary explains the violence of his feelings. "Attempted rising of slaves in some parts of the Island. The above quickly suppressed—the immediate shewing of discipline taking excellent and speedy effect—but at the same time a general anxiety thus engendered by no means, even now, wholly allayed." Four years later the British Parliament passed the act which put an end to the slave trade, with effective criminal penalties. Robert Haynes continued for twenty-five years longer to enjoy an uneasy dominion over his slaves on the island. But he lived long enough to see the Quakers finally victorious, his slaves freed, and the old order of society on the island overthrown. Handsomely compensated with a cash payment for his slaves by the Act of Parliament of 1833, he moved to England and lived the rest of his life at Reading in comfortable retirement.

What were the ingredients of the Quakers' success? First of all, moral conviction. They never had any doubt that slavery was a moral evil which they were called upon to oppose. Second, patience. They continued their work, decade after decade, undiscouraged by setbacks and failures. Third, objectivity. A large part of their work consisted of careful collection of facts and statistics which both sides in the dispute came to accept as accurate. It was the fact-gathering activities of the Quakers in Barbados which particularly infuriated my great-great-great-uncle. Fourth, willingness to compromise. The Quakers were concerned to free the slaves, not to punish the slave-owners. They accepted the fact that slaves were an economic asset and that the owners were entitled to fair compensation for the loss of their property. The slave-owners were not to be humiliated. As a result, even my great-great-great-uncle in the end swallowed his pride and quietly pocketed his cash settlement. The willingness of the British abolitionists to buy out the slave-owners made the crucial difference between the peaceful liberation of the West Indian slaves in 1833 and the bloody liberation of the American slaves thirty years later. The British government paid the slave-owners twenty million pounds. The cost of the American Civil War was considerably higher.

The abolition of nuclear weapons is a task of the same magnitude as the abolition of slavery. Nuclear weapons are now, as slavery was two hundred years ago, a manifestly evil institution deeply embedded in the structure of our society. People who hope to push the fight against nuclear weapons to a successful conclusion must bring to their task the same qualities which won the fight against slavery, moral conviction, patience, objectivity, and willingness to compromise. Those who fought against slavery two hundred years ago made a historic compromise which opened the way to their victory; they decided to concentrate their efforts upon the prohibition of the slave trade and to leave the total abolition of slavery to their successors in another generation. They saw that the slave trade was a more glaring evil than slavery itself and more vulnerable to political attack. They were able to mobilize against the slave trade a coalition of moral and economic interests which could not at that time have been brought together in the cause of total abolition. There is a lesson here for the peace movements of today. The ultimate aim of peace movements is the total abolition of war. All war is evil, but the use of nuclear weapons is a more glaring evil, and the abolition of nuclear weapons is a more practical political objective than the abolition of war. Modern pacifists, like the Quakers of the eighteenth century, would be well advised to attack the more vulnerable evil first. After we have succeeded in prohibiting nuclear weapons, the abolition of war may become a feasible objective for later generations, but from here it is out of sight.

Pacifism as a political cause has suffered from the fact that its greatest leaders have been men of genius. People of outstanding genius, transcending the beliefs and loyalties of the tribe in which they happen to be born, tend naturally toward pacifism. Unfortunately, people of genius do not usually make good politicians. Gandhi was one of the rare exceptions. Genius and the art of political compromise do not sit easily together. Except for Gandhi, the great historic figures of pacifism have been prophets rather than politicians. Jesus in Judea, Tolstoy in Russia, Einstein in Germany, each in turn has set for mankind a higher standard than political movements can follow.

When Tolstoy wrote *War and Peace,* he was a Russian patriot, sympathetic to the martial spirit of his soldier characters and proud of their bravery. His skeptical realism belongs squarely, as Alexander Blok's fevered romanticism does not, in the mainstream of Russian patriotic literature. But Russian patriotism was too narrow a frame for Tolstoy's genius. At the age of fifty he experienced a religious conversion to the gospel of peace. He repudiated the sovereignty of all national governments, including his own. He cut himself off from the aristocratic society in which he had formerly lived. And for the last thirty years of his life he preached the ethic of nonviolence in its most uncompromising form. He demanded that we not only refuse to serve in armies and navies but also refuse to cooperate in any way with coercive activities of governments. Revolutionary action against governments was forbidden too; those who oppose a government with violence cannot lead the way to the abolition of violence. He called us to follow a way of life based on strict obedience to the words of Jesus: "Ye have heard that it hath been said, an eye for an eye and a tooth for a tooth: but I say unto you, that ye resist not evil; but whosoever shall smite thee on thy right cheek, turn to him the other also."

The Czar's government was wise enough not to lay hands on Tolstoy or to attempt to silence him. Only the young men who followed his teaching and refused military service were put in prison or exiled to Siberia. Tolstoy himself lived unmolested on his estate at Yasnaya Polyana with his faithful disciples and his disapproving wife. He corresponded with the young Gandhi. He became a prophet and spiritual leader for pacifists all over the world. Wherever he saw cruelty and oppression, he spoke out for the victims against the oppressors. He warned the wealthy and powerful in no uncertain terms of the explosion of violence to which their selfishness was leading: "Only one thing is left for those who do not wish to change their way of life, and that is to hope that things will last my time—after that, let happen what may. That is what the blind crowd of the rich are doing, but the danger is ever growing and the terrible catastrophe draws nearer." The wealthy and powerful listened politely to his warnings and continued on the course which led to the cataclysms of 1914 and 1917. The situation of Tolstoy at the end of his life was similar to the situation of Einstein fifty years later, the venerable white-bearded figure, wearing a peasant blouse as a symbol of his contempt for rank and privilege, universally respected as a writer of genius, disdained by practical politicians as a cantankerous old fool, loved and admired by the multitude as spokesman for the conscience of mankind.

A hundred years have now passed since Tolstoy's conversion, and the power of nationalism over men's minds is as strong as ever. There was perhaps a chance, at the end of the nineteenth century and the beginning of the twentieth, that the working people of Europe would unite in a common determination not to be used as cannon fodder in their masters' quarrels. This was the dream which Tolstoy dreamed, and it was shared by many of the leaders of workers' organizations in various European countries during the years before 1914 when these organizations were growing rapidly in membership and power. The dream was an international brotherhood of workers united in loyalty to socialist and pacifist principles.

The dream was an international general strike which would become effective on the day of declaration of war and would leave the generals of the belligerent armies without soldiers to command. Among the leaders who believed in international brotherhood as a practical political program for the workers of the world, Jean Jaurès of France was outstanding. Jaurès was an experienced politician, representing the French Socialist party in the Chamber of Deputies, and reelected repeatedly by his constituency of miners. He was a patriotic Frenchman and never advocated unilateral disarmament or unconditional pacifism. He knew personally the socialist leaders in Germany and Austria and understood the ambiguities of their position. But he believed with passionate conviction in the possibility that an international general strike against war could be successful. This dream collapsed on July 31, 1914, when the German, Austrian, and Russian armies were already mobilizing for war, the workers in each country had forgotten their international brotherhood and were marching obediently to the frontiers to defend their respective fatherlands, and Jean Jaurès, sitting disconsolate at his supper in a public restaurant in Paris, was shot dead by a fanatical French patriot.

Tolstoy's radical pacifism never became a serious political force in Europe, and least of all in Russia, either before or after the revolution. The only effective action of workers against war occurred in 1917, when Lenin encouraged the soldiers of Kerenski's government to desert from the front lines where they were fighting the Germans. But this desertion was not the fulfillment of Jaurès's dream of an international strike against war; it was merely an opening move in the new war for which Lenin was preparing. As soon as Lenin had seized power, he organized a new army and used it to defend his territory against the remnants of the old army in the civil war of 1918–1921. Neither the Czar before the revolution, nor Lenin afterward, hesitated to spill blood; neither had difficulty in finding an ample supply of young Russians willing to kill or to die for the defense of Russia against her enemies. The seeds of Tolstoy's gospel of nonviolence fell mostly upon stony soil as they were carried all over the world, and nowhere was the soil stonier than in his native Russia.

The great blossoming of nonviolence as a mass political movement was the work of Gandhi in India. For thirty years he led the fight for Indian independence and held his followers to a Tolstoyan code of behavior. He proved that satyagraha, soul-force, can be an effective substitute for bombs and bullets in the liberation of a people. Satyagraha, a word and a concept invented by Gandhi, means much more than nonviolence. Satyagraha is not merely passive resistance or abstention from violent actions. Satyagraha is the active use of moral pressure as a weapon for the achievement of social and political goals. Gandhi used satyagraha impartially to castigate the British governors of India and his own followers, whenever they strayed from the path of nonviolence. With his Hindu background and his London lawyer's training, he understood the psychology of Indian peasants and of imperial government officials, and succeeded in bending them both to his will. The chief tools of satyagraha were civil disobedience, the peaceful but ostentatious breaking of laws imposed by the alien authorities, and the fast unto death, a personal hunger strike in which Gandhi repeatedly wagered his life in order to compel friends and enemies alike to attend to his demands. The tools worked. There were many setbacks and occasional lapses into violence, but the campaign of satyagraha succeeded in winning independence for India without any war between the native population and the occupying power. British administrators found Gandhi absurd and exasperating, but they could not either shoot him or keep him permanently in prison. When he fasted unto death they dared not let him die, knowing that no one who might take his place would be able so well to control the violent temper of his followers. Satyagraha was an effective weapon in Gandhi's hands because he was, unlike Tolstoy, an astute politician. For thirty years Gandhi was, in effect, collaborating with the British authorities in keeping India peaceful, while at the same time defying them publicly so that he never appeared to his followers as a British stooge. Successful use of satyagraha requires, besides courage and moral grandeur, also a talent for practical politics, an understanding of the weak points of the enemy, a sense of humor, and a little luck. Gandhi possessed all these gifts and used them to the full.

Gandhi's luck ran out at the end of his life, when the campaign against British rule was won and he was trying to bring India to independence as a united country. He then had to deal with quarrels between Hindu and Moslem, deeper and more bitter than the power struggle between European and Asian. Satyagraha failed to subdue Hindu and Moslem nationalism as it had subdued British imperialism. Five months after the violent birth of independent India and

Pakistan, the scene of Jaurès's death was reenacted in Delhi. Like Jaurès, Gandhi was shot by a nationalist who considered him insufficiently patriotic.

With Gandhi, as with Jaurès, died the hope of a continent turning decisively away from war. Nehru, prime minister of newly independent India, had never been a wholehearted believer in nonviolence. The rulers of Pakistan believed in nonviolence even less. Within thirty years after independence, three wars showed how little Gandhi's countrymen had learned from his example. India and Pakistan fought over the disputed province of Kashmir as France and Germany had fought over Alsace and Lorraine. Together with the regiments and warships of the colonial army and navy, the governments of India and Pakistan inherited an addiction to the old European game of power politics. Gandhi's satyagraha was an effective weapon for a subject people to use against their oppressors, but his followers discarded it promptly as soon as they gained control of their own government and stood in the oppressors' shoes.

The moral of Gandhi's life and death is that pacifism as a political program is much more difficult to sustain than pacifism as a personal ethic. Being himself a leader of extraordinary charisma and skill, Gandhi was able to organize a whole people around a program of pacifism. He proved that a pacifist resistance movement can be sustained for thirty years and can be strong enough to defeat an empire. The subsequent history of India proved that political pacifism was not strong enough to survive the death of its leader and to withstand the temptations of power.

During the years between the two world wars, while Gandhi was successfully organizing his nonviolent resistance in India, political pacifism was also popular in Europe. European pacifists were encouraged by Gandhi's example and hoped to revive Jaurès's dream of an international alliance of nonviolent resisters against militaristic national governments. The pacifist dream in Europe failed disastrously. There were three main reasons for the failure: lack of leadership, lack of a positive objective, and Hitler. The European pacifists never produced a leader comparable to Gandhi. Einstein was a pacifist, and lent his name and prestige to the pacifist cause until the rise of Hitler led him to change his mind, but he had no wish to be a political leader. Like Tolstoy, he was more of a hero to the world at large than to his own countrymen. Pacifism, even at the peak of Einstein's popularity, was never strong in Germany. It was strongest in England, where George Lansbury, a Christian Socialist with firm pacifist convictions, was leader of the Labour party from 1931 to 1935. Lansbury was capable of courageous action in the Gandhi style. In 1920, when he was mayor of Poplar in the East End of London, he went to prison rather than submit to government policies which he considered oppressive. He remained a hero to his constituents in East London. But he never attempted to dominate the European scene as Gandhi dominated the scene in India. Gandhi had the tremendous advantage of a positive objective, the cause of Indian independence, around which he could mobilize the enthusiasm of his followers. Lansbury and the other European pacifists had no similar objective; they supported the League of Nations as an international peace-keeping authority, but the League of Nations was an inadequate focus for a mass political movement. The League was widely perceived as nothing more than a debating society for elderly politicians. Nobody could take seriously the picture of millions of Europeans defying their governments in a gesture of loyalty to the League. Gandhi was swimming with the tide of nationalism; Lansbury and his followers were swimming against it. As a result, the foreign policy of the British Labour party under Lansbury's leadership was wholly negative; no rearmament, no action against Hitler, and no wholehearted commitment to pacifism.

It was Lansbury's fate to preside over the British pacifist movement at the peak of its popularity during the same years which saw Hitler's rise to power in Germany. A few weeks before Hitler became chancellor, the undergraduates of Oxford debated the proposition "That this House will under no circumstances fight for its King and Country," and approved it by a substantial majority. This vote received widespread publicity and may in fact, as the opponents of pacifism later claimed, have encouraged Hitler to pursue his plans of European conquest more boldly. Whether or not Hitler paid attention to the Oxford students' vote, there is no doubt that his aggressive policies were encouraged by the existence of strong pacifist sentiments in England and France. In October 1933, Hitler felt confident enough to withdraw from the international Disarmament Conference which had been meeting since before he became chancellor; this action was an official notification to the world that he intended to rearm Germany. Four days later, George Lansbury spoke for the Labour party in the House of Commons:

> We will not support an increase in armaments, but we shall also refuse to support our own or any other government in an endeavour to apply penalties or sanctions against Germany. No one will ask for these if the great nations immediately, substantially disarm and continue until universal disarmament is accomplished.

The great nations were not about to disarm, as George Lansbury well knew. His policy meant that England would simply do nothing, neither arm nor disarm. He was caught in the tragic dilemma of political pacifism. The pacifists of England and France, by announcing their unwillingness to fight, made Hitler more reckless in risking war and made the war more terrible when it came. There is no easy answer to this dilemma. A country facing an aggressive enemy must decide either to be prepared to fight effectively or to follow the path of nonviolence to the end. In either case, the decision must be wholehearted and the consequences must be accepted. The example of England in the 1930s proves only that a halfhearted commitment to pacifism is worse than none at all. Halfhearted pacifism is in practice indistinguishable from cowardice. European pacifism became finally discredited when World War II began and halfhearted pacifists could not be distinguished from cowards and collaborators. The debacle of European pacifism has at least one clear lesson to teach us: Pacifists, if they are to be effective in the modern world, must be as wholehearted and as brave as Gandhi.

In 1935 Lansbury was forced to choose between his pacifist principles and his position as leader of the Labour party. Being an honest man, he stuck to his principles and handed over the leadership of the party to Clement Attlee, the same Attlee who became prime minister ten years later and made the decision to arm Britain with nuclear weapons. Pacifism as an effective political force in England was dead. But it was still alive in India. Young Englishmen who were against the establishment acclaimed Gandhi as a hero. We greatly preferred the flamboyant Gandhi to the powerless Lansbury and the colorless Attlee. Our conversation was sprinkled with the rhetoric of pacifist doctrine. If only we had a leader like Gandhi, we said, we would fill the jails and bring the warmongers to their senses.

We continued to talk in this style, while Hitler filled his concentration camps in Germany and silenced those who opposed his policies. Then in 1939 Hitler attacked and overran Poland. We were face to face, as Lansbury had been in 1933, with the classic pacifist dilemma. We still believed theoretically in the ethic of nonviolence, but we looked at what was happening in Poland and decided that nonviolent resistance would not be effective against Hitler.

Now, forty years later, a book called *Lest Innocent Blood Be Shed* has been written by Philip Hallie, telling the story of a French village which chose the path of nonviolent resistance against Hitler. It is a remarkable story. It shows that nonviolence could be effective, even against Hitler. The village of Le Chambon sur Lignon collectively sheltered and saved the lives of many hundreds of Jews through the years when the penalty for this crime was deportation or death. The villagers were led by their Protestant pastor, André Trocmé, who had been for many years a believer in nonviolence and had prepared them mentally and spiritually for this trial of strength. When the Gestapo from time to time raided the village, Trocmé's spies usually gave him enough warning so that the refugees could be hidden in the woods. German authorities arrested and executed various people who were known to be leaders in the village, but the resistance continued unbroken. The only way the Germans could have crushed the resistance was by deporting or killing the entire population. Nearby, in the same part of France, there was a famous regiment of SS troops, the Tartar Legion, trained and experienced in operations of extermination and mass brutality. The Tartar Legion could easily have exterminated Le Chambon. But the village survived. Even Trocmé himself, by a series of lucky accidents, survived.

Many years later, Trocmé discovered how it happened that the village survived. The fate of the village was decided in a dialogue between two German soldiers, representing the bright and the dark sides of the German soul. On the one side, Colonel Metzger, an appropriate name meaning in German "butcher," commander of the Tartar Legion, killer of civilians, executed after the liberation of France as a war criminal. On the other side, Major Schmehling, Bavarian Catholic and decent German officer of the old school. Both Metzger and Schmehling were present at the trial of Le Forestier, a medical doctor in Le Chambon who was arrested and executed as an example to the villagers. "At his trial," said Schmehling when he

met Trocmé many years later, "I heard the words of Dr. Le Forestier, who was a Christian and explained to me very clearly why you
were all disobeying our orders in Le Chambon. I believed that your
doctor was sincere. I am a good Catholic, you understand, and I can
grasp these things. . . . Well, Colonel Metzger was a hard one, and
he kept on insisting that we move in on Le Chambon. But I kept
telling him to wait. I told Metzger that this kind of resistance had
nothing to do with violence, nothing to do with anything we could
destroy with violence. With all my personal and military power I
opposed sending his legion into Le Chambon."

That was how it worked. It was a wonderful illustration of the
classic concept of nonviolent resistance. You, Dr. Le Forestier, die
for your beliefs, apparently uselessly. But your death reaches out
and touches your enemies, so that they begin to behave like human
beings. Some of your enemies, like Major Schmehling, are converted into friends. And finally even the most hardened and implacable of your enemies, like the SS colonel, are persuaded to stop
their killing. It happened like that, once upon a time, in Le Chambon.

What did it take to make the concept of nonviolent resistance
effective? It took a whole village of people, standing together with
extraordinary courage and extraordinary discipline. Not all of them
shared the religious faith of their leader, but all of them shared his
moral convictions and risked their lives every day to make their
village a place of refuge for the persecuted. They were united in
friendship, loyalty, and respect for one another.

Sooner or later, everybody who thinks seriously about the meaning of nuclear weapons and nuclear war must face the question
whether nonviolence is or is not a practical alternative to the path
we are now following. Is nonviolence a possible basis for the foreign
policy of a great country like the United States? Or is it only a
private escape route available to religious minorities who are protected by a majority willing to fight for their lives? I do not know
the answers to these questions. I do not think that anybody knows
the answers. The example of Le Chambon shows us that we cannot
in good conscience brush such questions aside. Le Chambon shows
us what it would take to make the concept of nonviolent resistance
into an effective basis for the foreign policy of a country. It would
take a whole country of people standing together with extraordinary courage and extraordinary discipline. Can we find such a coun-

try in the world as it is today? Perhaps we can, among countries which are small and homogeneous and possess a long tradition of quiet resistance to oppression. But how about the United States? Can we conceive of the population of the United States standing together in brotherhood and self-sacrifice like the villagers of Le Chambon? It is difficult to imagine any circumstances which would make this possible. But history teaches us that many things which were once unimaginable nevertheless came to pass. At the end of every discussion of nonviolence comes the question which Bernard Shaw put at the end of his play *Saint Joan:*

O God that madest this beautiful earth, when will it be ready to receive Thy Saints? How long, O Lord, how long?

PART IV

·——⟡——·

CONCEPTS

I know that most men—not only those considered clever, but even those who really are clever and capable of understanding the most difficult scientific, mathematical or philosophic problems—can seldom discern even the simplest and most obvious truth if it be such as obliges them to admit the falsity of conclusions they have formed, perhaps with much difficulty—conclusions of which they are proud, which they have taught to others, and on which they have built their lives.

LEO TOLSTOY, 1896

17

The Importance of Being Stuck

"Stuckness. That's what I want to talk about today," says Robert Pirsig in his book *Zen and the Art of Motorcycle Maintenance*. "If your mind is truly, profoundly stuck, then you may be much better off than when it was loaded with ideas. The solution to the problem often at first seems unimportant or undesirable, but the state of stuckness allows it, in time, to assume its true importance. . . . Stuckness shouldn't be avoided. It's the psychic predecessor of all real understanding."

The theme of stuckness followed by illumination is familiar to almost everybody who tries to do creative work in science or in the arts. There may have been a few darlings of the gods who could like Mozart pour out streams of celestial music uninterrupted by intervening periods of dryness. Among scientists it seems to be an inexorable rule that discoveries come interspersed with long stretches of frustration. Einstein gave a classic description of the working of scientific invention at the highest level. He was describing, twenty years after the event, the gestation and birth of the general theory of relativity:

Once the validity of this mode of thought has been recognized, the final results appear almost simple; any intelligent undergraduate can understand them without much trouble. But the years of searching in the dark for a truth that one feels, but cannot express; the intense desire and the alternations of confidence and misgiving, until one breaks through to clarity and understanding, are only known to him who has himself experienced them.

In his search for a satisfactory theory of gravitation Einstein was stuck, on and off, for seven years. After the time of stuckness was over and he had started moving along the right path, he finished the working out of the theory in seven weeks. But the unconscious rhythm of the creative process cannot be hurried. Without the seven years of patient struggling and exploring of blind alleys, he could never have arrived at the seven weeks of illumination.

In the literature of religious experience we find descriptions of a similar rhythm. William James writes of the process of religious conversion in words which might have been used to describe the slow approach to scientific understanding:

> Yet all the while the forces of mere organic ripening within him are going on towards their own prefigured result, and his conscious strainings are letting loose subconscious allies behind the scenes, which in their way work towards rearrangement; and the rearrangement towards which all these deeper forces tend is surely pretty definite, and definitely different from what he consciously conceives and determines. It may consequently be actually interfered with—jammed, as it were, like the lost word when we seek too energetically to recall it—by his voluntary efforts slanting from the true direction.

The anonymous author of "The Cloud of Unknowing," writing five hundred years earlier and in a less convoluted style than William James, uses the metaphor of a storm-tossed boat to tell the same story:

> For suddenly, or even thou knowest, all is away and thou left barren in the boat, blowing with blundering blasts now hither and now thither, thou knowest never where nor whither. Yet be not abashed; for he shall come, I promise thee, full soon, when he liketh, to relieve thee and doughtily deliver thee of all thy dole, far more worthily than ever he did before. Yea! and if he go again, again will he come; and each time, if thou wilt bear thee by meek suffering, will he come more worthlier and merrylier than other. And all this he doth because he will have thee made as pliant to his will ghostly as a Roan glove to thy hand bodily.

We find a remarkable unanimity among religious writers, Moslem and Buddhist as well as Christian, that enlightenment comes at the end of a long dark road, that the soul must wander aimlessly before it unexpectedly finds fulfillment.

There are many examples of the same psychological rhythm, prolonged frustration followed by swift and decisive action, in the political history of mankind. The American revolution of 1775 followed this pattern. So did the German revolution which brought Hitler to power in 1933. As the old religious writers well knew, the experience of sudden illumination may come from the devil as easily as from God. Saint Theresa of Ávila, greatest of Christian mystics, was for a time unsure whether her visions came from above or below. Our psychological rhythms are ethically neutral. If a people has been politically frustrated for a long time and is ready for radical change, radical change will come when the time is ripe, and the people's political leaders have then the responsibility to choose whether the change shall be for good or for evil. The moment of maximum opportunity, the moment when people are ready to change the direction of their thinking, is also a moment of maximum danger.

The Americans in 1775 showed extraordinarily good judgment in entrusting their destinies to George Washington. The Germans in 1933 showed extraordinarily poor judgment in entrusting theirs to Hitler. In both cases, the decision was impelled by a public consensus that a continuation of the existing state of political frustration would be intolerable. People will endure stuckness for a decade or two, but then the time comes when they would rather do anything than nothing. The time is then ripe for revolution, and a leader who promises change will be followed. I saw this happen myself in England in 1939 when our Prime Minister Neville Chamberlain turned suddenly from appeasing Hitler to fighting him. Chamberlain was not as great a statesman as Washington, nor as great a demagogue as Hitler, but he understood how to get England moving. He understood that in 1939, after ten years of economic depression and political indecision, the people of England were ready for drastic change. With extraordinary speed and efficiency, he equipped the entire civilian population of the country within a year with forty million gas masks. The technical effectiveness of our gas masks was widely questioned, but nobody doubted their political effectiveness as a symbol of the sudden shift in mood of the British government and people. Our French cousins in Paris told us in the autumn of 1939 that they were sure that their government was not serious about the war;

they knew this because they had not been given gas masks.

The official historian of the British civil defense programs in World War II interjects into his narrative of these events a quotation from the poet Milton: "For Britain (to speak a truth not often spoken) as it is a land fruitful enough of men stout and courageous in war, so it is naturally not over-fertile of men able to govern justly and prudently in peace, trusting only in their mother-wit." He remarks that Milton's words were as true in 1939 as they had been three hundred years earlier. They are still true today, not only in Britain but in other countries around the world. And therein lies a major source of danger.

The great danger inherent in the cycle of stuckness followed by impulsive change arises from the fact that the most readily available vehicle of impulsive change in the political sphere is war. Traditionally, war has been the easiest way for societies to break loose from the restraints of law and habit. The fatal attractiveness of war results from the psychological need of mankind for occasional periods of recklessness alternating with longer periods of routine. More often than not, the leader who promises change after a period of stuckness is a war leader. I happened to be in England during the weeks in May 1982 when the British fleet was sailing south to do battle with Argentina over the Falkland Islands. The mood of the country was the same as it had been in September 1939 when Neville Chamberlain declared war on Hitler and we were waiting to do battle with Germany. I felt as if I had never been away, as if the intervening forty-two years had changed nothing. The Falklands affair was a small thing compared with World War II. But the psychology of it, from the British point of view, was the same. In 1982 as in 1939, the mood of the country was tragic rather than jingoistic. People were not expecting a cheap victory or an advantageous outcome. The mood could be summed up in the words which I heard in a casual street conversation in Oxford: "Well, this is going to be a bloody mess, and nobody is going to thank us for it, but at least it is better than sitting and doing nothing." These words distill the essence of the problem of war psychology in the modern era. The outcome, both in 1939 and in 1982, turned out to be less disastrous than we had expected. But we had been ready to take the chance, to accept the risk of disaster, rather than sit and do nothing. I am not here arguing the merits of the Falklands campaign or of Britain's part in World War II. I am merely saying that both were accepted by the British public in the same spirit and for the same reason, because it is our nature as human beings to accept tragedy more readily than frustration.

And yet war is not the only cure for stuckness in international relations. There are also examples in history of stuckness dissolved by courageous acts of peace. One conspicuous example is the Marshall Plan of 1947, which put an end to a period of acute economic distress and political uncertainty in Western Europe. George Kennan considers his part in the conception of the Marshall Plan to be "the most significant constructive contribution I was ever able to make in government." Another example is the test ban treaty of 1963, which put an end to a period in which Soviet-American arms control negotiations seemed to be stuck forever on technical problems of verification. A third example was John Kennedy's decision in 1961 to launch a peaceful expedition to explore the moon. The Apollo project was consciously intended by Kennedy to provide a psychological relief from the frustrations caused by intractable Soviet-American disagreements. Apollo was to be what William James had called for long ago, a moral equivalent of war. The idea was to escape from the stuckness of Soviet-American political quarrels by beating the Russians in a bloodless technological competition instead of by beating them in battle. The idea was a good one, and up to a point it worked. It stopped working when the symbolic battle of Apollo was displaced from the focus of public attention by the real battles of Vietnam. Unfortunately, nobody since 1961 has repeated Kennedy's tactic of deliberately committing a country to a daring nonmilitary enterprise as a substitute for the excitements of war. It is a tactic which we could profitably use again on future occasions when international frustrations threaten to break out into tragedy. The arena chosen for nonmilitary adventures need not be as remote as the moon.

I am writing in the year 1983, at a time when international affairs are pervaded by a feeling of stuckness more intense than at any time since the end of World War II. The immobility of Soviet-American relations is only one aspect, though undoubtedly a central aspect, of the general malaise. The SALT II treaty may stand as a symbol of the stuckness of the world. That treaty, which was supposed to put an end to the multiplication of offensive nuclear weaponry, emerged after seven years of painful negotiation, covering twenty-four pages of small print, crammed with technical details unintelligible to the

nonexpert reader, and permitting the two sides to deploy almost all
the nuclear armaments which they would have wished to deploy in
the absence of a treaty. Although the treaty was never formally
ratified, both sides have abided by its terms since it was signed in
1979. The nuclear arms race is slowly grinding to a halt, not because
of the treaty but because the immense quantity of existing weapons
diminishes the importance of any additional deployments.

People all over the world have become aware that we are stuck
and are looking impatiently for a way out. The stuckness which
they are feeling is not a transient thing. It did not begin with the
SALT II treaty, and it will not end with the next arms control treaty
or with the next international crisis. It has been building up slowly
over the last thirty years, since the international upheavals associated
with World War II were completed and the political landscape of
the world became effectively frozen. For thirty years the governments of the United States and the Soviet Union have been mind-
lessly accumulating nuclear weapons while endeavoring to keep the
other countries of the world in a state of political immobility. The
people of the world, in the United States as well as elsewhere, are
increasingly convinced that the continuation of existing habits of
thought and action offers them no hope of a happier future. The
feeling of stuckness brings with it a readiness for radical change.
Radical change is dangerous, and the leaders of government are
right in sensing danger in any disturbance of our precarious equilibrium. But radical change can also be creative, and Robert Pirsig is
right in saying that stuckness is the forerunner of understanding.

The Pastoral Letter on War and Peace, approved in 1983 by the
Roman Catholic bishops of the United States, speaks eloquently of
our stuckness and of the radical shift in political attitudes which this
stuckness has engendered in the Catholic hierarchy.

> We see with increasing clarity the political folly of a system which
> threatens mutual suicide, the psychological damage this does to
> ordinary people, especially the young, the economic distortion of
> priorities—billions readily spent for destructive instruments while
> pitched battles are waged daily in our legislatures over much
> smaller amounts for the homeless, the hungry and the helpless here
> and abroad. But it is much less clear how we translate a no to
> nuclear war into the personal and public choices which can move
> us in a new direction, toward a national policy and an international

system which more adequately reflect the values and vision of the kingdom of God. . . . Soviet behavior in some cases merits the adjective reprehensible, but the Soviet people and their leaders are human beings created in the image and likeness of God. To believe we are condemned in the future only to what has been the past of U.S.-Soviet relations is to underestimate both our human potential for creative diplomacy and God's action in our midst which can open the way to changes we could barely imagine.

From their reexamination of Christian doctrine in the context of nuclear strategy, the bishops draw two practical consequences of great importance. They condemn any strategy of assured destruction which involves indiscriminate targeting of civilian populations. And they condemn any strategy which allows first use of nuclear weapons under any circumstances. The condemnation of assured destruction and first use strikes at the heart of our existing nuclear policies. When the bishops of a traditionally conservative hierarchy feel themselves impelled to demand radical changes of policy, the time must surely be ripe for radical changes to begin.

The present epoch of stuckness is coming to an end and the time of change is approaching. We now have an opportunity to choose in which direction we wish change to go. We cannot predict the accidents of political life which will make change possible, but we can prepare ourselves to take advantage of these accidents so as to push change into directions which we consider hopeful. Fundamental change is always slow. Historical accidents which trigger change may happen quickly, but the time scale of change in the ways of thinking of mankind cannot be hurried. It took us thirty years to build up to our present condition of stuckness. We should expect that it will take another thirty years to complete the cycle of changes by which our stuckness may be dissolved. We should look for remedies which attack the basic causes of our malaise, not for quick cures which attack only the symptoms.

The earlier parts of this book described pieces of the technological and historical background out of which the present predicament of mankind has grown. The last part, which now begins, is concerned with our response to our predicament. It is not enough to understand how we came to be where we are; we must also understand the nature of the choices which are open to us as we move from where we are into the future. In this last part I will be trying to answer the central questions of our time: Where is safer ground to be found, and how do we reach it? I do not have new answers to these questions. I shall examine various answers which others have proposed, and explore their strengths and weaknesses. At the end I offer the reader a list of alternative answers with my own judgment of their merits. The answers which I judge to be wisest are similar to those which the Catholic bishops are advocating in their Pastoral Letter. Which of these answers, if any, turn out to be the right ones will depend upon the unforeseeable march of history.

18

The Quest for Concept

I borrowed the title of this chapter from George Kennan. He wrote an essay with this title sixteen years ago. I decided that Kennan's way of looking at things is the best way to come to grips with the problems of nuclear weapons, and so I have adopted Kennan's title as my own. This does not mean that Kennan is responsible for my conclusions. It means that I have accepted Kennan's fundamental standpoint, that we shall not succeed in dealing with the political and technical problems of controlling our weapons until we have agreed upon a coherent concept of what the weapons are for.

First I go back into history to illustrate what the word "concept" means. As a schoolchild in England I was taught the fundamental concept of British foreign policy. The concept is this: whoever happens to be the strongest power in continental Europe shall not be allowed to dominate the narrow seas around Britain. The leading continental power was Spain in the sixteenth century, Holland briefly in the seventeenth, France in the eighteenth and nineteenth, Germany in the first half of the twentieth, and Russia in the second half of the twentieth century. England fought wars against every one of these powers. Perhaps we fought too many wars. But our wars had at least the virtue of being fought for a concept which was clear, and practical, and feasible. Because the wars were fought for a limited objective, it was possible to win most of them without any total humiliation of our adversaries. One may agree or disagree with the concept. One may think it is moral or immoral, necessary or unnecessary. But one at least has to admit that it is durable. It served pretty well as a basis for British policy for four hundred years, surviving the rise and fall of a great empire, and surviving the growth and decline of England as a world power. During all this time, the narrow seas stayed open and England stayed free. The concept remained the same, whether we were dealing with Philip II or with Louis XIV or with Napoleon or with Hitler. It remains the same today. It has nothing to do with ideology and little to do with moral principles or legal obligations.

Kennan was arguing, and still is arguing, for a similarly clear and limited concept upon which to base American foreign policy. He observes that American policy once had a clear conceptual basis. This basis lasted for about a hundred years after the founding of the republic. It comprised two concepts. One was the Monroe Doctrine, saying that any new annexation of territory by a European power in either North or South America would be regarded as "endangering the peace and happiness of the United States." The other was the doctrine of the open frontier, saying that the United States should be free to expand westward all the way to the Pacific. These two concepts were sufficient as a basis for American policy, until shortly before the end of the nineteenth century. But thereafter, as Kennan describes it,

> there crept into the ideas of Americans about foreign policy something that had not been there in the earlier days. It was a histrionic note—a note of self-consciousness, or pretension. There was a desire not just to *be* something but to *appear* as something: to appear as something greater perhaps than one actually was. It was inconceivable that any war in which we were involved could be less than momentous and decisive for the future of humanity. . . . As each war ended, and it became necessary to talk about the world political future, we took appeal to universalistic, utopian ideals, related not to the specifics of national interest but to legalistic and moralistic concepts that seemed better to accord with the pretentious significance we had attached to our war effort.

This was the situation as Kennan saw it in 1947 when he became director of the Policy Planning Staff in the State Department. Under his guidance the staff defined a new concept which they proposed as a basis for American policy in the world that emerged from World War II. Their concept was modest and realistic. It said simply that the major centers of industrial strength then existing outside the United States and the Soviet Union, namely Britain,

Germany, and Japan, should not be allowed to fall under Soviet control. Nothing was said about China. Nothing was said about Cuba, Iran, or Afghanistan. Nothing was said about leading a world crusade against communism. The concept was that the vital interests of the United States would be adequately protected so long as the main concentrations of population and industry capable of producing modern weapons remained in independent hands. As a concept, this idea had some similarity to the British concept of keeping open the narrow seas. In both cases, the concept had the purpose of establishing a limited area within which our vital interests were confined. The limited area could be, and must be, defended from annexation by rival powers. Outside the limited area, we should be under no obligation to act as policemen in other people's quarrels.

Kennan's concept of limited liability did not become the policy of the United States. Instead, the United States government adopted a concept called containment, which was based on Kennan's ideas but missed the essential point. The concept of containment, as it evolved in practice, meant that the United States would be committed to oppose the territorial expansion of communism with equal fury, no matter where it occurred and no matter who might be responsible for it. It was the concept of containment in this expanded sense which led us to disaster in Vietnam and came close to leading us into an even greater disaster in Cuba.

Kennan wrote his "Quest for Concept" in 1967, when the Vietnam tragedy was still unfolding and no end was in sight. His final sentences express the hope that sustained him through those dark days, a hope that should also sustain us today as we struggle to deal with the enduring problems of nuclear armaments:

It remains my hope that if the Vietnam situation takes a turn that permits us once again to conduct our affairs on the basis of deliberate intention rather than just yielding ourselves to be whip-sawed by the dynamics of a situation beyond our control, we will take up once more the quest for concept as a basis for national policy. And I hope that when we do, what we will try to evolve is concept based on a modest unsparing view of ourselves; on a careful examination of our national interest, devoid of all utopian and universalistic pretensions; and upon a sober, discriminating view of the world beyond our borders—a view that takes account of the element of relativity in all antagonisms and friendships, that sees in others neither angels nor devils, neither heroes nor blackguards; a concept, finally, which accepts it as our purpose not to abolish all violence and injustice from the workings of international society but to confine those inevitable concomitants of the human predicament to levels of intensity that do not threaten the very existence of civilization.

If concept could be based on these principles, if we could apply to its creation the enormous resources of intelligence and ingenuity and sincerity that do exist in this country, and if we could refine it and popularize it through those traditional processes of rational discussion and debate on the efficacy of which, in reality, our whole political tradition is predicated, then I could see this country some day making, as it has never made to date, a contribution to world stability and to human progress commensurate with its commanding physical power.

In this book I am trying to carry forward into the areas of weapons and strategy the process of rational discussion and debate upon which Kennan rested his hope for the future. We now possess weapons of mass destruction whose capacity for killing and torturing people surpasses all our imaginings. The Soviet government has weapons that are as bad or worse. We have been almost totally unsuccessful in halting the multiplication and proliferation of these weapons. Following Kennan's lead, I want to ask some simple questions. What are these weapons for? What are the concepts which drive the arms race, on our side and on the Soviet side? Since the existing concepts have led us into a situation of mortal danger with no escape in sight, can we find any new concepts which might serve our interests better? Can we find a concept of weaponry which would allow us to protect our national interests without committing us to threaten the wholesale massacre of innocent people? Above all, a concept should be robust; robust enough to survive mistranslation into various languages, to survive distortion by political pressures and interservice rivalries, to survive drowning in floods of emotion engendered by international crises and catastrophes.

General Sir Archibald Wavell, who commanded British forces in the Middle East in World War II, published an anthology of poetry and also a book on generalship. I quote now from his book on generalship. "Whenever in the old days a new design of mountain gun was submitted to the Artillery Committee, that august body had it taken to the top of a tower, some hundred feet high, and thence dropped onto the ground below. If it was still capable of functioning it was given further trial; if not, it was rejected as flimsy." Wavell remarked that he would like to be allowed to use the same method when choosing a general. His suggestion applies equally well to the choice of strategic concepts. Any concept which is to succeed in regulating the use of weapons must be at least as robust as the weapons themselves or the generals who command them. A test of robustness for a concept, roughly equivalent to Wavell's hundred-foot drop for a mountain gun, is the process of verbal mauling which occurs in the public budgetary hearings of the committees of the United States Senate and House of Representatives.

The nuclear strategy of the United States was based for many years upon a concept which was definitively stated by Secretary of Defense McNamara in 1967:

"The cornerstone of our strategic policy continues to be to deter deliberate nuclear attack upon the United States or its allies by maintaining a highly reliable ability to inflict an unacceptable degree of damage upon any single aggressor or combination of aggressors at any time during the course of a strategic nuclear exchange, even after our absorbing a surprise first strike."

A year earlier, McNamara had given a less formal definition of the concept:

"Offensive capability or what I will call the capability for assuring the destruction of the Soviet Union is far and away the most important requirement we have to meet."

The concept is called "assured destruction" because of McNamara's choice of words. It is also sometimes called "mutual assured destruction," with the implication that the Russians possess the same capability for destroying us as we possess for destroying them and that Soviet strategy should be based on the same concept as our strategy. I will discuss Soviet strategy a little later. One thing that emerges clearly from Soviet doctrines is that the Soviet Union does not accept mutual assured destruction as a strategic goal. The word "mutual" is therefore misleading. It is better to call McNamara's concept assured destruction and to let the Russians speak for themselves.

Assured destruction has at least the virtue of robustness. McNamara never had any difficulty in explaining it to congressional

committees. It survived untouched the Vietnam War and the attendant political upheavals which changed so many other aspects of
American life and incidentally put an end to McNamara's tenure as
secretary of defense. It still survives today as an important component of American strategy and of American conduct of arms control
negotiations. The words "assured destruction" are clear and unambiguous, and their meaning survives translation into Russian. The
ability to survive translation is an essential virtue. Endless trouble
and misunderstanding were caused by the word "deterrence,"
which is a slippery concept in English and is usually translated into
Russian as *ustrashenie*. It turns out that the word *ustrashenie* really
means "intimidation," and so it was not surprising that discussions
with Russians about deterrence proved frustrating to all concerned.
There is no such difficulty with "assured destruction." Assured
destruction means exactly what it says. It means that no matter what
you do and no matter what happens to us, we retain the capability
to bomb you back into the Stone Age.

I make a sharp distinction between assured destruction as a fact
and assured destruction as a concept. It is a fact that we can as-
suredly destroy any country in the world, including our own, any-
time we feel like it. It is a fact that the Soviet Union can do the same.
These are facts which everybody must accept. But the concept of
assured destruction means something else. The concept means that
we adopt as the ruling principle of foreign policy the perpetuation
of this state of affairs. The concept means that we actively desire and
pursue the capability for assured destruction, with a priority overriding all other objectives. That is what McNamara said: "Assured
Destruction is far and away the most important requirement we
have to meet." Assured destruction must come first; everything else,
including our own survival, second. The concept requires that we
maintain at all times an assortment of offensive nuclear weapons so
numerous and so invulnerable that their ability to destroy the Soviet
Union is mathematically guaranteed. The fact of assured destruction is at the moment inescapable. The concept of assured destruction as a permanently desirable goal is only one of many concepts
which we are free to accept or to reject. The concept was accepted
as the basis of American policy during the McNamara era and is still
preferred by most of my friends in the American academic world
who are experts in strategy and arms control. But many political and
military leaders within the American government have always been

dissatisfied with assured destruction and are now pursuing other concepts.

One of the alternative concepts of the function and purpose of nuclear weapons is limited nuclear war. The concept of limited nuclear war was concisely stated in 1956 by Paul Nitze, the same Paul Nitze who is in 1983 negotiating with the Soviet Union the reduction of intermediate-range nuclear forces in Europe:

"It is to the West's interest, if atomic war becomes inevitable, that atomic weapons of the smallest sizes be used in the smallest area, and against the most restricted target systems possible, while still achieving for the West the particular objective which is at issue."

Oppenheimer believed in the same concept in 1951 when he campaigned for the initial deployment of nuclear weapons to defend Europe against invading armies. The concept of limited nuclear war has always been inherent in American doctrines for the use of tactical nuclear weapons; to that extent it has always been a part of American nuclear strategy. But when Nitze discussed the concept in 1956 he was not thinking only of tactical weapons. Like many people professionally involved with weaponry, Nitze believed that limited nuclear war should apply to strategic weapons too. Especially in the subterranean world of war planners who draw up lists of targets for strategic weapons, the concept of limited war has had a strong influence even during the years when the publicly proclaimed purpose of strategic deployments was assured destruction only. People who carry the responsibility for aiming weapons of mass destruction prefer to believe that the destruction for which they are responsible is directed at some specific military objective rather than at mere destruction for destruction's sake. Furthermore, as strategic weapons became more numerous and more accurate, the mission of assured destruction no longer provided enough targets for the available warheads. The professional targeters have been compelled, whether they believed in limited nuclear war or not, to assign warheads to missions of a more limited character than assured destruction. In this fashion the concept of limited nuclear war became unofficially embodied in the target lists long before it was officially acknowledged as a determining factor of strategic policy.

From time to time, successive secretaries of defense referred guardedly to limited nuclear war in their public statements. Finally, in August 1980, President Carter approved a document called Presidential Directive 59, which formally confirmed the fact that the

concepts of limited nuclear war and assured destruction now have
equal standing in American nuclear strategy. The Reagan administration accepted the doctrine of PD 59 and continued to put it into
practice. I cannot discuss PD 59 in detail, because I do not know
precisely what it says. Secretary of Defense Brown's description of
PD 59 stated that it leaves intact the concept of assured destruction
as the ultimate purpose of our strategic forces. PD 59 adds to assured
destruction a number of preliminary stages, so that we can theoretically carry out a variety of limited nuclear attacks on military and
political targets in the Soviet Union while keeping in reserve the
weapons needed for assured destruction. Secretary Brown emphasized that the new doctrine described only an evolutionary change
and not a radical departure from previous concepts. The change
consisted mainly in bringing the theory of strategic deployments
into line with the long-established realities of targeting. Our public
doctrine is now, as our targeting has always been, a compromise
between assured destruction and limited nuclear war.

One of the major defects of the concepts of assured destruction
and limited nuclear war is that they are not shared by the Soviet
Union. Soviet leaders have told us repeatedly in no uncertain terms
that they reject them both. They have told us that they consider the
concept of limited nuclear war to be an illusion, and that any attempt from our side to wage a limited nuclear war will be met from
their side by a full-scale nuclear response. They have told us that
they consider the concept of deliberate destruction of civilian populations to be barbarous, and that their strategic forces will never be
used for that purpose. We have good reason to believe that the
Soviet leaders mean what they say. The counterpart to McNamara's
statement of our concept of assured destruction is the statement
made in 1971 by the Soviet minister of defense, the late Marshal
Grechko. Here is Marshal Grechko speaking:

"The Strategic Rocket Forces, which constitute the basis of the
military might of our armed forces, are designed to annihilate the
means of the enemy's nuclear attack, large groupings of his armies,
and his military bases; to destroy his military industries; and to
disorganize the political and military administration of the aggressor
as well as his rear and transport."

Marshal Grechko's concept may not be gentler or more humane
than McNamara's, but it is certainly different. Grechko did not
target his forces with the primary mission of doing unacceptable

damage to our society. Their primary mission is to put our military forces out of action as rapidly and as thoroughly as possible. Unacceptable damage to our population will be a probable consequence of their use, but it is not their main purpose. The technical name for Marshal Grechko's concept is counterforce. Counterforce means that your ultimate purpose is to ensure the survival of your own society by destroying the enemy's weapons. Your immediate objective is to disarm him, not to destroy him.

There are many cultural and historical reasons why the counterforce concept fits better into the Russian than into the American way of thinking about war. The first and most important fact to remember about Russian generals is that they start out by reading Tolstoy's *War and Peace.* Their whole experience of war and peace in the years since 1914 has confirmed the truth of Tolstoy's vision. War according to Tolstoy is an inscrutable chaos, largely beyond human understanding and human control. In spite of terrible blunders and terrible losses, the Russian people in the end win by virtue of their superior discipline and powers of endurance. All this is entirely alien to the American view of thermonuclear war as a brief affair, lasting a few hours or days, with the results predictable in advance by a computer calculation like a baseball score, so many megadeaths on one side and so many megadeaths on the other. Assured destruction and limited nuclear war make sense if war is short, calculable, and predictable. Counterforce makes sense if war is long-drawn-out and unpredictable, and the best you can do is to save as many lives as you can and go on fighting with whatever you have left. I happen to believe that the Russian view of war, being based on a longer historical experience, is closer to the truth than ours. That is not to say that their concept of counterforce is free of illusions. Neither assured destruction nor limited nuclear war nor counterforce is to me an acceptable concept. If I had to make a choice between assured destruction and counterforce, I would choose counterforce as less objectionable on moral grounds. But neither assured destruction nor limited nuclear war nor counterforce answers our most urgent need, which is to find a concept which both sides can understand and accept as a basis for arms control negotiations.

The tragedy of the SALT negotiations arose out of the basic incompatibility of American and Soviet strategic concepts. The Soviet concept of counterforce says: "Whatever else happens, if you drive us to war, we shall survive." The American concept of assured destruction says: "Whatever else happens, if you drive us to war, you shall not survive." It is impossible to find, even theoretically, any arrangement of strategic forces on the two sides which satisfies both these demands simultaneously. That is why no satisfactory treaty can emerge from arms control negotiations so long as the concepts on the two sides remain as they are. The SALT II treaty is better than no treaty at all, but it is a miserable thing, unloved even by its friends, demonstrating the bankruptcy of the strategic concepts that gave it birth. If that is the best that our present concepts can do for us, then let us in God's name look for some better concepts.

I have drawn up a list of seven strategic concepts. Each of them might be a basis for a possible future. Three of them, assured destruction and limited nuclear war and counterforce, provided a basis for American and Soviet policies in the past and the present. As the examples of assured destruction and limited nuclear war make clear, it is possible for us to espouse two concepts simultaneously, but the resulting confusion and ambiguity of our intentions is in itself a source of danger. We would be well advised in future to choose a single concept and to make our policies as unambiguous as possible. We would also be well advised to choose a concept which is compatible, if not identical, with the concept preferred by the Soviet Union.

My list of concepts contains, in addition to the three already mentioned, four others, to which I give the names nonviolent resistance, non-nuclear resistance, defense unlimited, and live-and-let-live. This list makes no claim to completeness. I chose these additional concepts to represent four different directions in which we might decide to depart radically from the patterns of the past. I am thinking of a span of time extending twenty or thirty years into the future, within which radical changes are possible and perhaps inevitable. Each of the concepts might be adopted in a more extreme or a less extreme version. It is also possible that we shall avoid radical change and stay with our existing concepts for another thirty years. I shall try to weigh the advantages and disadvantages of each of these alternatives.

Nonviolent resistance means the concept of active pacifism as it was put into practice by Gandhi and Trocmé. *Non-nuclear resistance* means unilateral nuclear disarmament combined with vigorous deployment of non-nuclear weapons and a willingness to use them. *Defense unlimited* means a massive shift of emphasis from offensive to defensive weaponry, with defensive weapons of all kinds deployed as rapidly as technology will allow. *Live-and-let-live* is a compromise concept, designed to achieve a decisive turning away from dependence on nuclear weapons with the least possible disturbance of existing patterns of thought and behavior. Each of these concepts will be defined more precisely in the following chapters 19 to 22. Chapter 19 is concerned with assured destruction and with the reasons why this concept has always fitted better into the theoretical schemes of arms control experts than into the practical requirements of the real world. Chapter 20 is concerned with the three concepts, limited nuclear war and counterforce and defense unlimited, which require that we believe in the feasibility of actually fighting a nuclear war. Chapter 21 is concerned with the two concepts, nonviolent resistance and non-nuclear resistance, which require the unconditional rejection of nuclear weapons. Chapter 22 is concerned with live-and-let-live, which may be regarded as a middle way between nuclear war fighting and unilateral disarmament.

I excluded deterrence from my list of concepts, because that word has too many meanings. Any deployment of weapons by one country, with the aim of dissuading another country from doing something disagreeable, is a form of deterrence. Except for nonviolent resistance, every concept on my list involves deterrence in one form or another. One might even include under the label of deterrence the forty million gas masks deployed by the British civil defense organization in 1939; those gas masks may be given some credit for deterring Hitler from using poison gas when he attacked the civilian population of London in 1940. A deterrent in the widest sense of the word is any weapon which can be effective without being used. On the other hand, some experts in arms control give deterrence a narrow meaning roughly synonymous with assured destruction, while in popular American usage a deterrent simply means an offensive nuclear weapon system. Herman Kahn in his book *On Thermonuclear War* tried to bring order out of this confusion by carefully defining three concepts which he called Type I Deterrence, Type II Deterrence, Type III Deterrence. I prefer to call my concepts by names which do not need numbers to identify them.

Another word which does not appear in my list of concepts is "freeze." At the time when I am writing, the nuclear freeze is the main political objective of the peace movement with which I am associated. If in the next few years a consensus should develop in the United States population and government in favor of a freeze, this would have important consequences. The Soviet government already expressed its willingness to negotiate the conditions of a freeze. If the United States were wholeheartedly in favor of a freeze, it is likely that a treaty could be negotiated which would achieve to a large extent the stated objective of the peace movement: stopping the nuclear arms race. There are various possible versions of a freeze treaty, but they have in common the essential feature of prohibiting manufacture, testing, and deployment of new nuclear weapons and delivery systems. Such a treaty would be a major achievement. Why should I not consider it worthy of inclusion in my list? I exclude it because it is an action rather than a concept, a means rather than an end. Concerning the purpose of nuclear weapons and the conditions for their use, the freeze is silent. The freeze says only that we have enough weapons; it does not say what the weapons are for, and it does not say why we need as many as we have. One of the virtues of the freeze as a political objective is that people of widely differing viewpoints unite in supporting it. The freeze is compatible with every concept on my list except defense unlimited. One may support the freeze even if one believes, as I do, that it is valuable as a political symbol of opposition to nuclear weapons rather than as a substantial step toward the prevention of nuclear war.

In 1981, when our local peace group in Princeton, the Coalition for Nuclear Disarmament, was debating the choice of its objectives, some of us wanted to make the freeze the main objective while others wanted us to campaign for a United States policy of no first use of nuclear weapons. I belonged to the no-first-use party. I argued that a United States commitment to no-first-use would directly reduce the risk of nuclear war, whereas a commitment to the freeze would not. I argued that the no-first-use issue goes to the heart of our strategic policy, whereas the freeze affects only the details of the hardware. But the politically experienced members of our group told us that the freeze was the only objective which had a chance of nationwide support. No-first-use was useless as a political campaign issue, they said, because the ordinary citizen would not understand what it meant. So our group decided to leave no-first-use aside and work for the freeze. They helped to get the freeze referendum put on the ballot for the 1982 election in the state of New Jersey, and they helped to get it approved by a large popular majority. No doubt the political experts in our group were right in choosing an objective which could attract public support quickly and impressively. The popular vote in favor of the freeze probably influenced the New Jersey representatives when they voted five weeks later in Congress on the funding of the dense pack deployment of the MX missile; they voted fourteen to one to deny funding. This defeat of the MX deployment was an important tactical victory for the peace movement. Such tactical victories are the essential mechanism by which public opinion forces a reluctant government to pay attention to its demands. I do not deny the importance of the freeze as a tactical goal. But it is a short-range goal, having little to do with the quest for concept. After we have negotiated and ratified a treaty establishing a nuclear freeze, we shall still be living under the shadow of nuclear annihilation and we shall still be searching for a concept which will define our aims on a longer time scale.

It would be unfortunate if the concentration of the efforts of the peace movement upon the freeze should divert attention from longer-range objectives. The major part of the danger of nuclear war comes from the misuse of old weapons rather than from the production of new ones. That is why I consider no-first-use to be an issue of greater substance than the freeze. But no-first-use is also absent from my list of concepts; it is a policy rather than a concept. No-first-use is an essential component of the concept which I call live-and-let-live, and I will come back to it when I discuss that concept in detail.

Another item missing from my list of concepts is world government. World government is undeniably a concept. The wisest and most realistic exposition of it is the book *World Peace Through World Law* by Grenville Clark and Louis Sohn. Theoretically, world government provides a complete solution to our security problems. But it is difficult to imagine either Americans or Russians willingly accepting a world government which they did not dominate. Herman Kahn remarked in a footnote in his book on thermonuclear war, apropos the Clark-Sohn version of world government: "It is worth noting in this connection that it is easier to be a hero than a saint. It really would not be difficult to find thousands of Westerners willing to give up their lives for a world government of a satisfactory sort, but one would find very few willing to accept Chinese or

Indian standards of living, or any appreciable risk of this occurring, for either themselves or their families."

Whether we like it or not, world government may come into existence, one way or another, in the real world. Edward Teller was promoting world government in the 1940s while he was also promoting the hydrogen bomb, and it may be true, as he said then, that hydrogen bombs will in the end make world government inevitable. The reason I reject world government as a concept to guide our policies is that it violates Kennan's requirement that a concept should be modest and devoid of utopian and universalistic pretensions. An American foreign policy based upon the concept of world government would sooner or later degenerate, either into a pious ritual divorced from reality, or into a cold-blooded attempt to impose our will upon mankind by military force.

All through the history of ideological movements in international life runs a tragic theme, the terrible dissonance of thought and action. Again and again, we see thought leading to action which clashes with thought and results in folly and disaster. The pious and well-meaning doctrines of the Holy Alliance led in 1830 to the bloody suppression of Poland. The concept of the balance of power led the rulers of Europe into the catastrophe of 1914. Karl Marx's doctrine of the liberation of the workers of the world from their chains led in 1917 to the establishment of a regime as repressive as the Holy Alliance. In the nuclear era, Oppenheimer's concept of limited nuclear war as a comparatively humane strategy for defending Europe led to the dangerous proliferation of nuclear warheads overseas in exposed and vulnerable positions. Finally, the concept of assured destruction, which was supposed by the theorists of arms control to give us strategic stability at a fixed level of armament, has led in reality to unending fears of vulnerability and ever-increasing deployments. After looking at this dismal record of unfulfilled hopes, one might well conclude that all concepts are a delusion, that the dissonance of thought and action will always turn our concepts into traps. If the concepts which we have put into practice led us to such disasters, what reason have we to expect that concepts which we have not yet put in practice will not run into equally deadly snags?

In answer to this question I can only say yes, we must never put an absolute trust in concepts. We must always be aware that concepts may betray us. We must never let concepts overrule common sense. But we cannot avoid concepts altogether. Every nuclear policy must have some conceptual basis, realistic or unrealistic, wise or foolish. The option of acting without concepts is not open to us. The only alternative to wise concepts is foolish concepts. In spite of the failures of concepts in the past, we still must have concepts for the future, and we cannot avoid the responsibility of choosing our concepts in the light of whatever wisdom we can derive from conscience and from history.

The experience of the past has not been uniformly bleak. There have been some happier historical examples of wise concepts leading to good results. The British concept of the freedom of the seas led in the nineteenth century to an era of widespread peace and prosperity. Gandhi's concept of nonviolent resistance led to a peaceful transfer of power in India. Kennan's concept of limited liability led to the Marshall Plan in Europe and to a generous peace settlement in Japan. Both the Marshall Plan and the Japanese settlement were directly influenced by Kennan, and both have been lastingly beneficial. A comparison of this list of conceptual successes with my earlier list of failures shows that the concepts which failed were generally those which violated Kennan's principle of avoiding universalistic pretensions and apocalyptic overtones. Doctrinaire concepts usually prove disastrous. Modest and empirical concepts are more often successful. The Holy Alliance and Marxist historical determinism are prime examples of universalistic concepts which failed. Assured destruction is an example of a failed concept with apocalyptic overtones. The disaster of 1914 is an exception to the rule; the concept of the balance of power is modest according to Kennan's criteria, and it still failed. This exception may be explained by remarking that several of the rulers of Europe in 1914 had lost sight of the balance of power and were pursuing dreams of military glory. There is no guarantee that any concept, no matter how modest and well grounded in practical experience, will save us from the consequences of human folly.

The quest for concept promises us no sure road to survival. But it gives us solid ground for hope that a road will be found. We have seen that concepts modest in scope and careful in execution, keeping thought and action in harmony, can sometimes answer the needs of mankind with unexpected ease. Kennan, with his unrivaled double experience in the worlds of action and of thought, recently addressed a message to his colleagues in the world of thought, urging them not to abandon their efforts to bring light and reason into the world of action:

> If we, the scholars, with our patient and unsensational labors, can help the statesmen to understand these basic truths—if we can help them to understand not only the dangers we face and the responsibility they bear for overcoming these dangers but also the constructive and hopeful possibilities that lie there to be opened up by wiser, more restrained, and more realistic policies—if we can do these things, then we will be richly repaid for our dedication and our persistence; for we will then have the satisfaction of knowing that scholarship, the highest work of the mind, has served, as it should, the highest interests of civilization.

19

Assured Destruction

The concept of assured destruction defines the purpose of our nuclear weapons to be readiness at any time, before or during or after
a Soviet attack, to destroy the Soviet Union as a functioning society.
Assurance and destruction, the two components of the concept, are
equally essential. Destruction means demolishing cities and killing
people. Assurance means that the sufficiency of our weapons for this
purpose must be reliably guaranteed. The proponents of assured
destruction like to use the euphemism "unacceptable damage" in
order to avoid explicit mention of poisoned earth and burned bodies.
They calculate in various ways the number of cities which have to
be demolished and the number of people who have to be killed to
do "unacceptable damage to Soviet society." Unacceptable damage
seems generally to require a few tens of millions of corpses.

Anybody possessing normal human feelings and imagination
has difficulty in reacting with intellectual detachment to the literature of strategic analysis. The difficulty was well described twenty
years ago by the British physicist Patrick Blackett: "When I come
to study in detail some of the arguments of these new military
writers about nuclear war, I will necessarily have to adopt many
aspects of their own methods and terminology, that is, I will have
to meet them on the methodological ground of their own choosing.
I want therefore to apologise in advance for the nauseating in-
humanity of much of what I will have to say." Like Patrick Blackett,
I am compelled to suppress feelings of disgust while I am discussing
theories of nuclear strategy; like him, I trust the suppressed feelings
more than I trust the theories.

The dissonance of thought and action is nowhere sharper than in the doctrine of assured destruction. On the one hand, the concept of assured destruction as taught by academic theorists with their euphemistic jargon—stable deterrence and invulnerable second-strike forces and counter-value targeting. On the other hand, the reality of weapons held constantly in readiness to wipe out of existence tens of millions of people and to destroy forever the monuments of our cultural heritage.

The theory of assured destruction is simple and logical. The theory says that we need only to maintain a force of offensive nuclear weapons satisfying three conditions: the force must be powerful enough to destroy Soviet urban society, inaccurate enough not to threaten Soviet strategic weapons, and invulnerable enough to survive a Soviet attack. If these conditions are satisfied, then we have achieved a stable equilibrium. The situation is stable in two senses. We have crisis stability, meaning that even if we and the Soviet Union become involved in an intense crisis, neither side has any incentive to attempt a disarming first strike. We have arms race stability, meaning that the forces required to carry out the assured destruction strategy have a limited size and need not grow constantly larger. That is the theory. According to the theory, stability is the key to survival. If we can maintain both crisis stability and arms race stability, then the world can continue living with nuclear weapons indefinitely and the weapons will never be used.

The concept of assured destruction has other advantages besides theoretical simplicity. It has been tested in the real world. United States weapon deployments have been guided for thirty years, in theory and to a large extent in practice, by the requirements of assured destruction. The fact that we are still alive is evidence of the concept's practical success. At least up to the present moment, it has worked. During these thirty years the world has lurched from one crisis to another; bitter wars have been fought in many countries; but none of our local wars has grown into World War III, and our nuclear weapons have sat since 1945 unused. There is no way to measure how much the doctrines of assured destruction have contributed to our survival. American citizens and politicians, seeing that we survived with these doctrines for thirty years, tend to give the assured destruction strategy a large share of the credit. Even I, opposed as I am in principle to assured destruction, have to admit that the concept has helped to keep the world at peace.

Assured destruction has another advantage in the real world of people and politics. It separates nuclear weapons from other political and military activities. It keeps nuclear weapons isolated in a separate corner of our minds. There is much to be said for a concept which makes nuclear war seem unreal and apocalyptic. There is much to be said for a concept which encourages us to forget about nuclear weapons. For most of the time during the last thirty years, assured destruction has been disconnected from the problems of daily life. It is good for our psychological health not to worry about irremediable disasters. The concept of assured destruction, placing the mythological hell of nuclear war at a great distance from the everyday world of jobs and children, makes it easier for us not to worry. If we are not worrying about nuclear weapons, we may have more time and attention to spare for the real needs of suffering humanity, for the economic development of poor countries, and for the preservation of the biosphere.

The strategy of assured destruction is seen in its purest form in the nuclear policies of Britain and France. Britain and France deploy offensive missile forces with the ostensible purpose of destroying Moscow and a few other Soviet cities in case of a Soviet attack upon Britain or France. For this purpose, the British and French weapons do not need to be numerically comparable with Soviet forces. They need only to be mobile and well hidden so that they can survive a Soviet attack long enough to be fired. If they are ever fired, Britain or France will have committed suicide. The apocalyptic purpose of these weapons has made them seem irrelevant to the ordinary citizens of Britain and France. Life continues almost as if they did not exist. The politicians who maintain and control them seem to regard them as abstract symbols of national status rather than as real instruments of destruction.

Lord Zuckerman, who was for many years scientific adviser to the British defense establishment, argues the case for independent British and French nuclear forces in his recent book *Nuclear Illusion and Reality*. He is a strong believer in assured destruction, not only for Britain and France but for the United States too. He likes the concept of assured destruction because it permits nuclear forces to remain small and invisible. He believes that the United States and the Soviet Union could reduce their forces drastically if only they would both keep strictly to the assured destruction strategy. One of his arguments for the maintenance of a British nuclear force is that "its continued possession could help in the process of world disarmament, not because the UK might be allowed to argue the case in the conference chamber, but because the scale of what it has, and what the French have, is an indication to the two super-powers of the forces that are adequate to maintain a deterrent threat."

Zuckerman is deluding himself if he seriously imagines that the British and French nuclear forces might impress American political leaders as worthy examples for the United States to follow. Americans who have to deal with strategic issues tend to regard the British and French forces as unimportant nuisances, contributing nothing to international security and complicating the negotiation of arms control agreements. They speak disparagingly of the British nuclear force as a useless relic of vanished great-power status. The idea that the United States has anything to learn from the British example never enters their minds. Nevertheless, Zuckerman has a valid point. It is true, as he says, that the size of the British and French forces—at the moment (1983) sixty-four British warheads and ninety-eight French—is adequate for countries pursuing a pure assured destruction strategy. It is true that the United States force of ten thousand warheads and the Soviet force of seven thousand warheads are grossly excessive for this purpose. If both the United States and the Soviet Union could be persuaded to adopt assured destruction as the only mission of their nuclear forces, the road to drastic disarmament would be open, and there would be a possibility of reducing American and Soviet forces to sizes comparable with the existing British and French forces. The world of which Zuckerman dreams, the world of small, stabilized, invisible nuclear forces dedicated to a pure assured destruction mission, is a possible future for mankind and a valid long-range objective for arms control negotiations.

Unfortunately, Zuckerman's world is very far from the world in which we are living. The Soviet Union has never believed in assured destruction. And the United States has never believed in it exclusively. The United States has always maintained, behind the official doctrine of assured destruction, a variety of nuclear forces devoted to other missions. Herman Kahn's *On Thermonuclear War*, published in 1960, was important and unpopular because it revealed the glaring discrepancies between the theory of assured destruction and the actual course of events in the real world. Kahn also annoyed people by speaking plainly of killing and cancer instead of using the customary euphemisms. He pointed out that the assured destruction strategy was incompatible with two American habits which were already well established by 1960: the habit of regarding nuclear weapons as a substitute for non-nuclear forces in the defense of Europe, and the habit of worrying publicly about every real or imagined Soviet technological advance. During the years which have passed since 1960, these two habits have continued to erode the assured destruction component of American strategy. Gradually, the fraction of our weapons dedicated to limited nuclear war objectives has increased. And at the same time the assurance demanded by the assured destruction strategy has been diminished by constant worries about the vulnerability of our weapons to a Soviet first strike and about the alleged ability of Soviet civil defense to nullify their destructive effects.

As a result of these processes of erosion, we are left in 1983 with an American assured destruction strategy which is weakened in two ways. It provides neither the crisis stability nor the arms race stability which are theoretically supposed to be its advantages. Crisis stability is lost because of the mixture of assured destruction with limited nuclear war objectives. Many of our nuclear weapons are deployed overseas with an operational doctrine permitting first use; these weapons, intended for fighting limited nuclear war, are inherently crisis unstable, and their use in a crisis would probably lead to an unconstrained nuclear exchange. The limited nuclear war weapons infect the assured destruction weapons with their own crisis instability. Arms race stability is lost because the demand for absolute assurance of assured destruction can never be satisfied so long as the Soviet Union continues to believe in the possibility of survival. The Soviet first-strike threat and the Soviet civil defense program are not, in my opinion, technically capable of defeating our assured destruction strategy. But they are politically important as a statement of the fact that the Soviet Union will never acquiesce in its own extinction. So long as the Soviet Union refuses to agree to assured destruction, Soviet counterforce weapons and Soviet civil defense will continue to create alarm in American minds, and doubts about the assurance of assured destruction will persist. So long as doubts about assurance persist, our assured destruction weapons will be considered insufficient and arms race stability will continue to elude us.

Herman Kahn was one of the first Americans to worry seriously about Soviet civil defense. His worries always seemed to me misplaced and exaggerated. Several times I argued with him about this, saying that it would take the Russians many decades to bring their civil defense system up to Swiss standards, and asking why we should grudge the Russians whatever thin shreds of comfort they might derive from digging holes in the ground. Failing to convince him that his worries were unfounded, I ended by saying, "Oh, it's no use talking with you. You're paranoid." "Of course I'm paranoid," he replied cheerfully. "Didn't you know that? I make it my business to be paranoid. You had to be paranoid in 1933 to believe Hitler would exterminate the Jews, and you had to be paranoid in 1941 to believe the Japanese would attack Pearl Harbor."

Kahn's criticism of the assured destruction strategy was based on historical analogies which may or may not be valid. But he was right in stressing the incompatibility between the assumption of rational behavior upon which the theory of assured destruction is based and the many examples of irrational, paranoid, and unpredictable action which fill the pages of history. In 1967 Kahn organized a conference at his Hudson Institute to discuss the political and economic development of the world up to the year 2000. For two days we listened to learned academicians prognosticating the growth of industry, the consumption of electricity, and the world price of wheat, basing their calculations on the standard techniques of economic forecasting with allowance for probable technological innovations. On the last day of the meeting Kahn said, "You have heard what the experts think the future will be like. Now I am going to show you what the future will really be like." He then introduced three surprise speakers. The first was a white revolutionary, preaching death to capitalism. The second was a black revolutionary, telling us of cities burning and blood flowing in our streets. The third was a hippie with flowers in his hair, describing the universal peace and brotherhood that would follow from the universal use of LSD. Unfortunately, these surprise talks were not included in the official record of the conference which the Hudson Institute afterward published. They left a powerful impression on those who heard them. They made us aware of the enormous gulf which separates the world of economic theory from the world of human passion. An even wider gulf separates the human world from the world of strategic analysis. The central message of Kahn's book on thermonuclear war is contained in one sentence: "History has a habit of being richer and more ingenious than the limited imaginations of most scholars or laymen."

The concept of assured destruction failed to provide a stable basis for American strategy because it required human beings to forget their humanity. Assured destruction became diluted and confused with limited nuclear war objectives because the men whose job it is to target weapons insist on trying to target them humanely. Assured destruction lost its mathematical assurance because the Soviet leaders insist on trying to save their people's lives as best they can with counterforce deployments and with civil defense, and because Americans insist on regarding these Soviet countermeasures, in spite of their technical inadequacy, as evidence of a lasting Soviet unwillingness to accept the premises upon which the assured destruction doctrine rests. Assured destruction would be a stable strategy in a world of computers. In a world of human beings, it fails to bring stability because it lacks the essential ingredients which human beings require: respect for human feelings, tolerance for human inconsistency, adaptability to the unpredictable twists and turns of human history.

The case against the concept of assured destruction rests on three counts. First, it is not shared by the Soviet Union. Second, it is immoral. Third, it is in the long run suicidal. I have already explained why assured destruction does not fit, and is not likely in the future to fit, into the Soviet concept of war. So long as the Soviet Union does not accept the concept of assured destruction, our insistence upon it stands in the way of any satisfactory and permanent arms control agreement.

I do not need to spell out why it is immoral to base our policy upon the threat to carry out a massacre of innocent people greater than all the massacres in mankind's bloody history. But it may be worthwhile to remind ourselves that a deep awareness of the immorality of our policy is a major contributory cause of the feelings of malaise and alienation which are widespread among intelligent Americans, and of the feelings of distrust with which the United States is regarded by people overseas who might have been our friends. An immoral concept not only is bad in itself but also has a corrosive effect upon our spirits. It deprives us of our self-respect and of the good opinion of mankind, two things more important to our survival than invulnerable missiles.

I also do not need to spell out why the concept of assured destruction is ultimately suicidal. The concept rests on the belief that if we maintain under all circumstances the ability to do unacceptable damage to our enemies, our weapons will never be used. We all know that this idea makes sense so long as quarrels between nations are kept under control by statesmen weighing carefully the consequences of their actions. But who, looking at the historical record of human folly and accident which led us into the international catastrophes of the past, can believe that careful calculation and rational decision will prevail in all the crises of the future? Inevitably, if we maintain assured destruction as a permanent policy, there will come a time when folly and accident will surprise us again as they surprised us in 1914. And this time the guns of August will be shooting with thermonuclear warheads.

20

Nuclear War Fighting

The great conceptual advantage of the assured destruction strategy is that it does not require us to believe in the feasibility of actually fighting a nuclear war. The purpose of assured destruction weapons is only to prevent nuclear war, not to fight it. The weapons achieve their purpose by not being used. The assured destruction strategist is not supposed to worry about what happens if the weapons are used. When we threaten to use the weapons of assured destruction, our threat depends for its credibility upon our not worrying about the consequences. This is the central paradox of assured destruction. Its success requires us to blind ourselves deliberately to the consequences of its failure.

Assured destruction is politically popular because most people in civilian life do not believe that nuclear war fighting makes sense, and they feel comfortable with a strategy which tells them not to worry about it. Soldiers, and people who have had personal experience of war, tend to feel uncomfortable with assured destruction, because life has taught them to worry about unpleasant possibilities. The first instinct of a soldier confronted with an unfamiliar machine or idea is to ask, "What happens if it doesn't work?" As soon as professional soldiers came into possession of nuclear weapons, they began looking for concepts which would give nuclear weapons a rational purpose even if they should fail in their primary mission of preventing war. A rational purpose for nuclear weapons in war requires a concept which makes nuclear war fighting feasible. Both in the United States and in the Soviet Union, the soldiers developed concepts of nuclear war fighting: in America, limited nuclear war, and in the Soviet Union, counterforce. These concepts differ from each other in detail, but they have in common an insistence that nuclear wars can be rationally fought, that nuclear weapons do not fundamentally change the traditional principles of strategy and tactics. Both concepts begin with the belief that nuclear weapons differ only quantitatively but not qualitatively from weapons of other kinds.

The American plans for actually fighting nuclear war are contained in a compilation known as the Single Integrated Operation Plan—SIOP for short. The SIOP contains detailed lists of targets which might be attacked under various circumstances. It allows the commander to choose between a finite set of alternatives, ranging from carefully circumscribed limited nuclear war attacks to the most comprehensive version of assured destruction. The concept of limited nuclear war says that we should prefer the smaller attacks whenever possible, and that by choosing the smaller attacks we give ourselves a realistic chance of bringing a nuclear war to a negotiated end before either the Soviet Union or our own country is destroyed.

I was recently listening to a talk by an American air force major about the vulnerability of various air force facilities to Soviet attack. He droned on for a while about the ability of existing Soviet forces to destroy our machines. This was a familiar story, a collection of bad news which I had often heard before. But then the major dramatically changed his tone as he started to tell us the good news. After the SIOP is executed, he said, things will be different. After the SIOP is executed, he said, we will have eliminated most of our vulnerabilities. After the SIOP is executed, we will have machines that we can rely on. After the SIOP is executed, vulnerability will really not be a problem anymore. Every time he said, "After the SIOP is executed," his voice became more lively as he described the splendid opportunities that would then lie open for the air force to exploit. It took me a while to grasp what he was saying. Then suddenly I understood. "Good God," I said to myself. "This fellow really believes that nuclear war fighting is fun. Not just feasible, but fun." For a moment my mind flashed back to the poet Rupert Brooke in the early months of World War I, a volunteer soldier in the Royal Naval Division, training himself for the battles to come. Before leaving England for Gallipoli, he wrote in a letter to an American friend, "It's all a terrible thing. And yet, in its details, it's great fun." He was dead before he even reached Gallipoli. The young American major was no poet, but his voice was the voice of Rupert Brooke. After the SIOP is executed. In its details, it's great fun.

This is the terrible danger of the limited nuclear war concept, that it gives to nuclear war a false image of reasonableness. It is too easy for air force officers, busy with the details of their operations, to forget what the execution of the SIOP would really mean, to imagine themselves bravely obeying orders and keeping machines running while the mushroom clouds float by. It is too easy to forget that the Soviet weapons stand ready, in the words of Marshal Grechko, "to disorganize the political and military administration of the aggressor."

Any valid concept of nuclear war must at least recognize one inescapable fact. Nuclear war, even if it could be kept to some extent limited, would bring overwhelming confusion and disorganization. In the chaos of broken communications, demolished buildings, death, sickness, and hunger, even the air force would have difficulty in keeping its machines operational. And even if the machines were still running, the responsible officers would have difficulty in finding out what they were supposed to do next. Ignorant as we are of the nature of nuclear war, we know at least this much: that it would not leave the routines of the air force untouched. Everybody, including even air force officers, would be faced with immediate and elemental problems of survival. The realities of nuclear war would quickly reveal the absurdity of our prewar concepts of nuclear war fighting.

The air force major reminded me of another voice from the past, the voice of Major King Kong, also an air force major, the commander of the bomber "Leper Colony" in the film *Dr. Strangelove.* "Leper Colony" has just received the coded radio signal to proceed to its target in the Soviet Union.

"When King spoke, it was with quiet dignity. 'Well, boys, I reckon this is it.' 'What?' Ace Owens said. 'Com-bat.' 'But we're carrying hydrogen bombs,' Lothar Zogg muttered. King nodded gravely in assent. 'That's right, nuclear combat! Toe-to-toe with the Russkies.' "

The voice of the real air force major, happily looking forward to the days after the SIOP is executed, proved that Kubrick's characterization of Major Kong was not altogether unrealistic. Such men exist, and the concept of limited nuclear war gives official support to their fantasies.

Soviet military doctrine also gives support to the idea that nuclear war fighting is feasible. But the Soviet concept of counterforce is very different from our concept of limited nuclear war. The Soviet concept comes much closer to being realistic. The counterforce concept accepts the fact that nuclear war is unpredictable and uncontrollable. It accepts the fact that nuclear war will be an unimaginable disaster for all concerned. The counterforce concept says that if the Soviet Union sees a nuclear attack coming or has reason to believe that an attack is about to be launched, the Soviet Union will strike first at the attacker's weapons with all available forces, and will then do whatever is necessary in order to survive. The essence of the concept is the doctrine of preemption, which means knowing beforehand when an attack is coming and forestalling it by striking first.

The counterforce concept assumes, in my opinion correctly, that nuclear attacks will not be launched against the Soviet Union without warning. It assumes that any nuclear war will be preceded by at least several days of intense crisis and desperate attempts to settle the crisis by negotiation; there will be time for the Soviet Union to prepare the preemptive strike and launch it before it is too late. Each country's concept of nuclear war is conditioned by its historical experience. The United States fears an attack coming unexpectedly like the Japanese attack on Pearl Harbor. The Soviet Union fears an attack coming like Hitler's attack in 1941, with massive preparation and plenty of warning. The Soviet generals still regret that Stalin would not allow them to preempt Hitler in 1941. Next time, if there is a next time, this mistake will not be repeated.

It is important for us to understand two facts about the Soviet concept of counterforce. First, that the Soviet Union intends to survive, if the worst comes to the worst, by striking first. And second, that this intention does not imply that the Soviet authorities believe they could come through a nuclear war without immense losses and catastrophic damage. They do not believe that they have a "first-strike capability," in the sense in which this phrase is used by American strategists, meaning an ability to strike first without getting seriously hurt. Yes, they believe they can fight and win a nuclear war, as Richard Pipes says, by striking first and disorganizing the attacker's forces. But no, they do not believe that any cause less compelling than the imminent threat of annihilating attack would justify the cost of such a victory.

A Russian friend once described to me in simple terms his understanding of the counterforce strategy. He said it is like a vicious dog trained to guard a house from intruders. When a burglar comes to the house, the dog runs out and bites him without waiting until he comes close enough to break down the door. The dog is executing a preemptive strike. But the burglar can easily avoid trouble by keeping at a safe distance from the house. This homely analogy does not accurately reproduce all the technical intricacies of the counterforce concept. But I believe it correctly describes the way the concept is viewed by ordinary Soviet citizens. I would not be surprised if the Soviet leaders look at it in the same way. The shooting-down of the Korean airliner over Sakhalin in September 1983 showed us the vicious dog in action.

It is important for us also to understand the difference between the concept of first use of nuclear weapons and the concept of first strike. First use refers to tactical nuclear weapons, first strike to strategic weapons. The American doctrine of limited nuclear war says that we are prepared to use tactical nuclear weapons first if this is necessary to stop a non-nuclear invasion of Western Europe, but that we do not contemplate using strategic weapons first in a direct attack on the Soviet Union. That is to say, American doctrine allows first use but forbids first strike. Mr. Andropov and other Soviet leaders have said on various occasions that the Soviet Union will not be the first to introduce nuclear weapons into a non-nuclear war, but the Soviet counterforce doctrine says that the Soviet Union is prepared to respond with a full-scale preemptive attack on the United States if any Soviet forces anywhere are attacked with nuclear weapons. That is to say, Soviet doctrine forbids first use but allows first strike. There are good and valid geographical reasons why first use seems good to us and bad to them, while first strike seems good to them and bad to us. Unfortunately, the general public and the politicians on both sides do not understand the difference. Our people feel threatened when they hear that Soviet doctrine allows first strike, and the Russians feel threatened when they hear that our doctrine allows first use. Much of our reciprocal fear might be dispelled if we took the trouble to understand each other's concepts.

Misunderstanding of Soviet motives has led to exaggerated American fears of the Soviet counterforce concept. But not all our fears are exaggerated. We have good reason to be afraid of the counterforce concept, even when we understand it correctly, because it is crisis unstable. Whenever the Soviet Union is involved in an intense crisis, there will be a danger that real or imagined threats will be perceived as requiring a preemptive response. The purpose of the counterforce strategy is not only to discourage direct attacks on Soviet territory. The purpose is also to discourage countries hostile to the Soviet Union from stirring up political crises near to Soviet borders where they might endanger Soviet security. If the enemies of the Soviet Union insist on stirring up such a crisis, they must be afraid that nuclear vengeance may descend upon their heads. The fact that the counterforce strategy is crisis unstable serves to protect the Soviet Union from political as well as from military threats. The Soviet leaders probably view this crisis instability as a virtue of their strategic doctrine. It is a good way to make sure that no serious security problems arise in areas close to their borders. It is a good way to make sure that crises severe enough to threaten the power structure of the Soviet regime will never happen.

Unfortunately, the limited nuclear war strategy of the United States, with the attendant doctrine allowing the possibility of first use, is equally crisis unstable. And we rely on the crisis instability of our strategy, as the Soviet leaders rely on the crisis instability of theirs, to discourage any rash moves which might endanger the existing political equilibrium of Europe. On each side, a crisis-unstable strategy helps to perpetuate the status quo by persuading the other side that any major crisis would bring with it uncontrollable risks. This system of bilateral brinksmanship might indeed preserve the peace of Europe forever, if the only possible crises were those deliberately precipitated by one side or the other. But history is full of examples of crises which arose, like the crisis of July 1914, unplanned by either side of the quarrel. Against unplanned and unexpected crises the crisis-unstable strategies offer no protection. They offer only a slippery slope leading from such crises to disaster.

The world would probably be substantially safer than it is if both the United States and the Soviet Union believed in limited nuclear war or if both sides believed in counterforce. If both sides believed in limited nuclear war, then there would be a better chance that a crisis which crossed the threshold into nuclear war could in fact be kept limited. If both sides believed in the Soviet counterforce strategy, then we would not be deluding ourselves with plans for limited nuclear war fighting, and there would be a better chance that local wars and invasions could be stopped without reaching the nuclear threshold. The existing situation, with one side believing in limited nuclear war and the other side in counterforce, combines the worst features of both concepts. Our doctrine of first use of tactical weapons in local conflicts makes the nuclear threshold easy to cross, and the Soviet doctrine of massive counterforce response brings us quickly from the first crossing of the threshold to total disaster. The combination of the two doctrines is more crisis unstable than either doctrine by itself.

It is not in our power to change Soviet doctrines, but it is in our power to change our own. The most useful immediate step which we could take to reduce the crisis instability which threatens our existence is to abandon the concept of limited nuclear war. I do not advocate that we adopt instead the Soviet concept of counterforce, although that would be in many ways a change for the better. Counterforce is still crisis unstable and is therefore no solution to the problem of survival. Our quest for concept is not yet at an end.

The next concept on my list claims to provide an escape from crisis instability. I call the concept defense unlimited, because its main thrust is an attempt to outrun the Soviet Union in defensive technology. Its proponents are mostly military officers and their friends in the American aerospace industry. They speak of the concept, with a metaphor taken from the American football field, as a "technological end-run on the Soviets." Their doctrines are summarized in a book, *High Frontier: A New National Strategy*, published in 1982, with lavish illustrations in the style of military briefing charts. The following sentences convey the flavor of their thinking.

A bold and rapid entry into space, if announced and initiated now, would end-run the Soviets in the eyes of the world and move the contest into a new arena where we could exploit the technological advantages we hold. . . . When we look to space for the technological end-run on the Soviets, we find all factors call for an emphasis on strategic defense. . . . Defensive systems hold the only promise to break out of the Mutual Assured Destruction doctrine.

In short, the concept is to drive the arms race as vigorously as possible in the direction of defensive weaponry, mainly or entirely non-nuclear. The existing nuclear offensive deployments are not to be abandoned. As the defensive systems grow, the offensive weapons will gradually lose their preeminence. The defense need not be perfectly effective in order to be militarily useful. The function of defenses is described in terms of old-fashioned military analogies:

> With regard to impermeable or invulnerable defenses, there never has been nor ever will be a defensive system which could meet such criteria. Such perfectionist demands ignore the purposes of defenses and the effects of strategic defense on deterrence. Defenses throughout military history have been designed to make attack more difficult and more costly—not impossible. Defenses have often prevented attack by making its outcome uncertain. General Grant put a cavalry screen in front of his forces, not because the cavalry was invulnerable to Confederate bullets or because he thought it could defeat General Lee, but because he did not want the battle to commence with an assault on his main forces or his headquarters.

The defense unlimited strategy hopes to achieve an equilibrium which is crisis stable because neither side can be sure that its own attack would be successful or that the enemy's attack would be unsuccessful. Defenses create uncertainty and uncertainty creates stability. As the defenses become more capable, the danger of a disarming first strike becomes more remote. The authors of *High Frontier* assert, with a certain technological arrogance, that the United States can outrun the Soviet Union in the building of defenses, and they would like to maintain American defensive superiority for as long as possible. But they recognize that the Soviet Union will in time learn to build defenses as good as ours, and they welcome the prospect of a new strategic equilibrium with strong defenses in place on both sides:

> We should abandon this immoral and militarily bankrupt theory of Mutual Assured Destruction and move from Mutual Assured Destruction to Assured Survival. Should the Soviet Union wish to join us in this endeavor—to make Assured Survival a mutual endeavor—we would, of course, not object. We have an abiding and vital interest in assuring the survival of our nation and our allies. We have no interest in the nuclear devastation of the Soviet Union.

In spite of the inclusion of these fine moral sentiments, with which I heartily agree, I still classify defense unlimited as a nuclear war fighting concept. Defense unlimited does not imply that offensive nuclear weapons will be neglected. Offensive deployments are to be maintained with roughly the same mixture of purposes that they have now, partly assured destruction and partly limited nuclear war. As the defenses grow, the assured destruction mission is supposed to fade out while the limited nuclear war missions become dominant. The concept depends for its validity on the belief that good defenses will make nuclear war fighting feasible. Since offensive nuclear forces with war fighting missions will be retained, there is little justification for the claim that this concept puts us on the road toward assured survival. Any concept deserving the name assured survival must begin with the recognition that nuclear war fighting is a delusion.

Defense unlimited has some theoretical advantages over our existing strategies. It diminishes the crisis instability of our deployments, and it drives the technological arms race in a desirable direction away from weapons of mass destruction. Whether these advantages are real depends on whether the dreams of defense unlimited can be embodied in technically feasible hardware. Defense unlimited makes practical sense only if a non-nuclear defense against ballistic missiles can be built with reasonable effectiveness at reasonable cost. I have discussed some of the technical aspects of ballistic missile defense in Chapters 6 and 7. I came to the conclusion there that non-nuclear defenses are promising in the long run but unpractical in the short run. I described three possible futures for defense technology: the arms controllers' future, in which defense is permanently forbidden; the defense-dominated future, in which offensive nuclear forces are forbidden and defense runs free; and the technical-follies future, in which both offensive and defensive weaponry proliferate. The concept of assured destruction aims to bring us to the arms controllers' future. The concept of defense unlimited, if it would be put into operation with the existing balance of forces in the world, could bring us only to the technical-follies future. To bring us to the defense-dominated future we require another concept, which I will describe in Chapter 22.

The fundamental flaw in the concept of defense unlimited is that, even if all the technical difficulties of non-nuclear defense could be overcome, the effects of nuclear war fought with existing offensive weapons would still be catastrophic. The concept does little to diminish the chance that nuclear war might begin as a result of miscalculation or accident. And it introduces a new danger, that nuclear war might be triggered by some overenthusiastic spaceman starting a shooting match in the sky. Any concept which retains large offensive forces and regards nuclear war fighting as feasible will lead sooner or later to disaster. In this respect, defense unlimited is no better than counterforce or limited nuclear war. The designing of space defenses is great fun, like the preparation for the Gallipoli expedition about which Rupert Brooke wrote in 1914. The fact that it is fun makes the concept of defense unlimited all the more dangerous.

Violet Asquith, the daughter of the British prime minister, was a close friend of Rupert Brooke. She was given a special pass to see the ship *Grantully Castle* depart from Avonmouth on February 28, 1915, on its way to Gallipoli with Rupert on board. In the evening of the same day she described the scene in her diary:

> The gangway was raised and the ship moved slowly out, the Hood trumpeters playing a salute on their silver trumpets as it passed the mouth of the harbour. The decks were densely crowded with young, splendid figures, happy, resolute and confident—and the thought of the Athenian expedition against Syracuse flashed irresistibly through my mind.

The Athenian expedition against Syracuse set sail in the year 415 B.C. in a similar mood of joy and confidence. It was the turning point of the thirty-year-long Peloponnesian War between Athens and Sparta. Thucydides, the historian of that war, tells how the expedition ended:

> Of all the Hellenic actions which took place in this war, or indeed, I think, of all Hellenic actions which are on record, this was the greatest—the most glorious to the victors, the most ruinous to the vanquished; for they were utterly and at all points defeated, and their sufferings were prodigious. Fleet and army perished from the face of the earth; nothing was saved, and of the many who went forth few returned home. Thus ended the Sicilian expedition.

Of the fifteen officers of Rupert Brooke's battalion who sailed on the *Grantully Castle*, four were alive four months later, two at the end of the war.

The spirit of the Athenians who sailed to Sicily, the spirit of Rupert Brooke and his friends on the *Grantully Castle*, is still alive in the technological warriors of today, in the air force major with his enthusiasm for executing the SIOP, in the young space engineers with their enthusiasm for the high frontier. It is still true, as it was true in 415 B.C. and in A.D. 1914, that the details of preparing for war are great fun, that the happy warriors cannot imagine the totality of the disaster toward which they are headed. Only the number of the victims has changed.

21

Unilateral Disarmament

When one contemplates the barbarity and insanity of our existing weapons and the plans for their further multiplication, one is tempted to say that there is no hope of salvation in any concept that does not reject them unconditionally. Perhaps it is true that we would be better off rejecting nuclear weapons unilaterally and unconditionally, irrespective of what other countries may decide to do. But unilateral disarmament is not by itself a sufficient basis for a foreign policy. Unilateral disarmament needs to be supplemented by a concept stating clearly what we are to do after we have disarmed, if we are confronted by hostile powers making unacceptable demands. There is a concept which deals with this question in a morally and intellectually consistent way, namely the concept of nonviolent resistance. Nonviolent resistance is not the same thing as surrender. Morally, nonviolent resistance and surrender are at opposite poles. The concept of nonviolent resistance says simply: "You shall not obey unjust laws, you shall not collaborate with unjust authorities, and you shall not shed any man's blood except your own."

This was the concept with which Gandhi defied the British rulers of India and André Trocmé defied the German rulers of France. Gandhi and Trocmé proved that the concept sometimes works, that it can be practical as well as noble. But those who succeeded in putting nonviolent resistance into practice all agree that it is difficult, uncertain of success, and not to be undertaken lightly. Pastor Édouard Theiss, who was right-hand man to Trocmé in the organization of nonviolent resistance in Le Chambon, was asked afterward whether the Soviet Union should have used the same methods to resist Hitler's invasion. "No," he replied. "They had to use violence then. It was too late for nonviolence. . . . Nonviolence involves preparation and organization, methods patiently and unswervingly employed—the Russians knew nothing of all this. Nonviolence must have deep roots and strong branches before it can bear the fruit it bore in Le Chambon. Nonviolence for them would have been suicide; it was too late."

Is it too late for us now? If we decide that our existing weapons and concepts are morally unacceptable, then we must examine carefully every possible alternative, no matter how radical or difficult. Nonviolence is a possible alternative. Martin Luther King and others have demonstrated that nonviolent resistance can be successfully used in the United States as a tactic to win internal battles against injustice. Could it also be used by the United States to resist external enemies? Could nonviolent resistance become the guiding concept of American foreign policy? Most of us would answer no to these questions, but there is no reason why our no should be final and everlasting.

Three main obstacles stand in the way of nonviolent resistance as a practical concept for the United States. After we have defined the obstacles, we may be better able to judge whether they are permanently insuperable. The three obstacles are the problems of vicarious pacifism, robustness, and original sin.

A vicarious pacifist is one who sits comfortably at a safe distance from a fight and preaches nonviolent resistance to those whose lives are threatened. Pacifism loses much of its moral grandeur when it is vicarious. For geographical reasons, a United States policy of nonviolent resistance would in practice be a policy of vicarious pacifism. The people who would have to carry the burdens of resisting the Soviet Union nonviolently would not be Americans but citizens of allied countries nearer to the Soviet borders. The situation of American pacifists today is similar to the situation of English pacifists in 1938. The Munich agreement, which compelled Czechoslovakia to submit peacefully to Hitler's demands, was a victory for the English pacifists insofar as it kept England out of war, but it was a victory at other people's expense. An American policy of pacifism today would be difficult to distinguish from a policy of imposing surrender upon allies. If a policy of nonviolent resistance to the Soviet Union is to be successful, it must be initiated and sustained by the allies rather than by us.

Next comes the problem of robustness. The concept of nonviolent resistance is easily misrepresented as a concept of weakness and surrender. It would easily be torn apart by the divisive processes of American political life. It is difficult to imagine it standing up well when exposed to the sniping of congressional committees as they go about their political business as usual. It is difficult to imagine it lasting through changes of administration and through international crises as assured destruction has lasted. What would the representatives of Texas say if it were seriously suggested that they should nonviolently resist a Mexican army of occupation?

Finally comes the problem of original sin. This is an old question, debated for centuries by theologians. Is man perfectible, or is original sin a part of our nature? If we believe in perfectibility, we may place our hopes in nonviolent resistance as a permanent substitute for war. If we believe in original sin, we must expect that war and violence are inseparable from the human condition. In this context, the evidence of history gives strong support to the doctrine of original sin. Warfare has been a dominant concern of every civilization since history began.

The few examples of successful use of nonviolent resistance have been local, short-lived, and precarious. Nonviolent resisters backslide all too easily into violence. Trocmé's nonviolent resistance in Le Chambon was conducted within a milieu of violent resistance in the countryside around him. Trocmé himself was well aware that his survival depended partly on the fact that the violent resistance occupied the major share of the German soldiers' attention. His village was to some extent sheltered and protected by the surrounding violence. And his success in maintaining the commitment of the village to nonviolence was made easier by the fact that he could tell any backsliders who wanted to fight the Germans to go away and do it somewhere else. It is not clear whether a nonviolent resistance in the style of Trocmé could have been successful if it had been extended to the whole of France. Similar reservations apply to Gandhi's campaign of nonviolent resistance in India. Gandhi's success depended entirely on his personal charisma. Backsliding into violence occurred frequently during his lifetime, and the discipline of nonviolence disappeared rapidly after his death. Little is now left in India of the soul-force which he alone knew how to organize. If Attlee's government had not had the wisdom to withdraw from

India peacefully while Gandhi was still alive, it is likely that Indian nationalism would have achieved the same result not much later by force and violence. Some Indians today have still not forgiven Gandhi for depriving India of the glory of winning its freedom properly in a national war of independence.

The most tragic example of backsliding from a successful campaign of nonviolent resistance occurred in Germany. When the French army occupied the Ruhr valley in 1923 in order to extract the reparations demanded from Germany by the Treaty of Versailles, the German population responded with widespread and well-disciplined passive resistance. The resistance diminished as time went on, but it achieved its purpose. The French withdrew a year later, frustrated and discouraged. Germany emerged from the ordeal politically and economically strengthened. France agreed to a modification of the reparations schedule in Germany's favor. The failure of the Ruhr occupation was long remembered in France, and was one of the main reasons why France made no move to oppose Hitler in 1936 when he openly violated the Versailles Treaty by sending German troops into the Rhineland. But in Germany, alas, the success of the nonviolent resistance was soon forgotten and its architects repudiated. The Germans remembered the French occupation as a time of national humiliation and took no pride in its failure. They resolved to defeat the French next time in a less gentle fashion. Hitler became popular because he showed them a way to do it. And sixteen years later they did it.

Sadly I have to draw from these examples the conclusion that the concept of nonviolent resistance demands for its success a combination of exceptional leadership and human virtue which few nations possess and none have ever maintained for long. The sins of envy, hatred, and malice, if not original in our souls, are deeply embedded in the fabric of our culture. So long as our political institutions remain as they are, nonviolent resistance cannot be a robust enough foundation on which to build either a stable balance of power or a new world order.

In spite of all difficulties and discouragements, I keep nonviolent resistance on my list of possible concepts for our future. The path of nonviolence will always be open, if not for nations and governments, at least for individuals to follow when all other concepts are unacceptable. I now pass on to another concept, less radical, less difficult for nations to put into practice, but still requiring a substantial act of unilateral disarmament. This is the concept of non-nuclear resistance. It is the concept accepted by some, but not all, of the European advocates of nuclear disarmament. Those who accept it say:

"We, for our part, will have nothing more to do with nuclear weapons. We consider that we can defend our interests and the interests of our allies better without nuclear weapons than with them. If anybody threatens us with nuclear weapons, we shall not yield. If anybody attacks us with nuclear weapons, we shall do whatever we can to ensure that the attacker derives no benefit from our destruction."

A country adopting the concept of non-nuclear resistance could do a great deal to mitigate the consequences of a nuclear attack by building non-nuclear defenses and, following the Swiss example, by building a serious nationwide system of shelters. But a country choosing this path must understand that ABM systems and shelters cannot by themselves guarantee survival. Non-nuclear resistance, like assured destruction and other nuclear strategies, is a policy based upon a judgment of relative risks. If we judge that a country without nuclear weapons is less likely than a country with nuclear weapons to be a target for nuclear attack, that is a good reason for preferring non-nuclear resistance to assured destruction. The example of Japan proves that non-nuclear status is no sure protection against nuclear attack. But it is a reasonable presumption that nuclear war in the future is more likely to be triggered by panicky fear of attack than by deliberate malice; if this is so, then we shall be safer without nuclear weapons. If we take at face value the Soviet doctrines of counterforce and preemptive attack, we shall be led to the same conclusion, that the risk of Soviet preemption is smallest when we give the Soviet Union nothing to preempt.

George Kennan once stated the argument for non-nuclear resistance in a more personal fashion. His wife comes from Norway, and he still maintains close contact with her Norwegian family. Norway follows a policy of non-nuclear resistance, remaining a loyal member of the NATO alliance, pledged to resist Soviet invasion with a well-equipped army and navy, but refusing to allow nuclear weapons to be stationed on Norwegian territory. Kennan was one day speaking to me of his grandchildren, and remarked that he would feel more confident of their survival if they lived in Norway rather than in the United States. In other words, he considers non-nuclear resistance to be a less risky gamble than assured destruction. There are many reasons why a concept which is good for Norway may not be good for the United States. Nevertheless, Kennan's offhand remark expresses a deeply held conviction that our nuclear weapons endanger us more than they protect us. Jesus said the same thing the night before he died: "Put up again thy sword into his place: for all they that take the sword shall perish with the sword."

On another occasion Kennan was discussing in a public interview the problem of nuclear blackmail. The interviewer put to him the familiar question which most Americans regard as a sufficient justification for the possession of nuclear weapons: What can a country without nuclear weapons do when threatened by a country with nuclear weapons? Kennan answered the question forthrightly, speaking from his many years of experience as a diplomat:

> Stalin said the nuclear weapon is something with which you frighten people with weak nerves. He could not have been more right. No one in his right senses would yield to any such thing as nuclear blackmail. In the first place, it would be most unlikely (as is the case with most forms of blackmail) that the threat would be made good if one defied it. Secondly, there would be no point in yielding to it. Any regime that has not taken leave of its senses would reject the nuclear threat. "Why in the world should we give in to this?" it would argue. "If we do what you want us to do today in the name of this threat, what are you going to ask us to do tomorrow? There is no end to this process. If what you want us to do is to part with our independence, you will have to find others to do your work for you, and that means that you will have to take ultimate responsibility for running this country. We are not going to be the people to turn this government into an instrument of your power." No one would give in to this kind of pressure; nor does anybody use this kind of blackmail. Great governments do not behave that way.

I must make it clear, when I quote Kennan in this context, that he is not advocating unilateral nuclear disarmament as a policy for the United States. So far as strategic weapons are concerned, he believes that drastic disarmament can and should be achieved by bilateral negotiation between the United States and the Soviet Union. His discussion of nuclear blackmail was addressed to the problem of the tactical nuclear weapons deployed in Western

Europe, to the question whether removal of these weapons would leave the European countries fatally exposed to Soviet blackmail. He believes in non-nuclear resistance as a wise policy for Western Europe. He is saying that the countries which practice non-nuclear resistance—for example, Norway, Sweden, Switzerland, and Yugoslavia—are able to defend their independence at least as effectively as countries such as Britain, France, and West Germany, which rely on nuclear weapons. Even Finland, peculiarly exposed by virtue of its history and geography to Soviet interference, practices non-nuclear resistance with considerable success. There is a spiritual toughness among the people in Scandinavia, a toughness which the Soviet leaders respect, and which belongs to people who intend to remain masters of their own destiny. This toughness is a more effective protection against Soviet pressure than any number of nuclear weapons. The possession of nuclear weapons gives people the impression that resistance is synonymous with suicide, and thereby weakens the will to resist. Kennan is convinced that a withdrawal of nuclear weapons from Western Europe, carried out not too abruptly and with diplomatic consultation among all the interested parties, would strengthen rather than weaken the capacity of the European peoples to stand firm against Soviet pressure. It would also improve the chances of survival for their grandchildren.

But I am here concerned with a more difficult question, whether the concept of non-nuclear resistance can be applied not only to the tactical situation in Western Europe but to the entire strategic policy of the United States. Non-nuclear resistance for the United States would mean a total dismantling of the nuclear weapon apparatus—warheads, missiles, Trident submarines, and bombers—with a concomitant building up of non-nuclear parts of the armed forces, ordinary airplanes and boats and satellites and computers and precision-guided munitions and education and training of soldiers. Is such a drastic shift of United States strategy conceivable? And if it is conceivable, is it desirable?

It is inconceivable that a shift to a non-nuclear strategy for the United States could be imposed by an idealistic peace movement upon an unwilling military establishment. So long as the leaders of the military establishment believe in nuclear weapons as the mainstay of national defense, they will always find enough support from the American people and Congress to keep their nuclear forces in place. In a political battle between the generals and the peace movement over an issue which the generals can construe as unilateral disarmament, the generals will always win. But a shift to non-nuclear strategy is conceivable if it has strong support inside the military establishment as well as outside. It is conceivable that a powerful voice could arise within the military establishment, saying that weapons which can never be used for any rational military purpose are not weapons, that the whole nuclear apparatus is merely a distraction from the serious business of national defense, that the United States armed forces would be fitter and stronger if the resources now squandered on nuclear systems were transferred to units which can actually fight. It is conceivable that a new generation of military leaders will arise, determined to heal the rift which weapons of mass murder have interposed between our armed forces and our idealistic and intelligent young people. It is conceivable that the military establishment will itself decide that a shift to a non-nuclear strategy is required, in order to restore honor and self-respect to the ancient profession of soldiering. If our leading soldiers were to become convinced, as most of the great soldiers of the past were convinced, that high morale and a sense of purpose are more essential ingredients of military strength than big bombs, then a shift of United States strategy to non-nuclear resistance is by no means inconceivable.

James Fallows in his book *National Defense* describes eloquently the poor state of morale in the American army of today, and the strong desire of many army officers for reforms which would encourage a return to the military virtues of the past. There is no doubt that the spirit of the army has deteriorated over the last twenty years, and that radical changes will be needed before the army's traditional pride and sense of purpose can be restored. Fallows is not saying that the army's problems are primarily caused by our overemphasis on nuclear weapons. The causes of the army's problems are mainly social and institutional. But our reliance on nuclear weapons must be counted as one of the negative factors which nourish feelings of futility in the minds of infantrymen on duty in Germany. It is difficult for a young man serving in a nuclear-equipped army to believe in the reality of the job he is trained to do. Nuclear weapons give the individual soldier the feeling that nothing he does really matters. If the time comes when reformers within the military establishment reach positions of power and impose the drastic changes which are needed to cure the army's malaise, it is at least conceivable that they may include within their program of reforms a shift to a non-nuclear strategy. If that should happen, then an alliance of military reformers inside the establishment and antinuclear activists outside might be strong enough to make unilateral nuclear disarmament politically viable. It is not likely, but it is possible.

If we suppose that unilateral nuclear disarmament is conceivable, we have next to ask whether it is desirable. Would it last? Would it introduce an era of peaceful relaxation, or would it throw the world into desperate turmoil? After we had got rid of our nuclear weapons, what would stop the Soviet Union from murdering us? These questions have no easy answers. Non-nuclear resistance implies acceptance of a certain risk that the Soviet leaders may decide to destroy us. Nothing would stop them from doing it, once they had made their decision. But our present strategy accepts a similar risk. Nothing stops them from destroying us today, except their sanity and good sense. The risk of destruction is there, so long as the Soviet Union has thousands of nuclear weapons, no matter what we do. The question is whether the dismantling of our weapons would make the risk greater or smaller. In other words, which is the greater risk: a preemptive strike launched in fear and haste in a moment of crisis in spite of the certainty of retaliation, or a deliberately murderous attack launched in cold blood with no necessity for haste and no fear of retaliation? To weigh these risks requires a deeper understanding of the psychology of Soviet leaders than any of us possesses. I have seen no convincing evidence that the risk which we are now accepting is smaller.

The strength of the United States, like the strength of the Soviet Union, is ultimately based on geography. We can be destroyed with nuclear weapons but we cannot be conquered. Even after an unopposed nuclear strike, the Soviet Union would not have enough soldiers to occupy and control our territory. Any attempt at an occupation would be met by the implacable hostility of a surviving population well armed with handguns. If the Soviet leaders were contemplating a nuclear attack upon a non-nuclear United States, they would recognize that we would in the long run remain a formidable political and military power and that our power could not be permanently suppressed. They would recognize that our destruction could bring to the Soviet Union neither political tranquillity nor lasting security.

Another argument for non-nuclear resistance as a strategy for the United States is that this may be the most practical way to disarm the Soviet Union. Our ultimate goal is to get rid of Soviet nuclear weapons, one way or another. To get rid of Soviet weapons we have a choice of methods, either negotiation or various kinds of unilateral action. The path of negotiation is slow and beset with political difficulties. Unilateral action may arrive at the goal more quickly and easily. Admittedly, unilateral action is a chancy thing. Why should our dismantling of our weapons cause the Soviet leaders to dismantle theirs? We cannot know what the Soviet leaders would do if they were left suddenly alone in the world with their gigantic nuclear deployments. There would be voices raised within the Soviet hierarchy arguing for the transfer of resources and skilled labor from the nuclear weapons empire to other military and civilian enterprises. Such voices might or might not prevail. Especially if the United States were pushing ahead with non-nuclear military technology, the Soviet military research and development establishment would be under strong pressure to follow suit. The maintenance of thousands of nuclear warheads with their elaborate delivery systems and command-and-control systems might come to be regarded by the Soviet leaders as an unnecessary extravagance. We should not count on any such benign reaction on the part of the Soviet leaders. But we should also not dismiss it as a possibility. In a world of unavoidable risks, a big gamble may in the end be the least risky.

To my mind, the strongest argument for non-nuclear resistance is the fact that this strategy is realistically matched to the actual style of Soviet expansionism. The Soviet Union has on many occasions overrun, annexed, or occupied neighboring countries, from the Baltic states in 1940 to Afghanistan in 1979. In every case the purpose of the operation was to dominate the neighboring country politically, not to destroy it physically. The instruments of domination were Soviet garrisons and native Communist regimes prepared to collaborate with the occupying forces. Nuclear weapons did not help the Soviet Union to establish domination, and nuclear weapons would not have helped the native populations to resist. Where resistance was tried and failed, it failed because the native population was unprepared or politically divided. In the two cases, Finland and Yugoslavia, where a native population was politically united and well prepared by a competent government to resist, resistance was successful and the government preserved its independence.

Whether Afghanistan will be a third example of successful resistance remains to be seen. But in all cases the pattern of Soviet aims and methods has been consistent. The aim is political control, the method is political penetration with the help of Soviet troops. The essential requirements for a successful defense are a population willing to fight and a political cohesion too tough to penetrate. So long as the nature of Soviet society remains as it has been for the last fifty years, the weapons of choice for a successful resistance will be non-nuclear.

Three of the arguments against non-nuclear resistance are similar to the arguments against nonviolent resistance. I give them the same labels as before: vicarious pacifism, robustness, and original sin. A policy of non-nuclear resistance, if adopted by the United States, would impose the same policy upon countries, such as West Germany, which are more directly exposed to Soviet threats. Our policy would indeed be a form of vicarious pacifism if it were imposed by us upon our allies. However, this objection to the policy disappears if the nuclear disarmament movement wins public support earlier in Europe than in the United States. It is more likely that the Western Europeans will ask us to remove nuclear weapons from their territory than that we will remove them unasked. If West Germany and the other European countries which house our nuclear weapons should decide to follow the Norwegian example and adopt a policy of non-nuclear resistance, we could adopt the same policy without fear of being called vicarious pacifists.

The problem of robustness exists for non-nuclear resistance as it does for nonviolent resistance, but not to the same degree. For non-nuclear resistance to be robust in the context of American political life, it is essential that it have the support of the soldiers. If (and, oh, what a big *if*) the military establishment once becomes persuaded of the virtues of non-nuclear resistance, the tradition of relying on non-nuclear fighting strength might prove to be as robust as the tradition which our armed forces have maintained since World War I of not using lethal gas. The robustness of our commitment to non-nuclear resistance would be tested every time we became involved in a quarrèl with the Soviet Union; the most severe test would arise if the Soviet Union should ever use or threaten to use nuclear weapons. Perhaps a desire not to test our commitment beyond the breaking point would be an important restraining influence, keeping the Soviet leaders from exploiting their nuclear monopoly in a threatening manner. If we cannot be sure of the robustness of our commitment to non-nuclear resistance, neither can they.

Non-nuclear resistance would gain considerably in robustness if we were successful in developing the technology of non-nuclear ABM systems. But the robustness of non-nuclear resistance depends more on politics than on technology. It depends on the behavior of the Soviet Union, on the extent to which the Soviet Union will reciprocate our nuclear disarmament with unilateral actions of its own, on the extent to which the world can forget about nuclear weapons and turn its attention to more constructive concerns. It depends ultimately on the extent to which the world can escape from the burden of original sin.

Non-nuclear resistance, like nonviolent resistance, requires for its success an improvement in the moral standards of mankind. We have good reason to be skeptical of the possibility of any such improvement. But the degree of improvement required is enormously less for non-nuclear resistance than for nonviolent resistance. To make nonviolent resistance into an effective basis for international order, the world would need a steady supply of leaders of the moral stature of Gandhi, together with populations willing to follow such leaders. To maintain the ethic of nonviolence among nations is almost as difficult as to abolish sin. On the other hand, to make non-nuclear resistance effective requires only that mankind abandon certain uniquely indiscriminate weapons and certain genocidal habits of recent origin, thereby returning to the traditional standards of military honor which were generally accepted by civilized nations in the nineteenth century and earlier. Non-nuclear resistance does not require an advance to a new level of human morality, but only the restoration of an old level of morality. It does not require a moral regeneration of mankind, but only a recovery from the unusual moral degeneration which has occurred within the present century.

The problem of original sin is not just an abstract theological question. It affects the feasibility of non-nuclear resistance in concrete and specific ways. For example, it affects the non-nuclear status of Germany and Japan. West Germany and Japan are powerful industrial states which have committed themselves to a policy of not manufacturing or deploying nuclear weapons of their own. Both rely for their security upon the presence of American military forces. One of the strong arguments against American nuclear disar-

mament is that as soon as we decided to get rid of our nuclear
weapons, Germany and Japan would feel impelled to provide for
their own defense by becoming independent nuclear powers, and
that a world with a nuclear-armed Germany and a nuclear-armed
Japan would be even more dangerous and unstable than the world
we live in. To what extent is this argument valid? Is it true that our
renunciation of nuclear weapons would cause an automatic reaction
in Germany and Japan to fill the nuclear vacuum with their own
weapons? Or would our decision to rely on non-nuclear strength
merely confirm in German and Japanese eyes the wisdom of their
own earlier commitment to non-nuclear status? Which way Germany and Japan would go depends upon the strength of the determination of German and Japanese leaders not to repeat the crimes
and follies perpetrated by their predecessors in the 1930s and 1940s.
In other words, it depends on the degree to which the disastrous
experiences of the 1940s have produced in Germany and Japan a
lasting moral improvement. In this context, the question of original
sin can have very practical consequences. It determines whether we
are condemned by the viciousness of our nature always to arm
ourselves with the most vicious weapons, or whether our choice of
weapons can be a matter for rational debate and decision.

The last and strongest argument against non-nuclear resistance
is that we need nuclear weapons to prevent non-nuclear wars, and
especially to prevent a recurrence of grand-scale non-nuclear wars
like World Wars I and II. Most people believe, rightly or wrongly,
that if we had not had nuclear weapons the world would already
have been devastated by World War III. People who lived through
World War II tend to be grateful to the hydrogen bomb for saving
us from a repetition of those years of terror and misery. This is
probably the main reason why nuclear weapons have been politically popular. And it is one of the main reasons why non-nuclear
resistance will be unpopular. Advocates of non-nuclear resistance
must face the argument that by getting rid of nuclear weapons, we
are removing the fear of retribution which keeps Europe peaceful
and saves the world from the horrors of World War III. Non-
nuclear resistance, so the argument goes, will leave Western Europe
exposed to invasion, and will leave us with the choice, when the
invasion takes place, of either backsliding into nuclear warfare or of
fighting a non-nuclear World War III under unfavorable circumstances. This argument must be answered if non-nuclear resistance

is ever to be more than a dream.

The answer must be to deny that nuclear weapons and non-nuclear world wars are exclusive alternatives, to say rather that both are twentieth-century aberrations which mankind can learn to avoid. The concept of non-nuclear resistance implies a renunciation not only of nuclear weapons but also of those large-scale deployments of aggressive non-nuclear weapons which characterized the era of the world wars. Non-nuclear resistance means that each country relies for its defense on weapons of predominantly defensive character, weapons which do not lend themselves to grand-scale aggression in the style of Hitler. It is important for the viability of non-nuclear resistance that the technology of defensive weaponry be pushed ahead vigorously. Local non-nuclear defense against invasion must be made technically feasible and credible. But it is even more important that the concept of non-nuclear resistance be supported by a worldwide political consensus opposing both nuclear weapons and non-nuclear wars of conquest. There is no reason why patriotic citizens and soldiers dedicated to the defense of their respective countries should not join in such a consensus. But the belief that such a consensus can prevail in the world of the twenty-first century requires a suspension, in this limited area of war and weaponry, of belief in the doctrine of original sin.

After reviewing the arguments for and against non-nuclear resistance, I arrive at no final verdict. The arguments on both sides are largely political. The weight of a political argument is determined not by logic but by the number of people who believe it. If a political consensus in favor of non-nuclear resistance could be achieved, there are no technical reasons why this concept could not be made the basis of a stable balance of power.

22

※

The Middle Way

I am now at the seventh and last stop on my quest for concept, looking once more for a concept which will satisfy simultaneously the demands of military realism and human decency. I am trying to find a middle way between the concepts of assured destruction and nuclear war fighting on the one side and unilateral disarmament on the other, between Robert McNamara and Marshal Grechko on one side and André Trocmé and Gandhi on the other. There is such a middle way, and my friend Donald Brennan knew roughly where it lies. Donald Brennan died a few years ago at the age of fifty-four. He was a professional military expert who worked at the Hudson Institute, the research institute founded by Herman Kahn.

In July 1969 the United States was in the process of making a crucial decision which led directly to a major exacerbation of the arms race and to the failure of the SALT negotiations to halt the multiplication of weapons. The decision which was then made was to introduce into our strategic forces the so-called MIRV, that is to say, multiple independently aimed warheads carried by a single launcher rocket. The public was at that time far more interested in the question of ABM deployment, which was vociferously and successfully opposed by well-organized groups of citizens. Amid the noise of the ABM debate, the deployment of MIRV attracted little attention. The importance of MIRV was understood by 107 members of Congress, who introduced resolutions calling for a moratorium on MIRV testing and deployment. The House Foreign Affairs Committee's subcommittee on national security policy held a series of public hearings in an effort to arouse a more widespread opposition to MIRV. Five congressmen and five arms control experts gave testimony against the MIRV deployment. One of the expert witnesses was Donald Brennan. The hearings did not succeed in arousing the nation. After the hearings were over, testing and deployment of MIRV continued with steadily increasing momentum.

The main obstacle which the congressmen opposing MIRV had to overcome was the fact that MIRV fitted well both into the strategy of assured destruction and into the strategy of nuclear war fighting. At that time the Soviet Union was putting much effort into the development of missile defense technology and was beginning construction of an operational ABM system around Moscow. Advocates of MIRV argued that MIRV was essential in order to ensure that the Soviet ABM could be defeated. The experts who testified against MIRV were all, except for Brennan, believers in assured destruction. They were hampered in their opposition to MIRV by their commitment to the necessity of penetrating the Soviet defenses. Brennan could oppose MIRV unconditionally, because he denied that the defeat of Soviet ABM was necessary. In order to oppose MIRV in an intellectually convincing fashion, Brennan explicitly repudiated the concept of assured destruction and formulated a new concept to replace it. I quote now from his testimony:

> Let us consider two principles. The first principle is that, in terms of strategic nuclear conflict, following any plausibly feasible Soviet attack, we should be able to do at least as badly unto the Soviets as they had done or could do unto us.

Donald Brennan liked to call this principle the "brass rule," meaning that it is a debased form of the golden rule, which says you should do unto others what you wish they would do unto you. Note that this principle does not require us to do very badly unto the Soviets if they cannot do very badly unto us.

> The second principle is that we should prefer live Americans to dead Russians, whenever a choice between the two presents itself. The Soviets may be expected to prefer live Russians to dead Americans, and therein resides the basis for an important common interest; we may both prefer live Americans and live Russians. This formulation may seem so simple as to sound facetious, and in a sense it is, but it conceals a point that is profoundly important and surprisingly controversial.

After some technical discussion, Brennan ends by explaining why his second principle, the preference for live Americans over dead Russians, is controversial. It is controversial because it says that an assured destruction posture is not desirable as a way of life. Assured destruction, he says, may be necessary when no alternative is available, but we should not prefer it.

The concept which Donald Brennan advocated is called by the experts in arms control "parity plus damage-limiting." I prefer to call it "live-and-let-live." Perhaps it may be important to use a name for it which the public can understand. Donald Brennan was unfortunately an experts' expert, expressing his opposition to MIRV in technical language which had little public impact. I believe the name live-and-let-live accurately describes his concept and does not conceal its profound moral implications. To summarize Brennan's statement once again, his concept says: "We maintain the ability to damage you as badly as you can damage us, but we prefer our own protection to your destruction." I believe that this concept fits, as assured destruction does not, George Kennan's requirement that a concept should be modest, unpretentious, and free from apocalyptic overtones.

The great virtue I see in live-and-let-live is that it is a concept for all seasons. We are now living in a wintry season of distrust and despair. Live-and-let-live is robust enough to flourish in winter. It does not require a mood of joyful magnanimity to make it politically acceptable. It could be implemented now, without waiting for a change for the better in Soviet society or in our own. The concept, as Brennan described it, deals with the harsh realities of the world of 1969 or of 1983. But the concept also opens a path to a better world and gives us a plan for getting there. It will still be valid in spring or in summer, guiding us in the task of keeping a better world stable.

Brennan did not speak in his testimony of the long-range implications of live-and-let-live. He spoke of its long-range promise on various occasions privately. If we take a long view, we can regard live-and-let-live as equivalent to non-nuclear resistance plus bargaining chips. That is to say, the long-range plan of live-and-let-live is to reach the same end which non-nuclear resistance hopes to reach, but to get there by negotiation instead of unilaterally. Live-and-let-live regards our nuclear weapons only as bargaining chips to be negotiated away as rapidly as possible. It commits us firmly to the path of negotiating nuclear weapons all the way down to zero, or as close to zero as the Soviet Union will allow. It says that we prefer the number zero to any other number as a target for negotiation. It says that we prefer, given the choice, to base our security upon non-nuclear resistance rather than upon nuclear deterrence. It says that we do not regard the possession of any fixed number of nuclear weapons as permanently necessary to our well-being.

In any assessment of the long-range consequences of live-and-let-live, the great unknown factor is the Soviet response. We cannot expect that the Soviet Union will agree to the dismantling of nuclear weapons on any rapid time scale. There as well as here, bureaucratic inertia and interservice rivalries will make substantial disarmament slow and difficult. However, the hope that the Soviet Union would in the long run negotiate drastic reductions in nuclear forces has a solid basis in Soviet military doctrine. The Soviet counterforce doctrine, unlike our assured destruction doctrine, is consistent with bilateral reductions down to any desired level. And the Soviet strategy of survival of nuclear war will gain in feasibility as the level is lowered. One of the major advantages of live-and-let-live is that it does not demand any substantial shift in Soviet doctrines or patterns of behavior.

Since the concept of live-and-let-live regards nuclear weapons as political bargaining chips rather than desirable military assets, it allows us to conduct disarmament negotiations with flexibility. We are to insist on parity between the two sides as disarmament proceeds, but we do not need to insist on any elaborate technical definition of the meaning of parity. We could, for example, be content with a definition which makes equal aggregate numbers of warheads or of delivery vehicles the criterion of parity, leaving each country free to choose which weapons to retain within these aggregates. We are to insist on verifiability of agreements, but we should accept verification criteria which allow reasonable margins of error and infrequent false alarms.

Far-reaching nuclear disarmament is an objective for the long-range future. I now come back to the present and discuss what effects live-and-let-live should have on our current policies. The first question to be addressed is how we should aim our strategic weapons while we are negotiating their disappearance. The answer to this question is simple: We should not aim them at all. Live-and-let-live excludes assured destruction targeting as inconsistent with the basic principle that live Americans are to be preferred to dead Russians. Limited nuclear war and counterforce targeting are excluded because they are crisis unstable, especially since we are assuming no change in the Soviet practice of counterforce targeting. What then are we to do with our strategic weapons? We must simply maintain them as best we can, making sure that they are as invulnerable as possible to Soviet attack and that they are not aimed at anything in particular. This is what it means to say that we value them as bargaining chips but not as usable military weapons. The SIOP will continue to exist, but the weapons will no longer be poised for its instant execution. It would be helpful to crisis stability if we could provide some technical assurance to the Soviet authorities that our weapons were in fact unaimed; but I do not know how this could be done without compromising their invulnerability. The fact that the weapons are unaimed, whether the Soviet authorities believe it or not, will not diminish their importance in Soviet perceptions as an enduring threat to Soviet power. The incentive for the Soviet Union to get rid of our weapons by negotiation will still exist.

The concept of live-and-let-live should rule over all areas of our foreign policy, not only over the technical issues of the strategic arms race between the United States and the Soviet Union. Live-and-let-live should have a major impact on the weapons we and our allies deploy in Western Europe and on the political problems which surround the control and use of these weapons. The tactical nuclear weapons in Western Europe are in theory intended for fighting limited nuclear war, but in reality they are a component of an assured destruction strategy. If they are ever used, they will bring assured destruction immediately to Western Europe, and with high probability to the Soviet Union and the United States too. The live-and-let-live concept implies that we no longer regard tactical nuclear weapons as a satisfactory solution to the problem of European security. The ultimate objective of our policy must be to get rid of tactical nuclear weapons altogether. We should have no illusion that we can get rid of them quickly or easily. But it is an even greater illusion to imagine that we can go on living with them forever.

Two technical factors ought to help us to move toward a live-and-let-live strategy in Europe. First, our professional soldiers recognize the cumbersomeness of the nuclear weapon command structure, and the extreme vulnerability of the whole tactical nuclear weapon apparatus to a Soviet preemptive strike. Second, the development of precision-guided munitions and of dispersed mobile forces capable of destroying tanks and airplanes offers a realistic substitute for tactical nuclear weapons in the defense of Europe against invasion. It is wrong to claim, as some enthusiasts for precision-guided munitions have claimed, that these are magic weapons which will solve our military problems in Europe overnight. There are no magic weapons. But there are good as well as bad military technologies. A good military technology is one which leads away from weapons of mass destruction, toward weapons which allow people to defend their homeland against invasion without destroying it. The technology of precision-guided munitions is good in this sense. It is reasonable to imagine a hopeful evolution of affairs in Europe, with the technology evolving away from nuclear weapons toward precision-guided non-nuclear weapons, and with the political authorities evolving away from assured destruction toward live-and-let-live. Technical and political development must go hand in hand, each helping the other along.

The defense of Western Europe lies at the heart of our involvement with nuclear weapons. Both tactical and strategic nuclear forces grew up in the context of the military confrontation between East and West in Europe. It is important to understand the difference between the Eastern and Western concepts of nuclear weapons as they relate to the European situation. The Western concept was mainly driven by fears of local Soviet invasion and subversion such as occurred in Poland in 1944 and in Czechoslovakia in 1948; out of these fears grew the concept of limited nuclear war and the doctrine of first use. The Soviet concept was mainly driven by fears of a grand-scale assault on the Soviet Union such as occurred in 1941; out of these fears grew the concept of counterforce and the doctrine of preemption. The fears on both sides were then intensified by each side's perception of the other side's doctrine. American politicians perceive the Soviet doctrine of preemption as clear evidence of malign intent, while Soviet leaders feel threatened by our tactical nuclear deployments close to their borders. Each side sees the other side's doctrine as peculiarly evil. In reality there is nothing peculiarly evil in the Soviet first-strike doctrine, just as there is nothing peculiarly evil in our first-use doctrine. Both grew naturally out of the different historical experiences of the two sides. Both are firmly rooted and will not be easily changed.

What hope is there of escape from this web of threats and misunderstandings? A useful first step would be to educate the public so that the public knows the difference between first use and first strike. After that, it might be possible to discuss strategic doctrines publicly with some degree of rationality. We might then be able to negotiate a bargain with the Soviet Union, in which we agree to dismantle weapons associated with the threat of first use while they dismantle weapons associated with the threat of first strike. A trade-off of first-use against first-strike capabilities would not only improve the security of both sides but would also diminish the psychological anxieties which drive the arms race. Such a trade-off should be one of the immediate objectives of a live-and-let-live strategy.

George Kennan has been the most thoughtful and consistent opponent of our first-use doctrine. "I would submit," he wrote in 1959, "that the first thing we have to do in order to put ourselves in a position to negotiate hopefully for an abolition of nuclear weapons, or indeed to have any coherent strategy of national defense, is to wean ourselves from this fateful and pernicious principle of first use." Kennan's words are as true now as they were twenty-four years ago. A simple no-first-use declaration by the United States would be of enormous importance in lessening the risk of outbreak of nuclear war. Recently a distinguished panel of military experts contemptuously dismissed the idea of a no-first-use declaration on the ground that "declarations like that get put aside in the first moments of conflict." This shows that the panel did not understand what a no-first-use declaration is designed to do. Its purpose is not to constrain the use of weapons in wartime but to constrain the deployment of weapons in peacetime. When Country A signs a no-first-use declaration, the effect is to compel the military authorities in Country A to take into account the possibility that the political authorities in Country A may actually mean what they say. This means that Country A is forced to go to the trouble of hardening and concealing its weapons or withdrawing them from exposed positions where they would be vulnerable to preemptive attack. The effect is to make Country A's deployments more survivable and at the same time less threatening to neighboring countries. The risk of war is reduced by these changes in peacetime deployments, not by any possible direct effect of a no-first-use declaration in wartime.

Now suppose that two hostile countries, A and B, both sign a no-first-use declaration. The effectiveness of the declaration in constraining Country A's deployments does not depend at all upon Country A's believing that Country B is sincere. On the contrary, the more Country A mistrusts Country B's intentions, the stronger the effect of the declaration in discouraging Country A from unstable deployments. For the declaration to be effective, it is necessary only that Country A considers Country B not entirely trustworthy and vice versa, a condition that is well satisfied in the real world in which we are living. In a situation of mutual distrust such as exists in Europe, a no-first-use declaration will push Western deployments strongly in the direction of stability but will detract hardly at all from the deterrent value of the NATO weapons as seen by the Soviet Union. The greater the distrust, the smaller the effect of a no-first-use declaration on deterrence. Our own generals have to take our declaration seriously, but the Soviet generals cannot rely on it.

The practical relevance of these considerations is clearly seen in the contrast between American deployment policies for strategic and tactical weapons. American strategic forces are deployed under our no-first-strike policy, with the result that there is strong emphasis on hardening and concealment. Our tactical nuclear weapons in Europe and elsewhere are not subject to no-first-use constraints, with the result that they are far more exposed and vulnerable. The tactical weapons are more likely than the strategic weapons to get us into bad trouble, and a no-first-use declaration covering the tactical weapons would substantially reduce the danger. A no-first-use declaration would imply a drastic change in the force structure and strategy of the NATO alliance, and would have to be preceded by intensive discussions among the allies. This shows incidentally that the declaration would not be as empty of meaning as the panel of military experts supposed.

Live-and-let-live will have other implications. One immediate implication is that we do not need the MX missile. We should not merely reject the race track or the dense pack deployment of MX, but reject the MX missile in any shape or form. MX is a step in the wrong direction from almost every point of view; it is, as we saw in Chapter 5, a prime example of a technical folly. Being large, expensive, and vulnerable, it is not even a good weapon for the purposes of assured destruction or nuclear war fighting. If we are moving to a live-and-let-live strategy, the most important function of our missiles is to be crisis stable, and in this function the MX fails miserably. Another implication of live-and-let-live is that we push vigorously ahead with negotiations in all the areas where the Soviet Union has been willing to negotiate. Live-and-let-live attaches no intrinsic military value to nuclear weapons, and we should be glad to negotiate them away in a rather indiscriminate fashion provided that the principle of parity is maintained. A freeze agreement might be a good way to begin, provided that it is clearly understood that the freeze is a beginning and not an end.

The most delicate question in formulating a live-and-let-live strategy is the proper role of ABM defenses. The long-range objective of live-and-let-live is a defense-dominated non-nuclear world. In principle, the substitution of non-nuclear ABM systems for offensive nuclear missiles would be, like the substitution of precision-guided munitions for tactical nuclear weapons in Europe, a giant step for mankind in the direction of sanity. In practice, any plan to move toward extensive ABM defenses runs into severe technical, political, and legal difficulties, which were described in Chapter 7. The most serious of these difficulties is the existence of the SALT I treaty forbidding the expansion of ABM systems beyond narrow limits. The treaty must be respected, and the disagreeable features of ABM which made the treaty possible must not be ignored. The live-and-let-live concept says that our purpose is to get rid of nuclear weapons of all kinds and to maintain effective non-nuclear forces for the defense of territory on the ground. ABM defenses are not necessary. The concept does not require ABM for its success. All that matters is that the nuclear weapons be negotiated away, one way or another, with or without the help of ABM. Until the negotiated reduction of offensive weapons has made substantial progress, it would be foolish to raise the question of ABM at all. Nevertheless, if we are ever fortunate enough to see offensive weapons reduced to low levels, ABM defenses would be helpful in giving us confidence to make the next big jump from low levels to zero, and it would be foolish then not to take advantage of whatever benefits ABM defenses have to offer. The proper role of ABM defenses in a live-and-let-live strategy is mainly a question of timing.

It was an unfortunate historical accident that the SALT I treaty was negotiated in the aftermath of the defeat of a particular nuclear ABM system which was widely regarded as ineffective, extravagant, and dangerous. There were good reasons for rejecting the deployment of that particular ABM system at that particular time. But the defects of that system in no way justified the signature of a treaty which committed us to a dogmatic insistence that defense against ballistic missiles would always and in all circumstances be undesirable. To achieve agreements drastically reducing numbers of offensive weapons, and to provide assurance against clandestine violation of such agreements, some deployment of missile defenses may be helpful. In the long run, the transition from a world of assured destruction to a world of live-and-let-live must be accompanied by a transfer of emphasis from offensive to defensive weapons.

When we are thinking about defensive weapons in general and about ballistic missile defense in particular, we should distinguish sharply between ends and means. Our experts in the arms control community have never maintained this distinction. They are so convinced of the technical superiority of offensive over defensive weapons that they let the means determine the ends. I say that we have no hope of escape from the trap we are in unless we follow ends which are ethically acceptable. The ends must determine the means, and not vice versa. The only acceptable end that I can see, short of a disarmed world, is a defensively oriented world. We must decide first whether the defensive world is an end worth striving for. This question must come first. Only afterward comes the question of means.

Defense is not technically sweet. The primal sin of scientists and politicians alike has been to run after weapons which are technically sweet. Why must arms controllers fall into the same trap? There is a terrible arrogance in the statement that defense is hopeless and should therefore be forbidden. Nobody can possibly foresee the state of the world ten years ahead, let alone fifty. If a defensively oriented world is an end worth striving for, and if we pursue it diligently with all the available means, especially with moral and political as well as technical means, we have a good chance of success. The burden is on the opponents of defense to prove that a defensive world is politically impossible. It is not enough for them to say our ABM technicians didn't solve the problem of discriminating warheads from decoys.

I have described the long-range ethical objectives of live-and-let-live and some of its immediate implications. It remains now to summarize the arguments for and against it. The first and most important argument for live-and-let-live is that it is negotiable with the Soviet Union. Unlike assured destruction and limited nuclear war, it does not stand in contradiction with Soviet concepts of security and survival. It therefore offers the possibility of deep and far-reaching negotiated agreements for dismantling of nuclear forces. The second argument, almost as important, is that live-and-let-live is internally negotiable among the various political constituencies of the United States. Unlike non-nuclear resistance, it is consistent with the traditional determination of the American military establishment to maintain weapons at least equal to those of our possible enemies. It requires no unilateral disarmament and no retreat from our commitment to an effective defense of our allies. It offers the possibility of working toward nuclear disarmament along a path acceptable to the Defense Department and the State Department. It offers to the soldiers well-equipped armed forces second to none in the world, to the diplomats a conservative policy of resistance to Soviet aggrandizement, to the peace movement a commitment to get rid of nuclear weapons as fast as reductions can be negotiated. It is a concept robust enough to have a chance of holding these three constituencies together while the talks with the Soviet Union are in progress.

Additional arguments for live-and-let-live are the same as the arguments for non-nuclear resistance: first, that the ultimate strength of the United States derives from geography and not from nuclear weapons; second, that non-nuclear resistance is a good way to pull the Soviet Union toward nuclear disarmament; third, that Soviet expansionism has a persistent style which is more effectively opposed by non-nuclear than by nuclear weapons. These arguments apply equally to live-and-let-live. Live-and-let-live has the same long-range objectives as non-nuclear resistance; it differs only in approaching them bilaterally instead of unilaterally.

In the end, the advantages of live-and-let-live depend upon the stability of a non-nuclear world. If we suppose that the live-and-let-live strategy has been carried successfully to its final conclusion and that nuclear weapons have been outlawed from the face of the earth, the stabilizing effect of the fear of nuclear weapons will still remain. Any country which feels tempted to embark upon a career of conquest, either by breaking the ban on nuclear weapons or by launching campaigns of non-nuclear aggression in the style of Hitler, will know that the knowledge of how to manufacture nuclear weapons is widely spread over the earth and that the initial advantage accruing to the aggressor will not be permanent. Since the knowledge of nuclear weapons and the fear of their destructive power will never disappear, the stability of the non-nuclear world is made paradoxically robust by the fact that everybody knows it to be fragile.

One of the disadvantages of live-and-let-live is that it ties the pace of progress in disarmament to the pace of negotiations. The pace of negotiations is usually slow. Negotiating positions must first be worked out laboriously in internal negotiations within the bureaucracies on each side before they can be mentioned in bilateral discussions. Progress may be halted at any stage if the Soviet Union loses interest in proceeding further, or if the political coalition supporting our own proposals disintegrates. It will be difficult to sustain on either side the steadiness of purpose necessary to reach far-reaching agreements. We cannot expect that, even if things go well, the negotiated demolition of the apparatus of nuclear destruction on the two sides can be accomplished in a time shorter than twenty or thirty years. And if things do not go well, the weapons may blow us to pieces before we reach agreement. The concept of non-nuclear resistance could, if we embraced it, allow us to shake the world by swift unilateral action. Live-and-let-live proceeds by means of negotiations which are bound to be tedious, complicated, and uncertain. Slowness is the price we pay for caution. Non-nuclear resistance takes big risks in order to move fast. Live-and-let-live may miss big opportunities by moving slowly.

The arguments which I raised against nonviolent resistance and non-nuclear resistance—the arguments of vicarious pacifism, robustness, and original sin—may also be raised against live-and-let-live, but against live-and-let-live they are less cogent. The problem of vicarious pacifism hardly arises, since live-and-let-live is only mildly pacifist in concept and does not impose much greater risks on our allies than on ourselves. The problem of robustness is more serious. Live-and-let-live is not an easy concept to explain. It is at present unfamiliar to the majority of the American people. Standing where it does in the middle, between the hawks and the doves, it will be difficult to defend against political attack from both extremes. Nevertheless, the concept is logically coherent and politically practical, and its central location may in the end be a source of strength rather than of weakness. The problem of original sin exists for live-and-let-live, as it exists for all concepts which seek to establish an international order based upon restraint in the use of weapons.

Another argument against live-and-let-live is that it mentions only Russians and Americans and pays no attention to the rest of the world. This is a valid criticism of Brennan's formulation of the concept. He discussed the problem of nuclear weapons as a bilateral problem between the Soviet Union and the United States. In reality the problem is not purely bilateral even now, and it will become less and less bilateral if we are successful in negotiating American and Soviet nuclear force levels down toward the levels existing in Britain and France and China. It is easy to translate the concept of live-and-let-live into a world with five or more nuclear powers. We need only say, instead of speaking of Americans and Russians, "We should prefer live friends to dead enemies, whenever a choice between the two presents itself." However, we run into a serious difficulty when we try to define the meaning of strategic parity in a multilateral world. Does parity mean that all nuclear powers are to be equal, or does it mean that each is to be equal to the combined strength of all its possible enemies? The Soviet Union has good reason to prefer the second interpretation. Shortly before his death, Chairman Brezhnev remarked to a Western visitor, "You must remember that every nuclear weapon in the world is either in the Soviet Union or aimed at the Soviet Union." Brezhnev's statement was only slightly exaggerated.

We can prove mathematically that if three or more nuclear powers demand that they must be allowed to deploy weapons equal in number to the combined strengths of their enemies, the only way to satisfy all their demands simultaneously is to make all the numbers equal to zero. This mathematical theorem expresses a human truth about disarmament in general and about live-and-let-live in particular: If we ever succeed in reducing numbers of weapons to the point at which minor nuclear powers become important, then it will be easier to go all the way to zero than to stop halfway. The implementation of live-and-let-live thus divides itself into two distinct phases. Phase One is the phase of bilateral negotiation, when the nuclear forces of the United States and the Soviet Union are still dominant and the notion of parity based on rough equality of numbers is still meaningful. Phase Two begins when the numbers of weapons are reduced to such a point that the strategic parity of the United States and the Soviet Union depends mainly on geographical and non-nuclear strength and the transition to a non-nuclear and defense-dominated world becomes possible. Phase Two is the phase of transition. In Phase Two, negotiations must be multilateral and the criterion of parity can no longer be equality of numbers. In Phase Two, non-nuclear strength becomes increasingly dominant and the object of negotiation is to reduce the nuclear strength of all parties as rapidly as possible to zero. As we move into Phase Two, we move into a new world of multilateral complications. We may derive some comfort from statements which the British and French and Chinese governments have made on various occasions to the effect that they would willingly enter multilateral negotiations aimed at the reduction of their respective nuclear forces, if the American and Soviet nuclear forces had first been reduced to more reasonable levels. The Israeli government has never made any such statement. But the cooperation of the Israelis is not crucial to our program. It is a wise rule in international politics not to try to solve all the world's problems at once.

In every grand design for the cure of the world's ills, it is always Phase One which is real, while the later phases are concocted out of a mixture of hope and moonshine. Live-and-let-live is no exception. Phase One tells us what we have to do now with the world we know. If ever we reach the end of Phase One, the state of the world will have changed in unpredictable ways. Phase Two will be dealing with the problems of a different world, whose shape we cannot now foresee. In assessing the value of live-and-let-live as a way out of the world's present predicament, it is Phase One which counts. If Phase One can start the world moving in the right direction toward a hopeful future, then live-and-let-live is doing all that we can reasonably ask any concept to do for us.

23

The Fateful Choice

I want in this chapter to pull together a number of ideas which arose in earlier chapters, and to arrive at some conclusions. In the end we have to make choices which will be important for the future of mankind. Fateful choices, rather than a single fateful choice. We should approach these choices with proper humility, remembering that we are not God almighty. Our task is not to choose the best possible path for the world to follow. The world will choose its own path, driven by forces which are largely beyond our control. Our task is to choose tools, people, and concepts which will enable us to give the world an effective push in the direction of survival, whenever it comes to a fork in the road.

The world seems now to be approaching a fork in the road, a fork with two ways out, marked by conspicuous signposts, one marked "Ban the Bomb!," the other marked "Don't Rock the Boat!" Chapter 1 described our task as a search for a common language which would enable warriors and victims to understand each other. "Ban the Bomb!" is the slogan of the victims, "Don't Rock the Boat!" the slogan of the warriors. "Ban the Bomb!" says that our existing weapons and strategy are unacceptably dangerous. "Don't Rock the Boat!" says that it would be unacceptably dangerous to upset the political equilibrium which has grown up around our existing weapons and strategy. Since both these statements are true, there is no escape from our dilemma. No matter whether we try to hold our world in place or to turn it upside down, we shall be living with danger. So long as independent sovereign states exist, the danger of nuclear destruction will not disappear. But there is also a middle way, a third way out of the fork, the way marked "Live-and-Let-Live." The middle way is not an escape from the dilemma. It does not abolish the danger. It promises only to diminish danger by bringing together in the cause of peace the skills of warriors and the moral indignation of victims.

Our dilemma is in essence the same as the dilemma of the diplomats which was described in Chapter 14. The diplomatic history of the last two centuries has been a story with two alternating themes: international order and balance of power. The purpose of international order is to keep the world peaceful; the purpose of the balance of power is to keep it stable. The dilemma of the diplomats arose because a peaceful world is usually not stable and a stable world is usually not peaceful. When diplomats created institutions of international order and neglected the balance of power, international order became impotent and there was no stability. When they pursued the balance of power and neglected international order, national power became irresponsible and there was no peace. So the world blundered repeatedly through the same tragic cycle, from a failed international order to emergence of a new balance of power, from a balance of power to competitive alliances and war, from the disasters of war to a new attempt at international order.

Nuclear weapons have arrested the cycle. That is the great blessing which nuclear weapons have brought us. Because we have nuclear weapons, the cycle is stuck. We have a balance of power with competitive alliances but no war. Instead of war, we have the threat of nuclear annihilation. The threat of annihilation keeps the cycle from turning. But the old dilemma of the diplomats is still with us. We know that we cannot live forever under the threat of nuclear annihilation. If we are to survive, the threat must be removed sooner or later. "Ban the Bomb!" says that we must establish an international order to remove the threat before it destroys us. "Don't Rock the Boat!" says that we must preserve the threat in order to maintain the balance of power which keeps the world stable. The choice we face is the same choice the diplomats always faced: either an unstable international order or a stable balance based upon the threat of violence. Only the magnitude of the violence has changed.

The great diplomats, from Metternich to Harriman and Kennan, have known that wisdom lies in compromise, that the pursuit of international order without power is futile, and that the pursuit of power without international order is barbarous. To find the

workable compromise between international order and balance of
power is the diplomat's high art. And the same art is needed to find
the middle way through the dilemmas of nuclear policy. There is
no safe path. But the path of compromise is likely to be safer than
either the naive recklessness of "Ban the Bomb!" or the blind con-
servatism of "Don't Rock the Boat!" The diplomat's art consists
above all in understanding the purposes and personalities of the
enemy. It was in pursuit of this understanding that Metternich came
to Dresden and Harriman and Kennan to Moscow. It was through
the possession of this understanding that Metternich was able to
humble Napoleon, Harriman was able to negotiate a test ban treaty
in two weeks, and Kennan was able to build political strength
against Soviet penetration of Western Europe by designing the
Marshall Plan.

The fundamental flaw in our nuclear policies from the beginning has been our failure to understand the Soviet point of view. We
have never applied the diplomat's art to this most important of all
diplomatic problems. The failure of understanding has been equally
grievous among our military war fighters and among our civilian
experts in arms control. Our war fighters with their elaborate plans
of limited nuclear war have never been willing to face the fact that
the Soviet doctrine of massive preemption makes such plans meaningless. Our arms controllers with their fixation upon assured destruction have never been willing to understand that the driving
force of Soviet policy is a determination to survive, and that this
deeply rooted will to survive makes assured destruction unacceptable. Both the war fighters and the arms controllers, through their
failure to understand Soviet purposes, have made Soviet military
doctrine appear more evil and dangerous than it in fact is. Both
groups fear what they do not understand, and their fears have been
the driving force on our side of the nuclear arms race. Both groups
try to force the Soviet Union to accept their alien concepts, and then
become resentful when the attempt fails. Neither group takes the
trouble to look at the world through Soviet eyes. Neither group has
sufficient insight to see that for the leaders of a nation carrying the
cultural and historical heritage of Russia, the doctrines of preemption and survival are the logical and natural response to the American challenge. When we are deciding how to deal with the Soviet
Union, either militarily or diplomatically, the first necessity is to
understand the Soviet view of the world and to accept the fact that

Soviet concepts and doctrines have strength and durability equal to our own.

In our choice of people to guide us to a safer future, the diplomats come first in importance. But we also need soldiers and technologists. We became acquainted in Chapters 5 and 13 with the types of soldier we need and with the types we do not need. If we are trying to build a foundation for an international order, based on the negotiated elimination of weapons of mass destruction, and stabilized by the ability of all nations to defend themselves with weapons of limited destructive power, we shall need soldiers who have mastered the art of doing more with less. We shall not need soldiers who understand only how to conquer and destroy with massive armies and massive armaments. We shall need Hermann Balck with his mules and mobility, not Alfred Jodl with his timetables of conquest. We shall need Sir George Milne with his doctrine of strategic moderation, not Sir Hugh Trenchard with his strategic bombers. We shall need Horatio Nelson with his proud little ships, not Napoleon with his grand army. In the difficult task of building a stable balance of power based on limited military means, we shall need all the help we can get from the Balcks, the Milnes, and the Nelsons, from the soldiers and sailors who will rise to the challenge of doing more with less. Fortunately, the men who know how to fight well with limited means are also the men who know how to sustain the morale and spirit of a peacetime army. There is here a natural convergence of interest between the needs of our armed forces, beset by problems of recruitment and crumbling discipline, and the needs of a world trying to move away from dependence on nuclear weapons.

Last come the technologists. We have seen in Chapters 3 to 7 examples of good and bad technologies. The good technologies are those which defend with limited means. We need the good technologies, not only as military tools but as channels of communication with our enemies. Technologists are great teachers. Discussions with Soviet officials about political and social questions will not convert them to our way of thinking. We can argue with them for years about military doctrines and never reach agreement. But our technologists have no difficulty at all in persuading them to adopt our technology. When we deploy MIRV on our missiles, so do they. When we talk big about computers or high-energy lasers, so do they. When we collect intelligence with photographic reconnaissance satellites, so do they. More surprisingly, the force of our example is also sometimes effective in a negative direction. We phased out multimegaton warheads from our strategic weapons; so did they. We stopped large-scale deployment of missile defenses and decided to negotiate the SALT I treaty; so did they. Our technology, if we care to use it for this purpose, gives us a uniquely effective means for guiding Soviet policies into directions which we may consider desirable. This channel of communication has the advantage of being always open. Soviet leaders do not always wish to listen to our diplomacy, but they always listen to our technology. We cannot use technology to persuade them to move in directions which they consider contrary to their interests. But our technology can influence them effectively whenever, as often happens, we wish them to move in a direction where their interests run parallel to ours. The move to non-nuclear defense is a case in point. If our technologists lead strongly into non-nuclear defensive weaponry, it is a good bet that theirs will follow suit.

Our choice of people determines to a great extent our choice of direction for the future. If we choose diplomats to understand Soviet purposes and if we listen to what they have to say, if we choose soldiers to hold the balance of power steady with limited means, if we choose technologists to lead the way into a defensively oriented future, our direction is well set. But we need concepts as well as people to guide us. It is to concepts that we must turn for an understanding of the range of alternatives open to us and for a broadening of our mental horizons beyond the limits set by short-term political constraints.

In Chapters 18 to 22 I outlined seven concepts covering a wide range of viewpoints. It is important that we do not discard any of them totally. Whether we like them or not, whether we consider them practical or not, they are there for history to choose from. History's choice may not coincide with ours. Circumstances may arise in which each one of them becomes dominant. We should be prepared to understand and deal with each of them as the necessity arises.

One of the seven, nonviolent resistance, I set aside as insufficiently robust for present-day use. But it has been used effectively in France and in India, and the time may come when we shall find the moral strength to use it ourselves. Defense unlimited I set aside as technically foolish and dangerous. But it may nevertheless be put into operation if the ideology of the high frontier prevails. Counterforce I set aside as crisis unstable and therefore undesirable as a concept for American strategy. But it is of crucial importance for us to understand counterforce also through Soviet eyes, where it appears as a natural defensive strategy, fitting into the framework of a conservative military tradition, carrying forward into the nuclear age the hard-earned lessons of World War II, and well suited to the historical and geographical circumstances of the Soviet Union. Whatever we may think of it, counterforce is the concept preferred by the Soviet Union and is likely to remain so. Efforts from our side to shift the Soviet Union away from counterforce are unlikely to succeed. Furthermore, if we correctly understand the place of counterforce in the Soviet view of the world, we shall see that the Soviet preference for counterforce is not in itself contrary to our interests. The existence of large Soviet nuclear forces is contrary to our interests. But the Soviet concept of counterforce is consistent with the reduction of these forces by negotiation, simultaneously with the reduction of our own forces, all the way to zero.

Two of the seven concepts, assured destruction and limited nuclear war, I rejected for various reasons—assured destruction because it is immoral and suicidal, limited nuclear war because it is illusory, and both of them because they are incompatible with Soviet concepts and therefore incompatible with comprehensive arms control agreements. Nevertheless, assured destruction and limited nuclear war are the preferred concepts of the United States government and have been so for thirty years. They are as firmly rooted in the NATO alliance as counterforce in the Soviet Union. There is a strong case to be made for leaving our concepts as they are, just as there is a strong case for leaving Soviet concepts as they are. Our present concepts have kept us alive and have kept Western Europe free for thirty years. The fundamental fact of Western European politics is that nobody will take seriously the idea of fighting another major non-nuclear war to defend Europe. Our nuclear weapons have given us a way to avoid this problem. Any upsetting of the balance of power in Europe is inordinately risky. Why not leave well alone? This is the case for staying with the concepts of assured destruction and limited nuclear war, the case which is summed up in the slogan "Don't Rock the Boat!"

The opposing slogan, "Ban the Bomb!" belongs to the concept of non-nuclear resistance, a concept which holds that national defense is important but is best done without the encumbrance of nuclear weapons. Non-nuclear resistance is the quick way to get rid of our nuclear weapons. Just throw them away and see how much better we shall do without them. If I were running the United States as an absolute monarch, I would choose non-nuclear resistance as my policy. It is risky, it is hopeful, and in my heart I know that it is right. I would accept the risks of leaving the Soviet Union as the only major nuclear power in the world.

Fortunately, I am not an absolute monarch and do not have to take this responsibility. So long as the United States is a constitutional republic, non-nuclear resistance will not be adopted as national policy unless it has the support of the military establishment. To persuade a majority of soldiers to support it will take a long time and a revolution in military thinking. Non-nuclear resistance, in the context of United States strategic policy, is a concept for people who are willing to wait a long time to see their dreams come true.

Nobody knows what would really happen if the Soviet Union were suddenly left as the sole major nuclear power. One possibility is an intensification of Soviet expansionism, beginning with invasions and annexations of neighboring countries, and ending with a weakened Western alliance forced in desperation to fight a disastrous war; this is the 1939 scenario. Another possibility is the emergence of Germany, France, China, and Japan as major nuclear powers to fill the gap left by the United States, ending with a precarious balance of power based on unstable alliances; this is the 1914 scenario. A third possibility is a general pacification and relaxation of relations between Eastern and Western Europe, ending with a peaceful disintegration of the NATO and Warsaw Pact alliances; this is a scenario without historical precedent. At one time or another, I have heard each of these three scenarios put forward as the inevitable consequence if we should unilaterally discard nuclear weapons. My own opinion is that all three scenarios are unlikely, and that after the withdrawal of our nuclear weapons the world would continue to behave in approximately the same way as it did before.

Of one thing we can be sure. Chairman Andropov and his colleagues in the Politburo do not spend much of their time thinking about what they would do in response to the unilateral nuclear disarmament of the United States. The simplest and most cogent argument against the concept of non-nuclear resistance is the same argument which Kennan used against nuclear blackmail. Great governments do not behave that way.

We are left with live-and-let-live, the last of my seven concepts and the one which I am advocating as the middle way, the best practical compromise between the conflicting imperatives of "Ban the Bomb!" and "Don't Rock the Boat!" Live-and-let-live combines a fundamental change in our long-range strategic objective with as little change as possible in our day-to-day tactics and in our commitment to the maintenance of a balance of power while negotiations with our adversary proceed. The fundamental change in objective is that we look to a defense-dominated balance of non-nuclear forces rather than to an offense-dominated balance of nuclear terror as the ultimate basis of our security. The choice between an offense-dominated world and a defense-dominated world is, in the end, the fateful choice which lies before mankind.

The greatest obstacle which the concept of live-and-let-live has to overcome is the belief, prevalent among ordinary citizens as well as among technologists and soldiers and arms controllers, that defensive weapons don't work. Whether this belief is valid depends on what we mean by the word "work." If we mean by "work" that a weapon should save our lives when we fight a nuclear war, then defensive weapons do not work and offensive weapons do not work either. If we mean by "work" that a weapon should save those targets which are not attacked, then defensive weapons work well and offensive weapons do too. In the real world, the question whether weapons "work" is equally ambiguous and uncertain, whether the weapons are offensive or defensive. We cannot be sure that weapons of any kind will save our skins if the worst comes to the worst. We cannot be sure that either defensive or offensive weapons will be useless in discouraging madmen from murdering their neighbors. There are no compelling technical grounds for choosing an offensive rather than a defensive strategy as a basis for our long-range security. The choice ought to be made on political and moral grounds. Technology is a good servant but a bad master. If we decide on moral and political grounds that we choose a defense-dominated world as our long-range objective, the diplomatic and technological means for reaching the objective will sooner or later be found, whether the means are treaties and doctrines or radars and lasers.

Chapter 22 described in brief and inadequate fashion a possible route by which we might move from an offense-dominated to a defense-dominated world, from a world of assured destruction to a world of live-and-let-live. This great and difficult transition can only be consummated after the strategic deployments of the United States and the Soviet Union have been enormously reduced by long and tough negotiations. But even now, we shall be in a safer and more stable situation if we immediately move to a live-and-let-live policy than if we stay with assured destruction and limited nuclear war. If we now adopt the strategy of live-and-let-live, that does not mean that we let down our strategic guard or that we put our trust in Soviet good will or that we change our opinions of the nature of Soviet society. It merely means that we change the underlying concept of our strategy from the assured destruction of Soviet society to the assured survival of our own.

In 1947 the Policy Planning Staff of the American State Department formulated the concept of limited liability which I mentioned in Chapter 18. They proposed this concept as a basis for a coherent foreign policy. George Kennan, director of the staff, described their concept in his essay "The Quest for Concept" twenty years later:

> We in the Planning Staff were concerned to restore an adequate balance of power in Europe and eventually in Asia. We thought that once such a balance had been restored, we would negotiate a military and political Soviet retirement from Central Europe in return for a similar retirement on our part. We saw no virtue in keeping our military forces nose to nose with those of Russia. We welcomed the prospect of the emergence, between Russia and ourselves, of a Europe that would be neither an extension of Soviet military power nor of our own. We thought all this could be achieved by indirect, political means. It was our hope that if we could make progress along the lines I have described, there would be a good chance that the world would be carried successfully through the crisis of instability flowing from the defeat of Germany and Japan. New vistas might later open up—vistas not visible at that time—for the employment of our great national strength to constructive and hopeful ends.

This concept is as valid today as it was in 1947. Live-and-let-live is in essence only the extension of George Kennan's concept into the era of nuclear-equipped armies and intercontinental missiles. Kennan's concept was rejected by the American government in 1947.

If it had been accepted, it would have brought to devastated Europe the hope of continent-wide freedom from Soviet occupation. Today the concept of live-and-let-live carries with it an even greater promise, the promise of a first decisive step back from our fatal addiction to the technology of death.

24

---•◦◦◦•---

Tragedy Is Not Our Business

The dominant theme in the history of our century is the tragedy of the two world wars. The just cause with which each world war began, the fight for freedom, was corrupted and almost obliterated by the growth of the modern technology of killing. The heritage of this tragedy is the deployment of nuclear weapons in quantities so large as to obliterate any conceivable just cause in which they might be used. The cultural patterns of the past persist, and the safeguards regulating the use of these weapons are not proof against technical accidents and human folly. The concepts underlying our present strategic doctrines are morally repugnant and politically sterile. We are caught in a chain of tragic consequences, unfolding from the actions of our fathers like the force of inherited destiny in the old Greek myths.

The concept which I call live-and-let-live is a possible way of escape from our predicament. The essence of live-and-let-live is a determination to move away from nuclear weaponry toward defensive and non-nuclear weaponry. The means for bringing about this movement are moral, political, and technical, in that order. Morally, we must arouse the conscience of mankind against weapons of mass murder as we roused mankind against the institution of slavery a hundred and fifty years ago. Politically, we must negotiate international agreements, first to reduce deployments of nuclear weapons and later to eliminate them. Technically, we must push further the development of non-nuclear defensive systems to enhance the stability of a non-nuclear world.

There is a chance that we may now be at a historical turning point, with mankind as a whole beginning to turn decisively against nuclear weapons. If the turning is real, it will find appropriate political forms in which to express itself. If the turning is not real, no political program can succeed in bringing us to nuclear disarmament. So this last chapter is concerned with humanity and morality rather than with weapons and politics. Napoleon said that in war the moral factors are to the material factors as ten to one. The same ratio between moral and material factors should hold good in our struggle to abolish nuclear weapons. That is why the moral conviction must come first, the political negotiations second, and the technical means third, in moving mankind toward a hopeful future. The first and most difficult step is to convince people that movement is possible, that we are not irremediably doomed, that our lives have a meaning and a purpose, that we can still choose to be masters of our fate.

Polls taken among young people in American schools and colleges in recent years have shown that a consistently large majority believe, on the one hand, that their lives are likely to end in a nuclear war and, on the other hand, that there is no point in worrying about it since it is bound to happen anyway. We are all to some extent affected by this paralysis of the will, this atrophy of the moral sense. We shrug off with silly excuses our burden of responsibility for the impending tragedy. We behave like the characters in a Samuel Beckett play, sitting helplessly in our garbage-cans while the endgame of history is played out. Or we fritter away our days like John Osborne's Jimmy Porter, waiting for the big bang to come and convinced that nothing can be done about it, accepting the inevitability of a holocaust which is, as Jimmy says, about as pointless and inglorious as stepping in front of a bus. Why have we become so apathetic and fatalistic? What is wrong with us? Our most basic need is to restore a sense of meaning to the modern world. If we can recover a sense of meaning, then we may find the moral strength to tackle the institutions of nuclear weaponry as resolutely as our ancestors tackled the institutions of slavery.

The first step toward dealing effectively with the problem of meaninglessness in modern life is to recognize that it is nothing new. If people believe that their difficulties are new and never happened before, then they are deprived of the enormous help which the experience of past generations can provide. They do not take the trouble to learn how their parents and grandparents struggled with similar difficulties. They never acquire the long perspective of history which would let them see the littleness of their own problems in comparison with the problems of the past. If people lack a sense of proportion and a sense of kinship with past generations, then it is not surprising that they become anxious and confused and fall into that mood of self-pity which is one of the most unattractive aspects of the contemporary scene.

Past generations were as troubled as we are by the psychological disorientation associated with rapid change. I could give many examples to prove it, but since space is limited I give only one. Consider the Pilgrim fathers at Plymouth in Massachusetts, three hundred and fifty years ago. We all have a mental image of the society in which the Pilgrims lived after they settled in New England. The village clustered around the church, the hard work in the fields, the shared privations and dangers, the daily prayers, the old-fashioned Puritan virtues, the simple faith in divine providence, the ceremony of thanksgiving after harvest. Surely here was a society that was at peace with itself, a community close-knit through personal friendships and religious loyalties. This traditional image of the Pilgrim society is not entirely false. But the reality is stranger and more complicated.

Here is the reality. William Bradford, passenger on the *Mayflower* and historian of the Plymouth colony, is writing in the year 1632, twelve years after the first landing.

Also the people of the Plantation began to grow in their outward estates, by reason of the flowing of many people into the country, especially into the Bay of the Massachusetts. By which means corn and cattle rose to a great price, by which many were much enriched and commodities grew plentiful. And yet in other regards this benefit turned to their hurt, and this accession of strength to their weakness. For now as their stocks increased and the increase vendible, there was no longer any holding them together, but now they must of necessity go to their great lots. . . . By which means they were scattered all over the Bay quickly, and the town in which they lived compactly till now was left very thin and in a short time almost desolate.

So suburban sprawl and urban decay were already rampant within twelve years of the beginning. But let me go on with Bradford's account.

> To prevent any further scattering from this place and weakening of the same, it was thought best to give out some good farms to special persons that would promise to live at Plymouth, and likely to be helpful to the church or commonwealth, and so tie the lands to Plymouth as farms for the same; and there they might keep their cattle and tillage by some servants and retain their dwellings here. . . . But alas, this remedy proved worse than the disease; for within a few years those that had thus got footing there rent themselves away, partly by force and partly wearing the rest with importunity and pleas of necessity, so as they must either suffer them to go or live in continual opposition and contention. And other still, as they conceived themselves straitened or to want accommodation, broke away under one pretense or other, thinking their own conceived necessity and the example of others a warrant sufficient for them. And this I fear will be the ruin of New England, at least of the churches of God there, and will provoke the Lord's displeasure against them.

I leave William Bradford, already in 1632 lamenting the breakdown of the old moral standards and the disintegrating effects of rapid economic growth. These people who broke away from the Plymouth community were not yet the rebellious sons and daughters of the Pilgrims. The sons and daughters had not even had time to grow up. These people who broke away were the Pilgrims themselves, corrupted within twelve years of their landing by the temptations of easy money.

The next question is now: Granted that past generations shared our problems, what can past generations do to help us? The most helpful thing they did was to leave us their literature. Through the writings of the war poets we share the agonies of the two world wars. Literature ties us together. Through literature we know our roots. Through literature we become friends and colleagues of our predecessors. Through literature they talk to us of their troubles and confusions and give us courage to deal with our own. William Bradford understood this well. His purpose in writing his history of the Plymouth colony was, as he says, "that their children may see with what difficulties their fathers wrestled in going through these things in their first beginnings; and how God brought them along, notwithstanding all their weaknesses and infirmities. As also that some use may be made hereof in after times by others in such like weighty employments." Bradford also understood that if his account was to be useful to future generations it must be totally honest. That is the greatness of Bradford. He shows us the Pilgrims as they really were, not a group of pious saints but a bunch of people like ourselves, mixed up in their motives and purposes, feuding and quarreling with one another, keeping one eye on heaven and the other eye on the cash box, and finally, in spite of all their muddles and mistakes, building a new civilization in the wilderness. Proudly Bradford tells how in the eighteenth year of the settlement, standing firm against the murmuring of the rude and ignorant, they hanged three Englishmen for the murder of an Indian.

If we are searching for meaning in a world of shifting standards, literature is one place where we can find it. All of us have periods in our lives when meaning is lost, and other periods when it is found again. It is an inescapable part of the human condition to be borrowing meaning from one another. No man is an island. Or as William Blake said it:

> The bird a nest,
> The spider a web,
> Man friendship.

If we are lucky, we have friends or children or wives or husbands to lend us meaning when we cannot find it for ourselves. But often there come bad times when there are more borrowers than lenders, when a whole society becomes demoralized and finds meaning to be in short supply. Perhaps the present is such a time. In such times, those of us who have a taste for reading can turn to literature and borrow meaning from the past. Literature is the great storehouse where meanings distilled by all kinds of people out of all kinds of experience are preserved. From this storehouse we are all free to borrow. Not everybody reads books. Some cannot read and others prefer television. But enough of us love literature and know how to find meaning in it; we can take care of the needs of the rest by lending out what we have found.

I turn now to another writer, closer to us than William Bradford. I have been lucky enough to know her personally. She is Clara Park of Williamstown, Massachusetts, and her first book was called

The Siege. If I have anything to say worth saying on the subject of human values, I owe most of it to her. *The Siege* is the story of the first eight years of the life of Clara Park's autistic daughter. In the book the daughter is called Elly. It is a book about a particular autistic child and her family. And it is also, indirectly, a book about people in general and their search for meaning. We are still quite ignorant of the nature and causes of autism, but we know at least this much. The autistic child is deficient in those mental faculties which enable us to attach meaning to our experiences. We all from time to time have difficulty in grasping the meanings of things which happen to us. The autistic child has the same difficulty in an extreme degree. The siege by which Clara and her husband and her three older children battered their way into Elly's mind was only an extreme case of the struggle which all teachers must wage to reach the minds of their pupils. The task is the same, to bring a sense of the meaning of life to minds which have lost an awareness of meaning or never possessed it. The story of Clara's siege has many connections with the theme of human response to nuclear weapons. The metaphor of a siege is a good one to describe the struggle we are engaged in. We are trying to surround the sterile official discussions of nuclear strategy with an aroused public concern, to break down the walls of hopelessness and indifference which keep us from feeling the urgency of our danger. Clara is telling us that the search for human values is a two-sided thing. We must be borrowers as well as lenders. The measure of Clara's achievement is that she not only planted in Elly's meaningless solitude an understanding of the meaning of human contact and conversation, but also distilled out of Elly's illness insights which gave added meaning to her own life, to the life of her family, and to her work as a teacher.

Clara is a scholar and a teacher as well as a wife and a mother. Here is her own summing up, describing how a teacher is ready to receive as well as to give meaning.

I learn from Elly and I learn from my students; they also teach me about Elly. In the early years, I knew a student who was himself emerging from a dark citadel; he had been to the Menninger Clinic and to other places too, and he knew from inside the ways of thought I had to learn. "Things get too much for her and she just turns down the volume," he told me. I remembered that, because I have seen it so often since, in Elly and in so many others. Human beings fortify themselves in many ways. Numbness, weakness, irony, inattention, silence, suspicion are only a few of the materials out of which the personality constructs its walls. With experience gained in my siege of Elly I mount smaller sieges. Each one is undertaken with hesitation; to try to help anyone is an arrogance. But Elly is there to remind me that to fail to try is a dereliction. Not all my sieges are successful. But where I fail, I have learned that I fail because of my own clumsiness and inadequacy, not because the enterprise is impossible. However formidable the fortifications, they can be breached. I have not found one person, however remote, however hostile, who did not wish for what he seemed to fight. Of all the things that Elly has given, the most precious is this faith, a faith experience has almost transformed into certain knowledge: that inside the strongest citadel he can construct, the human being awaits his besieger.

Clara does not need to tell us, because anybody reading her book knows it already, that outside the first circle of her family and the second circle of her students there is a third circle, the circle of her readers, a great multitude of people, teachers, doctors, parents, friends and strangers, who all in their different ways can gather the gift of meaning from her story. And once again the gift works both ways. The book itself gave perspective and illumination and meaning to Clara's private struggle, a struggle which continued for many long years after the book was finished. Clara had always been a natural writer and a lover of literature. She had always believed in the power of written words to redeem the dullness of day-to-day existence. But it was Elly's illness and slow awakening which gave Clara a theme to match her capabilities as a writer. Elly gave Clara the strength of will and the understanding of human suffering which shine through the pages of her book. Through this book Clara reached out and touched the multitude in the third circle. She found herself embarked on a mission like the prophet in Pushkin's poem, who meets an angel at the crossroads and is sent out "Over land and sea, / To burn the hearts of people with a word."

When Elly was twelve years old, I had the impression that she came close to being a totally alien intelligence, such as we might expect to encounter if we were successful in finding an intelligent life form in some remote part of the galaxy. Astronomers have often asked themselves how we could hope to communicate with an alien

intelligence if we were lucky enough to discover one. Perhaps Elly
throws a little light on this question. At two years old she looked
through human faces as if they were panes of glass; she was eight
years old before she called her mother by name. Her mental world
must have been radically different from yours and mine. And yet she
could communicate quite well with us through the medium of
mathematics. While I was staying at her house, a letter arrived for
Elly from another autistic child. Elly opened the letter. It contained
nothing but a long list of prime numbers. I could see that the
numbers were all the primes between one and a thousand. Elly
glanced through the list rapidly, then took a pencil and gleefully
crossed out the number 703. She was laughing and singing with joy.
I asked her why she didn't like the number 703, since it looked to
me like a perfectly good prime. She wrote down in large figures so
that everyone could see, "703 = 19 × 37." With that there could
be no argument. So I knew that even the most alien intelligence has
something in common with us. Her prime numbers are the same as
ours.

One more public glimpse of Elly was provided by her father,
showing her a little later at a crucial stage in her search for meaning.
David Park and Philip Youderian published in the *Journal of Autism
and Childhood Schizophrenia* an article with the title "Light and
Number: Ordering Principles in the World of an Autistic Child."
They described a marvelously elaborate and abstract scheme by
which Elly at that time attached numbers to her emotions and to the
comings and goings of the sun and moon.

The numbers 73 and 137 are there, carrying their burden of
magic, and the concept of the days in general belongs to their
product 73 × 137 = 10001. What does it all mean? It is not hard
to share Elly's meanings to some extent. One may react much as
she does to sun and cloud. Some people respond to the individual
qualities of numbers and think it splendid that 70003 is a prime.
But these are only fragments of adult thought. For Elly they unite
into a harmonious whole, capable of profoundly influencing her
mood and her reaction to events. In essence, someone from whom
the gift of words has been largely withheld has built a world of
light and number. . . . It is clear if one talks with Elly that many
of the actions of the people around her, and most of their interests
and concerns, have no meaning at all for her. It is our conjecture

that Elly's system of ideas represents her effort to fill the deficiency by establishing her own kind of meaning. . . . Elly now talks more than she did when her system was new, though still with great effort and concentration, and she has begun to share with others what she has seen during the day and what has happened at school. Recently, when asked a question about her system, she smiled and said, "I used to care about that last year." Not that it is gone now, but only that there are more and more things to think about now that do not fit into the system.

Elly has come a long way in the years since these words were written. It took Elly's parents twenty years to nurture in her a sense of meaning and of human values so that she can now communicate with us as one human being to another. Perhaps in twenty years we can likewise break through our barriers of apathy and denial and face honestly the human implications of our nuclear policies. Just as Elly's family released Elly from her private world of light and number, we may be able to release our nuclear strategists from their closed-in world of theoretical destruction and unreal war fighting, by opening windows into their world from the outside until they, too, see "that there are more and more things to think about that do not fit into the system." Elly is now no longer a case history but a real person, a grown-up person whose privacy needs to be respected. If you want to see what she has been doing recently, you can buy one of her paintings, signed with her real name, Jessica Park.

But I have not finished with Clara. She recently published in the *Hudson Review* an article with the title "No Time for Comedy," which speaks more directly than *The Siege* to the problem of our moral paralysis. The *Hudson Review* is a writers' magazine, read mostly by people with a professional interest in literature. Clara is saying to her literary colleagues that modern literature in its obsession with gloom and doom has lost touch with reality. She quotes from the Nobel Prize speech of Saul Bellow, who stands on her side in this matter:

> Essay after essay, book after book . . . maintain . . . the usual things about mass society, dehumanization, and the rest. How weary we are of them. How poorly they represent us. The pictures they offer no more resemble us than we resemble the reconstructed reptiles and other monsters in a museum of paleontology.

We are much more limber, versatile, better articulated; there is much more to us; we all feel it.

Perhaps a restoration of our spirit may go hand in hand with a restoration of our literature. When we can write truly about ourselves, we shall also be better able to feel truly and act truly. In *The Siege,* Clara showed what it means to write truly. In the *Hudson Review* article she is saying that the fundamental malaise of our time is a loss of understanding of the ancient art of comedy. Comedy, not in the modern sense of a comedian who tries to be funny on television, but in the ancient sense of comedy as a serious drama ending in a mood of joy rather than sorrow. *The Siege* itself is, in this ancient sense of the word, a comedy. It is a classic drama of courage and love triumphing over obstacles, written in a style and language appropriate to our times.

Here is Clara's view of tragedy and comedy:

The Iliad and the Odyssey are the fundamental narratives of Western consciousness, even for those who have not read them: two masks, two modes, two stances; minor chord and major; two primary ways of meeting experience. The Iliad sets the type of tragedy, as Aristotle tells us, where greatness shines amid violence, error, defeat and mortality. The Odyssey celebrates survival among the world's dangers and surprises, and then homecoming, and order restored. It is the very archetype of a prosperous outcome, of Comedy. . . .

Tragedy and Comedy: though the words are paired, their order is not reversible. . . . We can imagine Iliad and Odyssey in only one sequence. To turn back from the long voyage home to the fall of the city, from Odysseus in Penelope's arms to Hector dead and Achilles' death to come, would be to turn experience upside down. . . . Historically indeed, but above all emotionally, the Odyssey comes last.

Last, as Sophocles at ninety, his proud city collapsing around him, in defeat returned to the bitter legend and brought old Oedipus to the healing grove of Colonus, insisting that though suffering is disproportionate, it is not meaningless but mysteriously confers blessing: last, as Matisse with crippled fingers cut singing color into immense shapes of praise. . . . Shakespeare's sequence makes the same statement; what comes last is not the sovereign Nothing of

King Lear but the benign vision of The Winter's Tale and The Tempest. . . .

Here on stage stand Ferdinand and Miranda, undertaking once more to live happily ever after—the young, our own, that simple investment in the future we're all capable of, our built-in second chance. For them the tragic past is only a story that grownups remember. Untendentiously, insouciantly, they will go about their business, the business of comedy, making new beginnings of our bad endings, showing us that they were not endings at all, that there are no endings. . . .

What is at issue today is whether we have grown too conscious and too clever for comedy's burst of good will. In every age but this the creators of our great fictions have regularly accorded us happy endings to stand beside those others that evoke our terror and our pity. Happy endings still exist, of course. But they have lost their ancient legitimacy. . . They awaken an automatic distrust. . . . And so for the first time since the beginning of our literature there is no major artistic mode to affirm the experience of comedy: healing, restoration, winning through. . . . It is a grand claim we make when we reject happy endings: that we are very special, that whatever songs previous ages could sing, in our terrible century all success is shallow or illusory, all prosperity a fairy-tale; that the only responses to our world which can command adult assent are compulsive ironies and cries of pain; that the world which seems to lie before us like a world of dreams, so various, so beautiful, so new, hath, in short, really neither joy nor love nor light, nor certitude, nor peace, nor help for pain, and we are here as on a darkling plain waiting for Godot.

Clara goes on to say that the essential feature of comedy is not the happy ending but the quality of the characters which enables them to earn a happy ending. Odysseus, the prototype of the comic hero, earned his happy ending by being clever, adaptable, devious, opportunistic, and not too much concerned with his own dignity. When it was necessary to escape from a bad situation in the Cyclops' cave, he was willing to take a ride hanging onto the underbelly of a sheep. Here is Homer's image of the human condition, an image which has helped to keep us sane for three thousand years and can still keep us sane if we do not close our eyes to it: the Cyclops stroking the back of his favorite ram, telling it how grievously

Odysseus has injured him and asking it where Odysseus has gone, while Odysseus precariously hangs on to the wool underneath, silently hoping for the best. The art of comedy is to make happy endings credible by showing us how they are earned. The heroes of comedy are people who do not pity themselves. They take the rough with the smooth. When they are lucky they are not ashamed of it. When they are unlucky they do not despair. Above all, they never give up hope.

There is in the literature of our own century another fine example of tragedy and comedy in action. In December of the year 1911 the Norwegian explorer Amundsen reached the South Pole. A month later the British explorer Scott arrived at the Pole. After heroic exertions, Scott and his companions died in a blizzard on the way home, only eleven miles from the depot where they would have found supplies and safety. The story of Scott's expedition was written ten years later by Apsley Cherry-Garrard. Cherry-Garrard was one of the survivors who went out in search of Scott and found him dead in his tent. Here is his description of the scene:

> Bowers and Wilson were sleeping in their bags. Scott had thrown back the flaps of his bag at the end. His left hand was stretched out over Wilson, his lifelong friend. Beneath the head of his bag, between the bag and the floor-cloth, was the green wallet in which he carried his diary. . . .
>
> We never moved them. We took the bamboos of the tent away, and the tent itself covered them. And over them we built the cairn.
>
> I do not know how long we were there, but when all was finished and the chapter of Corinthians had been read, it was midnight of some day. The sun was dipping low above the Pole, the Barrier was almost in shadow. And the sky was blazing—sheets and sheets of iridescent clouds. The cairn and Cross stood dark against a glory of burnished gold.

Cherry-Garrard ends his last-but-one chapter with the text of Scott's message to the public, found among the papers in the tent. After summarizing the causes of the disaster, Scott finishes on a more personal note:

> For four days we have been unable to leave the tent—the gale howling about us. We are weak, writing is difficult, but for my own sake I do not regret this journey, which has shown that Englishmen

can endure hardships, help one another, and meet death with as great a fortitude as ever in the past. We took risks, we knew we took them; things have come out against us, and therefore we have no cause for complaint, but bow to the will of Providence, determined still to do our best to the last. . . . Had we lived, I should have had a tale to tell of the hardihood, endurance and courage of my companions which would have stirred the heart of every Englishman. These rough notes and our dead bodies must tell the tale.

Those are the immortal words of the tragic hero Robert Scott. But Cherry-Garrard does not stop there. After those words he begins a new chapter, his last chapter, with the title "Never Again." It starts with a quotation from the poet George Herbert:

> And now in age I bud again,
> After so many deaths I live and write;
> I once more smell the dew and rain,
> And relish versing. O my onely light,
> It cannot be
> That I am he
> On whom thy tempests fell all night.

Then Cherry-Garrard goes on:

I shall inevitably be asked for a word of mature judgment of the expedition of a kind that was impossible when we were all close up to it, and when I was a subaltern of twenty-four, not incapable of judging my elders, but too young to have found out whether my judgment was worth anything. I now see very plainly that though we achieved a first-rate tragedy, which will never be forgotten just because it was a tragedy, tragedy was not our business. In the broad perspective opened up by ten years' distance, I see not one journey to the pole, but two, in startling contrast one to another. On the one hand, Amundsen going straight there, getting there first, and returning without the loss of a single man, and without having put any greater strain on himself and his men than was all in the day's work of polar exploration. Nothing more businesslike could be imagined. On the other hand, our expedition, running appalling risks, performing prodigies of superhuman endurance, achieving immortal renown, commemorated in august cathedral sermons and by public statues, yet reaching the Pole only to find our terrible journey superfluous, and leaving our best men dead on the ice. To

ignore such a contrast would be ridiculous; to write a book without
accounting for it a waste of time. . . .

The future explorer . . . will ask, what was the secret of
Amundsen's slick success? What is the moral of our troubles and
losses? I will take Amundsen's success first. Undoubtedly the very
remarkable qualities of the man himself had a good deal to do with
it. There is a sort of sagacity that constitutes the specific genius of
the explorer: and Amundsen proved his possession of this by his
guess that there was terra firma in the Bay of Whales as solid as on
Ross Island. Then there is the quality of big leadership which is
shown by daring to take a big chance. Amundsen took a very big
one indeed when he turned from the route to the Pole explored and
ascertained by Scott and Shackleton and determined to find a second pass over the mountains from the Barrier to the plateau. As it
happened, he succeeded, and established his route as the best way
to the Pole until a better is discovered. But he might easily have
failed and perished in the attempt; and the combination of reasoning and daring that nerved him to make it can hardly be overrated.
All these things helped him. Yet any rather conservative whaling
captain might have refused to make Scott's experiment with motor
transport, ponies and man-hauling, and stuck to the dogs; and it was
this quite commonplace choice that sent Amundsen so gaily to the
Pole and back, with no abnormal strain on men or dogs, and no
great hardship either. He never pulled a mile from start to finish.

John McPhee gives us another glimpse of Amundsen in his
recent book *Coming into the Country*. McPhee's book is about
Alaska. He describes how on a wintry day in 1905, with the temper-
ature at sixty below, Amundsen quietly walked into the post office
at Eagle, Alaska, to send a telegram home to Norway announcing
that he had completed the first crossing of the Northwest Passage.
The last four hundred miles he traveled alone with his sled and dog
team. No fuss, no cathedral sermons. That was six years before he
arrived at the South Pole.

Cherry-Garrard's final verdict on the two South Pole expedi-
tions was simple. "There is a sort of sagacity that constitutes the
specific genius of the explorer." Amundsen had it. Scott didn't. The
word "sagacity" is carefully chosen. Sagacity is not the same thing
as wisdom. Wisdom is the greater virtue, but it is too rare and too
solemn for everyday use. Sagacity is by comparison rather cheap,

rather slick, rather undignified, but nine times out of ten it is sagacity that will get you out quicker when you are stuck in a bad hole. The shipwrecked mariner in Kipling's Just-So story "How the Whale Got His Throat" was "a man of infinite resource and sagacity," and so he naturally knew how to trick the whale into giving him a free ride back to England. Three thousand years earlier, Odysseus showed the same sort of sagacity in dealing with the Cyclops. Sagacity is the essential virtue for the hero of a comedy. It is the art of making the best of a bad job, the art of finding the practical rather than the ideal solution to a problem, the art of lucking out when things look hopeless.

Cherry-Garrard gives Scott his due. It was true, as Cherry-Garrard says, that Scott's life and death made a first-rate tragedy. First-rate in every sense—in the nobility of character of the hero, in the grandeur of the geographical setting, in the epic quality of Scott's prose, and in the tragic flaw of Scott's nature, the pride and stubbornness which led him to demand more of himself and of his companions than was humanly possible. A first-rate tragedy indeed, worthy of all the fine speeches and sermons that have been devoted to it. And yet Cherry-Garrard, who lived through it, looks back on it with a cool eye. Tragedy, he says, was not our business. When all is said and done, Amundsen knew his business as an explorer and Scott didn't. The business of an explorer is not tragedy but survival.

It happened that the drama of Scott's last expedition and the text of his diaries became known to the British public in 1913, just a year before the outbreak of World War I. The surviving members of the expedition were, as Cherry-Garrard reports, submerged in a tide of hero worship. The dead were transmuted into mythical figures of superhuman virtue. The intensely emotional and uncritical reaction of the British public to their tragedy foreshadowed the equally emotional and uncritical reaction of England to the greater tragedy of 1914. The two tragedies had much in common. Many a young officer in the British Expeditionary Force carried a copy of Scott's diary with him in the trenches, and found in Scott's stoic spirit a source of courage and strength. The tragedy of the trenches, like the tragedy in the Antarctic, was a tragedy of a nation which valued self-sacrifice more highly than sagacity. The public which romanticized Scott was the same public which romanticized the young men marching off to die by the thousands in hideous and badly planned battles. Cherry-Garrard understood that the business of a soldier,

like the business of an explorer, is not tragedy but survival. Having
survived the Antarctic, he survived the Western Front too. Concerning the larger tragedy, he wrote: "That was a war which killed
ten million men; left a trail of misery, mental and physical, which
no man can measure; and settled nothing." The futility of the larger
tragedy helped him to see the smaller in true perspective. His judgment of Scott's tragedy and Amundsen's survival helps us to put
into perspective the tragedies of a later time.

The main thing I am trying to say in this book is that Cherry-
Garrard's judgment applies to us too. Tragedy is not our business.
Too much preoccupation with tragedy is bad for our mental health.
Tragedy is a real and important part of the human condition, but
it is not the whole of it. Some people try to make a tragedy out of
every aspect of modern life. In the end their mental state comes to
resemble the attitude of another famous character of modern fiction:

> Eeyore, the old grey Donkey, stood by the side of the stream, and
> looked at himself in the water.
> "Pathetic," he said. "That's what it is. Pathetic."
> He turned and walked slowly down the stream for twenty yards,
> splashed across it, and walked slowly back on the other side. Then
> he looked at himself in the water again.
> "As I thought," he said. "No better from this side. But nobody
> minds. Nobody cares. Pathetic, that's what it is."

The Eeyore syndrome is somewhere deep in the heart of each
one of us, ready to take over if we give it a chance. Anyone who
has to deal with mentally sick people will be familiar with the voice
of Eeyore. Those of us who consider ourselves sane often feel like
that too. The best antidote that we have against the Eeyore syndrome is comedy, comedy in the new-fashioned sense, making fun
of ourselves, and also comedy in the old-fashioned sense, the drama
of people like Odysseus and Amundsen who survive by using their
wits. Survival is our business, and in that business it is the heroes
of comedy who have the most to teach us.

Odysseus and his friends can teach us a trick or two which may
come in handy when we are in a tight spot. But the tricks are not
important. The important thing which comedy does for us is to
show us meanings. Just as the central theme of the *Iliad* is death,
the central theme of the *Odyssey* is homecoming. The homecoming
of Odysseus gives meaning to his adventures and his sufferings.

Homecoming is still in the modern world a powerful symbol and source of meaning. Millions of Americans come home each year for Thanksgiving. The homecoming of Jews to Jerusalem gave meaning to their two-thousand-year odyssey.

Homecoming is the reward for survival, but it is not the end of the story. There is no end, because homecoming means a new beginning. Homecoming means renewal and rebirth, a new generation growing up with new hopes and new ideals. Their achievements will redeem our failures; their survival will give meaning to our bewilderment. This is the lesson of comedy. No matter how drastically the institution of the family is changed, no matter how authoritatively it is declared moribund, the family remains central to our social and mental health. The children find meaning by searching for their roots; the parents find meaning by watching their children grow.

Clara Park's book *The Siege* is a celebration of the remedial power of the family. It is family love and discipline which breaks through the isolation of a sick child and gives meaning to the suffering of the parents. William Bradford's book *Of Plymouth Plantation* is also, in the same classic tradition, a comedy, and it is appropriate that it ends with a family chronicle, a list of the surviving Pilgrims and their descendants unto the third and fourth generations:

> Of these hundred persons which came first over in this first ship together, the greater half died in the general mortality, and most of them in two or three months' time. And for those which survived, though some were ancient and past procreation, and others left the place and country, yet of those few remaining are sprung up above 160 persons in this thirty years, and are now living in this present year 1650, besides many of their children which are dead and come not within this account. And of the old stock, of one and other, there are yet living this present year, 1650, near thirty persons. Let the Lord have the praise, who is the High Preserver of men.

Many of us do not share Bradford's religious belief, but we can all share his pride and his hope. Pride for what the old people have done, hope for what the young people will do. The most important lesson which comedy has to teach us is never to give up hope.

This lesson, not to give up hope, is the essential lesson for people to learn who are trying to save the world from nuclear destruction. There are no compelling technical or political reasons why we and the Russians, and even the French and the Chinese too, should not in time succeed in negotiating our nuclear weapons all the way down to zero. The obstacles are primarily institutional and psychological. Too few of us believe that negotiating down to zero is possible. To achieve this goal, we shall need a worldwide awakening of moral indignation pushing the governments and their military establishments to get rid of these weapons which in the long run endanger everybody and protect nobody. We shall not be finished with nuclear weapons in a year or in a decade. But we might, if we are lucky, be finished with them in a half century, in about the same length of time that it took the abolitionists to rid the world of slavery. We should not worry too much about the technical details of weapons and delivery systems. The basic issue before us is simple. Are we, or are we not, ready to face the uncertainties of a world in which nuclear weapons have been negotiated all the way down to zero? If the answer to this question is yes, then there is hope for us and for our grandchildren. And here I will let Clara Park have the last word:

> Hope is not the lucky gift of circumstance or disposition, but a virtue like faith and love, to be practiced whether or not we find it easy or even natural, because it is necessary to our survival as human beings.

Bibliographical Notes

General

Here is a list of works which influenced my thinking:

Einstein on Peace, edited by Otto Nathan and Heinz Norden (New York: Simon & Schuster, 1960).

John Erickson, *Soviet Military Power* (London: Royal United Services Institute for Defence Studies, 1971).

Amitai Etzioni, *The Hard Way to Peace: A New Strategy* (New York: Collier Books, 1962).

James Fallows, *National Defense* (New York: Random House, 1981).

Herman Kahn, *On Thermonuclear War* (Princeton University Press, 1960).

Fred Kaplan, *The Wizards of Armageddon* (New York: Simon & Schuster, 1983).

George F. Kennan, *Memoirs, 1925–1950* and *Memoirs, 1950–1963* (Boston: Little, Brown, 1967 and 1972); *The Nuclear Delusion: Soviet-American Relations in the Atomic Age* (New York: Pantheon Books, 1982).

Terence H. O'Brien, *Civil Defence,* History of the Second World War, United Kingdom Civil Series (London: H.M. Stationery Office, 1955).

Pastoral Letter of the United States Bishops on War and Peace, "The Challenge of Peace: God's Promise and Our Response," published in *Origins,* Vol. 13, pp. 1–32 (Washington: National Catholic News Service, 1983).

Noel Perrin, *Giving Up the Gun: Japan's Reversion to the Sword, 1543–1879* (Boulder: Shambhala Publications, 1980).

Tom Stonier, *Nuclear Disaster* (Cleveland: World Publishing Co., 1963).

These works will be cited in the following notes by author's name and year of publication.

I recently assigned Kahn 1960 and Stonier 1963 as required reading for a student seminar in arms control, and learned to my dismay that both were unobtainable. So the students who learn arms control will remain ignorant of the thinking of their predecessors.

Perrin 1980 is a well-documented historical study and also a parable of nuclear disarmament. The Japanese rejection of guns after a half century of intensive use and manufacture provides a precedent for a future worldwide rejection of nuclear weapons. The fact that the professional military class was the force effectively opposing guns in Japan suggests that we look to our professional soldiers for an effective opposition to nuclear weapons. Both in seventeenth-century Japan and in the world of today, soldiers have an incentive to get rid of weapons which make fighting excessively dangerous.

My title page quotation comes from an earlier draft of Pastoral Letter 1983, published in *Origins*, Vol. 12, p. 699 (April 1983). This book was almost finished when the Pastoral Letter appeared, but the bishops' main conclusions and recommendations coincide with mine.

The quotations heading Parts I–IV have the following sources:

    I.   H. G. Wells, "The Rediscovery of the Unique," Fortnightly Review, July 1891, quoted in *H. G. Wells*, a biography by Norman and Jeanne MacKenzie (New York: Simon & Schuster, 1973), p. 87.

    II.   Bertolt Brecht, "1940," in *Gedichte*, Vol. 4 (Frankfurt: Suhrkamp, 1961), p. 220 (my translation). For this quotation I am indebted to Philip and Phyllis Morrison.

    III.   Frederic Manning, *Her Privates We, by Private 19022* (London: Peter Davies, 1930), prefatory note.

    IV.   Leo Tolstoy, "What Is Art?" translated by Aylmer Maude, in Tolstoy's *Collected Works* (New York: Charles Scribner's Sons, 1902), Vol. 19, p. 468.

The following notes refer to individual chapters.

Preface

The Tanner Lectures on Human Values, Vol. 4, edited by Sterling M. McMurrin (Salt Lake City: University of Utah Press, 1983).

1. Agenda for a Meeting of Minds

For John von Neumann, see Eugene P. Wigner, *Symmetries and Reflections* (Bloomington: Indiana University Press, 1967), pp. 257–261.

    Helen Caldicott, *Nuclear Madness* (New York: Bantam Books, 1981).

    For Kennan and Pipes, see notes to Chapter 15.

    For world government, see Einstein 1960, p. 408.

    For nuclear theology, see Fallows 1981, p. 140.

2. The Question of Survival

Parts of this chapter are taken from a review of Stonier 1963 in *Disarmament and Arms Control*, Vol. 2 (1964), pp. 459–61.

    For the Los Alamos certificate and Oppenheimer's reply, see *Manhattan District History, Project Y, the Los Alamos Project, Vol. I*, by David Hawkins

(Report LAMS-2532, written 1946, distributed 1961, Office of Technical Services, U.S. Department of Commerce, Washington, D.C.), pp. ii, 293–94.

For prewar estimates of air raid casualties in Britain, see O'Brien 1955, pp. 95–6, and Kahn 1960, p. 376.

James R. Newman, review of Kahn 1960, *Scientific American*, Vol. 204 (March 1961), pp. 197–200, reprinted in *The Rule of Folly* (New York: Simon & Schuster, 1962).

Nuclear War, the Aftermath, edited by Jeannie Peterson and Don Hinrichsen (New York: Pergamon, 1982), a reprint of *Ambio*, Vol. 11, No. 2–3 (Stockholm: Royal Swedish Academy of Sciences, 1982). For effects of smoke, see Paul J. Crutzen and John W. Burke, pp. 114–25. For the editorial advisers' summary, p. 162.

Jonathan Schell, *The Fate of the Earth* (New York: Knopf, 1982).

My appraisal of Schell's thesis was influenced by Thomas Powers, "Choosing a Strategy for World War 3," *Atlantic Monthly*, Vol. 250 (1982), pp. 82–110. Powers is mainly concerned with the history of the American nuclear policy debate which resulted in the adoption of the war-fighting strategy embodied in Carter's Presidential Directive 59. His concluding paragraph touches the question of survival:

> Strategic planners hesitate to say what the world would be like after a nuclear war. There are too many variables. But they agree—for planning purposes, at any rate—that both sides would "recover," and that the most probable result of a general nuclear war would be a race to prepare for a second general nuclear war. As a practical matter, then, a general nuclear war would not end the threat of nuclear war. That threat, in fact, would be one of the very few things the pre-war and post-war worlds would have in common.

Bhagavad-Gita, the Song of God, translated by S. Prabhavananda and C. Isherwood (Hollywood: Marcel Rodd, 1947), p. 46.

3. Paradoxes of the Arms Race

For the text of the General Advisory Committee report and annexes, see Herbert F. York, *The Advisors: Oppenheimer, Teller and the Superbomb* (San Francisco: Freeman & Co., 1976), pp. 150–59. For Oppenheimer's letter to Conant, see p. 55.

Nevil Shute (Norway), *On the Beach* (New York: Signet Books, 1958).

For the Doomsday Machine, see Kahn 1960, pp. 145–48, and Peter George, *Dr. Strangelove or: How I Learned to Stop Worrying and Love the Bomb,* a novel based on the screenplay by Stanley Kubrick, Peter George and Terry Southern (New York: Bantam Books, 1964), pp. 96–99, 145.

4. David and Goliath

For David and Goliath, see I Samuel 17.

For the use of suckerfish to catch turtles, see David R. Moore, *Islanders and*

Aborigines at Cape York: An Ethnographic Reconstruction Based on the 1848–1850 Rattlesnake Journals (Canberra: Australian Institute of Aboriginal Studies, 1978), pp. 167–68. For this reference I am indebted to George B. Dyson.

Paul F. Walker, "Precision Guided Weapons," *Scientific American,* Vol. 245 (August 1981), pp. 37–45. See also letter by S. J. Deitchman and reply by Walker, *Scientific American,* Vol. 245 (November 1981), p. 10.

For von Neumann's view of weaponry, see Steve J. Heims, *John von Neumann and Norbert Wiener: From Mathematics to the Technologies of Life and Death* (Cambridge, Mass.: MIT Press, 1980). Heims's portrait of von Neumann is tendentious, but his quotations are accurate.

For Einstein's views, see Einstein 1960, pp. 95, 142, 495.

5. Technical Follies

Quotations from Hermann Balck are from an interview with Pierre Sprey, taped at Battelle Columbus Laboratories, Tactical Technology Center, Columbus, Ohio, in January 1979, published as an internal Battelle report. A second interview, taped in April 1979, is published in another report.

The official British history of the Second World War includes four volumes entitled *The Strategic Air Offensive Against Germany, 1939–1945,* by Sir Charles Webster and Noble Frankland (London: H.M. Stationery Office, 1961). The AGLT footnote is on p. 147 of Vol. 3. The Trenchard and Milne memoranda are in Vol. 4, Appendix 2, pp. 71–83.

For two examples of technical folly in the United States Army and Air Force, see Fallows 1981, Chap. 4.

6. Star Wars

A. T. Mahan, *The Influence of Sea Power upon the French Revolution and Empire, 1793–1812* (Boston: Little, Brown, 1919), Vol. 2, p. 118.

A good summary of the technical arguments against the effectiveness of laser weapons is "Laser Weapons" by K. Tsipis, *Scientific American,* Vol. 245 (December 1981), pp. 51–57. Tsipis demolishes lasers too easily by considering only the most ambitious missions. Lasers in space might be effective for less ambitious missions, for example for helping to discriminate warheads from decoys in conjunction with a conventional missile-defense system.

7. The ABM Problem

Two scholarly and well-documented histories of the political struggles surrounding ABM in the United States are available. *Ballistic Missile Defense,* by Benson D. Adams (New York, Elsevier, 1971), is a complete summary of events from the beginnings up to 1970. "Eggheads and Warheads: Scientists and the ABM," by Anne H. Cahn (MIT Thesis, 1971), is a detailed study of the opinions and actions of scientists involved in the decisive phase of the ABM debate from 1967 to 1969. Adams tends to be biased in favor of ABM, Cahn tends to be biased against it. The two accounts together give a balanced picture.

In connection with Count 1 of my case against ABM and the rebuttal to it, a penetrating analysis of the meaning of effectiveness of ABM systems was published a long time ago: "Strategy for Active Defense," by Thornton Read (Bell Telephone Laboratories Report, 1961). Read was, so far as I know, the first to explain clearly the distinction between technical effectiveness and military effectiveness, and the first to understand how an ABM system of surprisingly high military effectiveness can be put together out of components of dubious technical effectiveness.

8. Shelters

The old Swiss Shelter Handbook was published under the title *Handbuch der Waffenwirkungen für die Bemessung von Schutzbauten,* edited by G. Schindler and A. Haerter (Bern: Federal Civil Defense Office, 1964). It reproduced American published data on weapons effects, and applied this data to the calculation of performance of underground structures.

For a more recent account of Swiss shelters and their history, see Pierre A. Piroué, "Civil Defense in Switzerland," International Seminar on the World-wide Implications of a Nuclear War (Erice, Sicily: Ettore Majorana Institute for Scientific Culture, August 1981). I am indebted to Professor Piroué for reading an earlier draft of this chapter and correcting some errors.

For the history of the London underground station shelters, see O'Brien 1955, pp. 521–22, 543–45.

The Next Whole Earth Catalog: Access to Tools, 2d ed., edited by Stewart Brand (New York: Random House, 1981). For guns, see pp. 450–51.

9. Amateurs at War

Freeman Atkey's letters, manuscript copy by Mildred Atkey in the author's possession.

Obituary notice of Captain F. A. H. Atkey by G. L. Bickersteth in *The Marlburian,* probably 1916.

Beverley Nichols, *Father Figure* (London: Heinemann, 1972), pp. 124–27.

Lieutenant G. Dyson, *Grenade Warfare. Notes on the Training and Organization of Grenadiers* (London: Sifton, Praed and Co., 1915). American edition, *Grenade Fighting. The Training and Tactics of Grenadiers* (New York: George H. Doran Co., 1917).

G. Dyson, "Of All the World's Great Heroes," *The Spectator,* October 30, 1915, pp. 570–71. George's title would have been familiar to the readers of *The Spectator.* It comes from a popular patriotic song:

> Of all the world's great heroes
> There's none that can compare
> With the tow-row-row-row-row-row
> Of the British Grenadier.

The word "grenadier," by a curious twist of history, had become detached from its original meaning. The grenade had been an important infantry weapon until the eighteenth century, when the increasing range and accuracy of guns made it obsolete. It remained obsolete so long as infantry fought above ground. During the nineteenth and early twentieth centuries, grenadiers were elite infantry troops who had nothing to do with grenades. When trench warfare began in 1914, the obsolete weapon suddenly became essential and had to be reinvented. The British army restored the word "grenadier" to its old meaning by giving this elite title to anybody who could learn to throw a grenade.

Ronald W. Clark, in *JBS: The Life and Work of J. B. S. Haldane* (New York: Coward-McCann, 1969), pp. 44–46, describes how the biologist Haldane organized a grenade-fighting school at Nigg in Scotland in 1915. Haldane's school at Nigg and Dyson's at Tidworth were operating simultaneously. Haldane's methods were even more unorthodox than Dyson's, so it is not surprising that the army preferred to use Dyson's notes for the official handbook.

Paul Fussell, *The Great War and Modern Memory* (New York: Oxford University Press, 1975).

10. Education of a Warrior

This chapter was published with the title "The Sell-out" in *The New Yorker,* February 21, 1970. It was reprinted in Horace F. Judson, *The Techniques of Reading,* 3rd ed. (New York: Harcourt Brace Jovanovich, 1972), pp. 447–56.

W. H. Auden and Christopher Isherwood, *The Ascent of F6* (London: Faber and Faber, 1936), p. 16.

C. Day Lewis, *Overtures to Death* (London: Jonathan Cape, 1938), p. 25.

T. S. Eliot, *East Coker* (London: Faber and Faber, 1940), p. 14.

C. Day Lewis, *Word over All* (London: Jonathan Cape, 1943), p. 30.

11. Scientists and Poets

Parts of this and the next chapter appeared in *The Dial,* June 1982, pp. 38–43, with the title "The Oppenheimer Puzzle."

J. B. S. Haldane, *Daedalus, or Science and the Future* (London: Kegan Paul, Trench, Trubner and Co., 1924), pp. 1–2, 84. For Haldane, see also Clark's biography (cited in the notes to Chapter 9), p. 37.

The Poems of Wilfred Owen, edited by Edmund Blunden (London: Chatto and Windus, 1931; reprinted 1946), pp. 72, 66.

Robert Oppenheimer, Letters and Recollections, edited by Alice K. Smith and Charles Weiner (Cambridge, Mass.: Harvard University Press, 1980), pp. 156, 250, 286.

Erich Maria Remarque, *Im Westen Nichts Neues* (Berlin: Im Propyläen-Verlag, 1929), pp. 18–19. My translation.

T. E. Lawrence, *Seven Pillars of Wisdom, a Triumph* (New York: Doubleday Doran and Co., 1936), p. 5.

Charles Osborne, *W. H. Auden: The Life of a Poet* (New York, Harcourt Brace Jovanovich, 1979), p. 140.

U.S. Atomic Energy Commission, "In the Matter of J. Robert Oppenheimer, Transcript of Hearing before Personnel Security Board" (Washington: U.S. Government Printing Office, 1954), pp. 9, 10.

George Orwell, *Homage to Catalonia* (Boston: Beacon Press, 1952).

For Paul Fussell on trenches and on George Orwell, see *The Great War and Modern Memory* (cited in notes to Chapter 9), pp. 45, 109.

Richard Polenberg on Joe Dallet, personal communication to the author.

C. Day Lewis, *Overtures to Death* (cited in notes to Chapter 10), pp. 41–52.

John Osborne, *Look Back in Anger* (Chicago: Dramatic Publishing Co., 1957), p. 69.

12. The Scholar-Soldier

Oppenheimer Transcript (see notes to Chapter 11), pp. 497, 891–93.

U.S. Department of the Army, "Staff Officers' Field Manual FM 101-31-1, Nuclear Weapons Employment" (U.S. Government Printing Office, 1963), pp. 38, 50, 53, 55. A more recent unclassified handbook is FM 100-5, published in July 1976 with the title "Operations." FM 100-5 contains a short chapter (pp. 10–1 to 10–9) on tactical nuclear operations. I am indebted to Christopher Hallowell, editor of *The Dial*, for a copy of this chapter; it is far less detailed than FM 101–31–1, and I cannot judge whether the 1976 doctrine is really an improvement on the 1963 doctrine.

The discussion of "soldiers against nuclear war" at the end of Chapter 12 was influenced by Perrin 1980.

13. Generals

The details of Alfred Jodl's life and death are taken from the biography published by his widow, Luise Jodl, *Jenseits des Endes: Leben und Sterben des Generaloberst Alfred Jodl* (Vienna: Verlag Fritz Molden, 1976), pp. 25–26, 299–300, 330, 337–38. My translation.

The remark of Speer comes from Albert Speer, *Inside the Third Reich*, translated by R. and C. Winston (New York: Macmillan, 1970), p. 515.

T. S. Eliot, *Little Gidding* (London: Faber and Faber, 1942), ll. 31–38.

Hermann Balck's reminiscences were published in two Battelle reports. See notes on Chapter 5. The extracts quoted here are from the January report, pp. 18, 36, 56–57, and the April report, pp. 2–3, 30–31, 42.

For the battle of Maldon, see Michael Wood, *In Search of the Dark Ages* (London: BBC, 1981), pp. 180–84.

"The English Admirals" is a chapter (pp. 179–204) in *Virginibus Puerisque*, by Robert L. Stevenson (London: Chatto and Windus, 1897).

For the Soviet technocrats, see Erickson 1971, p. 14.

I am indebted to Lieutenant General Arthur S. Collins, Jr., U.S. Army, retired, for a copy of his essay "Strategy for Disaster" (unpublished, 1982). General Collins has published a summary of his conclusions in a shorter article, "Tactical Nuclear Weapons: Are They a Real Option?" *Army*, July 1982, pp. 36–39.

14. Diplomats

Metternich's Europe, edited by Mack Walker (New York: Harper & Row, 1968), contains the texts of Metternich's conversation with Napoleon (pp. 25–31) and Canning's speech to the House of Commons (pp. 139–43).

Kennan 1967, pp. 218–19, 332; Kennan 1972, pp. 158–59, 327–51; Kennan 1982, pp. 3–4, 179.

For Harriman's remarks about the test ban negotiation, see G. T. Seaborg, *Kennedy, Khrushchev, and the Test Ban* (Berkeley: University of California Press, 1981), pp. 235, 241, 251–52. For the text of the treaty, see pp. 302–305.

15. Russians

For an authoritative and well-documented summary of Soviet nuclear doctrine, see John Erickson, "The Soviet View of Deterrence: A General Survey," *Survival,* Vol. 24 (1982), pp. 242–51. Erickson 1971 is an older but still useful survey of Soviet military organization and doctrine.

The Thatcher-Brezhnev conversation was reported to me privately by a reliable source.

Richard E. Pipes, "Why the Soviet Union Thinks It Could Fight and Win a Nuclear War," *Commentary,* July 1977, pp. 21–34.

For Kennan's view of the Soviet leaders, see Kennan 1982, pp. 100–101. Kennan's 1944 essay with the title "Russia—Seven Years Later" is reprinted in Kennan 1967, pp. 503–31. For the circumstances in which the essay was written, see pp. 224–31.

Leo Tolstoy, *War and Peace,* translated by Constance Garnett (New York: Random House, Modern Library, 1931), pp. 723–25, 938.

Hilaire Belloc, *Selected Cautionary Verses* (Harmondsworth: Penguin Books, 1950), p. 19.

The Oxford Book of Russian Verse, edited and with introduction by Maurice Baring (Oxford: Clarendon Press, 1924). Blok's "On the Field of Kulikovo" is on pp. 177–82.

Alexander Blok, *The Twelve and Other Poems,* translated by John Stallworthy and Peter France (New York: Oxford University Press, 1970), pp. 35–36, 75–82, 141–60. I have not been able to find a satisfactory English translation of Blok. The German translation of "The Twelve" by Wolfgang E. Groeger (*Die Zwölf von Alexander Blok,* Berlin: Newa-Verlag, 1921) is, as Prince D. S. Mirsky remarks in his notes to *The Oxford Book of Russian Verse,* a masterpiece. Professor Emerson of Cornell University kindly sent me a copy of an English translation by her student Bob Strauss. The excerpts from "The Twelve" which I quote are a mixture of Stallworthy, Strauss and Dyson. I am indebted to Professor Emerson and Mr. Strauss for permission to quote from Strauss's version.

Ilya Ehrenburg, *The Thaw,* translated by Manya Harari (Chicago: Henry Regnery, 1955).

My 1956 visit to Moscow and Leningrad was described in an article, "Science and Freedom," in the *Baltimore Sun,* June 26, 1956.

16. Pacifists

The Barbadian Diary of General Robert Haynes, 1787–1836, edited by Everil M. W. Cracknell (Medstead: Azania Press, 1934), pp. 23–24. See note on page 62 for details of the events referred to in the diary.

Aylmer Maude, *Leo Tolstoy and His Works* (London: George Routledge and Sons, 1930), p. 48.

For the death of Jaurès, see Barbara W. Tuchman, *The Proud Tower: A Portrait of the World Before the War, 1890–1914* (New York: Macmillan, 1966), Chap. 8.

Philip P. Hallie, *Lest Innocent Blood Be Shed: The Story of the Village of Le Chambon and How Goodness Happened There* (New York: Harper & Row, 1979), p. 245.

John F. Kennedy, *Why England Slept* (New York: Wilfred Funk, 1940), describes the debacle of pacifism in England from the point of view of an unsympathetic but perceptive observer. For George Lansbury, see Chapter 3.

George Bernard Shaw, *Saint Joan* (New York: Random House, Modern Library), p. 172.

17. The Importance of Being Stuck

Robert M. Pirsig, *Zen and the Art of Motorcycle Maintenance: An Inquiry into Values* (New York: Bantam Books, 1975), pp. 250, 256, 257.

A. Einstein, "The Origins of the General Theory of Relativity," the Gibson Lecture given at Glasgow in 1933, reprinted in *The World as I See It* (New York: Covici-Friede, 1934).

William James, *The Varieties of Religious Experience: A Study in Human Nature,* the Gifford Lectures given at Edinburgh in 1901–1902 (London: Longmans Green, 1937), p. 206.

The Cloud of Unknowing, and Other Treatises, by an English mystic of the 14th century, edited by Dom Justin McCann (London: Burns Oates and Washbourne, 1924). The quotation is taken from "The Epistle of Privy Counsel," a postscript to "The Cloud of Unknowing," p. 123.

For civilian gas masks in Britain, see O'Brien 1955, pp. 61, 160, 330. The Milton quote is on p. 181.

Kennan 1967, p. 393.

Pastoral Letter 1983, pp. 14, 24.

18. The Quest for Concept

Kaplan 1983 is a history of American strategic concepts as they were developed at the Rand Corporation and implemented by the air force. This account, emphasizing the point of view of Rand Corporation veterans, is a useful corrective to the history of strategic thinking as seen in public political debates and in the literature of the arms control community. There was often a wide gap between inside and outside thinking. But Kaplan underrates the influence of outsiders. The Rand Corporation view did not always prevail.

Erickson 1982 (cited in notes to Chapter 15) not only explains Soviet strategic concepts accurately but also describes how American concepts appear through Soviet eyes.

George F. Kennan, "In American Foreign Policy: The Quest for Concept," *Harvard Today*, Autumn 1967, pp. 11–17.

General Sir Archibald Wavell, *Generals and Generalship* (New York: Macmillan, 1943), p. 3.

Robert S. McNamara, answer to question of Senator Saltonstall, U.S. Senate Defense Appropriations Hearing (1966), p. 229.

Robert S. McNamara, "The Dynamics of Nuclear Strategy," U.S. Department of State Bulletin, Vol. 57, No. 1476 (1967).

Paul H. Nitze, "Atoms, Strategy and Policy," *Foreign Affairs*, Vol. 34 (1956), pp. 187–98.

Thomas Powers 1982 (cited in notes to Chapter 2) gives an excellent account of the origin and significance of Carter's Presidential Directive 59.

A. A. Grechko, *Na Strazhe Mira i Stroitel'stva Kommunizma* (On Guard for Peace and the Building of Communism) (Moscow, 1971), p. 41.

Kahn 1960, p. 126 and footnote to p. 6.

Grenville Clark and Louis B. Sohn, *World Peace Through World Law* (Cambridge, Mass.: Harvard University Press, 1958).

Kennan 1982, p. 147.

19. Assured Destruction

P. M. S. Blackett, *Studies of War, Nuclear and Conventional* (New York: Hill and Wang, 1962), p. 130.

Solly Zuckerman, *Nuclear Illusion and Reality* (New York: Viking Press, 1982), p. 142.

Kahn 1960, p. 137.

Herman Kahn and Anthony J. Wiener, *The Year 2000: A Framework for Speculation on the Next Thirty-three Years* (New York: Macmillan, 1967).

20. Nuclear War Fighting

For a graphic account of the early history of American nuclear war fighting doctrines see David A. Rosenberg, "A Smoking Radiating Ruin at the End of Two Hours: Documents on American Plans for Nuclear War with the Soviet Union, 1954–1955," *International Security*, Vol. 6 (1982), pp. 3–38. For the later history, see Powers 1982 (cited in notes to Chapter 2) and Kaplan 1983.

John Lehmann, *The Strange Destiny of Rupert Brooke* (New York: Holt, Rinehart and Winston, 1981), pp. 127, 130–31, 163–64.

For Major Kong, see Peter George (cited in notes to Chapter 3), p. 19.

Lt. Gen. Daniel O. Graham, *High Frontier: A New National Strategy* (Washington, D.C.: High Frontier, Inc., 1982), pp. 3, 14, 23.

Thucydides, translated by Benjamin Jowett, Vol. 2 (Oxford: Clarendon Press, 1900), pp. 333–34.

21. Unilateral Disarmament

Hallie 1979 (cited in notes to Chapter 16), pp. 34–35, 184–85.

For nuclear blackmail, see Kennan 1982, p. 71.

For problems of morale in the U.S. Army, see Fallows 1981, Chapter 5.

22. The Middle Way

Donald Brennan, "Diplomatic and Strategic Impact of Multiple Warhead Missiles," Hearings Before the Subcommittee on National Security Policy and Scientific Developments of the Committee on Foreign Affairs, House of Representatives, 91st Congress, July 8–August 5, 1969 (Washington, D.C.: U.S. Government Printing Office), pp. 109–10. Testifying against MIRV were Congressmen Bingham, Cohelan, Foley, Moorhead, Anderson, and arms control experts Kistiakowsky, Brennan, Fisher, Coffee, and Scoville. In favor of MIRV were Congressman Hosmer and expert Foster. Three other witnesses took a neutral position.

George F. Kennan, *Reflections on Our Present International Situation* (Woodmont, Conn.: Promoting Enduring Peace, 1959), p. 6. There is an extensive literature discussing the first-use doctrine. For authoritative statements of the case against first use, see McGeorge Bundy, George F. Kennan, Robert S. McNamara, and Gerard Smith, "Nuclear Weapons and the Atlantic Alliance," *Foreign Affairs*, vol. 60 (Spring 1982), pp. 753–68, and Pastoral Letter 1983, p. 15.

23. The Fateful Choice

George Kennan, "The Quest for Concept" (see notes to Chapter 18).

Michael M. May, "U.S. Consensus Policy on Nuclear Weapons" (lecture given at the University of Chicago on the 40th anniversary of the first nuclear chain reaction, December 1–2, 1982), is the best short summary of the arguments for maintaining our present nuclear policies. May's discussion, unlike most of the literature of strategic analysis, is modest, unpretentious, simple and clear.

24. Tragedy Is Not Our Business

William Bradford, *Of Plymouth Plantation, 1620–1647*, edited by Samuel E. Morison (New York: Knopf, 1952), pp. 46, 252–54, 299–301, 447.

Apsley Cherry-Garrard, *The Worst Journey in the World: Antarctic 1910–1913* (London: Penguin Books, 1937), pp. 9, 479–81, 531, 534–36.

Clara Park, *The Siege: The First Eight Years of an Autistic Child. With an Epilogue, Fifteen Years Later* (Boston: Atlantic–Little Brown, 1982), pp. 274–75.

Clara Park, "No Time for Comedy," *Hudson Review,* Vol. 32 (1979), 191–200.

David Park and Philip Youderian, "Light and Number: Ordering Principles in the World of an Autistic Child," *Journal of Autism and Childhood Schizophrenia,* Vol. 4 (1974), pp. 313–23.

David Park, *Advocate,* Vol. 12, No. 2 (March 1980), pp. 5–6.

John McPhee, *Coming into the Country* (New York: Farrar, Straus & Giroux, 1977), pp. 361–65.

A. A. Milne, *Winnie-the-Pooh* (New York: E. P. Dutton, 1926), p. 70.

Index

Acknowledgments

Grateful acknowledgment is made for permission to reprint:

Excerpt from "Jim, Who ran away from his Nurse, and was eaten by a Lion" in *Cautionary Verses* (U.S.) and *Complete Verse* (Great Britain) by Hilaire Belloc. Copyright 1931 and renewed 1959 by Eleanor, Elizabeth and Hilary Belloc. Reprinted by permission of Duckworth and Company Limited, Alfred A. Knopf, Inc. and the author.

Excerpts from "East Coker" and "Little Gidding" in *Four Quartets* by T. S. Eliot. Copyright 1943 by T. S. Eliot; renewed 1971 by Esme Valerie Eliot. Reprinted by permission of Harcourt Brace Jovanovich, Inc., and Faber and Faber Ltd.

Excerpts from *Memoirs 1925–1950* by George F. Kennan. Copyright © 1967 by George F. Kennan. Reprinted by permission of Little, Brown and Company in association with The Atlantic Monthly Press.

The dedicatory poem of *The Seven Pillars of Wisdom* by T. E. Lawrence. Copyright 1926, 1935 by Doubleday and Company. Reprinted by permission of Doubleday and Company, the Seven Pillars Trust, and Jonathan Cape Limited.

Excerpt from *Father Figure* by Beverly Nichols. Copyright © 1972 by Beverly Nichols. Reprinted by permission of William Heinemann Limited and Eric Glass Ltd.

"Mental Cases" by Wilfred Owen in *The Collected Poems of Wilfred Owen* edited by C. Day Lewis. Copyright © 1963 by Chatto & Windus, Ltd. Reprinted by permission of New Directions Publishing Corporation and Chatto & Windus, Ltd.

"Where Are the War Poets?" in *Selected Poems* by C. Day Lewis (U.S. 1967) and in *Collected Poems* (Great Britain 1954). Copyright 1943 by C. Day Lewis. Reprinted by permission of Harper & Row, Publishers, Inc., and the Executors of the Estate of C. Day Lewis, Jonathan Cape Ltd., and Hogarth Press.

Excerpt from "The Nabara" in *Selected Poems* by C. Day Lewis (1967). Copyright 1938 by C. Day Lewis. Reprinted by permission of Harper & Row, Publishers, Inc.

"A Happy View" in *Collected Poems* by C. Day Lewis (1954). Reprinted by permission of the Executors of the Estate of C. Day Lewis, Jonathan Cape Ltd., and Hogarth Press.

Excerpt from *The Advisors: Oppenheimer, Teller and the Superbomb* by Herbert F. York (Freeman & Co.). Reprinted by permission of the author.

About the Author

Freeman Dyson has been a professor of physics at the Institute for Advanced Study in Princeton since 1953. Born in England, he came to Cornell University as a Commonwealth Fellow in 1947 and settled permanently in the U.S. in 1951.

Professor Dyson is not only a theoretical physicist; his career has spanned a large variety of practical concerns. In World War II he worked for the Royal Air Force doing operations research. Since that time he has been unable to stop thinking about the great human problems of war and peace. Inside the U.S. government, he has been a consultant to the Defense Department and the Arms Control and Disarmament Agency. Outside the government, he has spoken and written widely about the ethical dilemmas of the nuclear age. In 1979 he published *Disturbing the Universe*, a scientific autobiography interspersed with meditations on the human condition. *Weapons and Hope* is another meditation, attempting to understand in greater depth that part of the human condition which involves nuclear weapons and nuclear strategies.

In addition to his scientific work, Professor Dyson has found time for raising five daughters, a son, and a stepdaughter.